To Robert Steel for his courage,
determination, inspiration and love.

Charles Gwathmey and Robert Siegel

Charles Gwathmey and Robert Siegel
Buildings and Projects 1964–1984

Edited by Peter Arnell and Ted Bickford
Associate Editor, Ivan Zaknic

Icon Editions

Harper & Row, Publishers, New York

Cambridge, Philadelphia, San Francisco, London,
Mexico City, São Paulo, Sydney

Charles Gwathmey and Robert Siegel, Buildings and Projects 1964–1984. Copyright © Charles Gwathmey and Robert Siegel 1984. All rights reserved. Printed in Japan. No part of this book may be used or reproduced in any manner whatsoever without written permission except in the case of brief quotations embodied in critical articles and reviews. For information address Harper & Row, Publishers, Inc., 10 East 53rd Street, New York, N.Y. 10022. Published simultaneously in Canada by Fitzhenry & Whiteside Limited, Toronto.

First Edition

Library of Congress Catalog Card Number: 84–47564

ISBN: 0–06–433285–3
ISBN: 0–06–430145–1 pbk.

Printed and bound in Japan by Dai Nippon Printing Company

Set in Simoncini Garamond by Circle Graphics, Washington, D.C.

We would like to extend a special thanks to Mark Uhlig for his general help and goodwill; and of course to Charles Gwathmey, Robert Siegel, Ivan Zaknic and Cass Canfield Jr.
P.A. T.B.

Executive Editors:
Peter Arnell
Ted Bickford

Associate Editor:
Ivan Zaknic

Managing Editor:
Catherine Bergart

Editorial Assistant:
Scott Gutterman

Design:
Alessandro Franchini,
Arnell/Bickford Associates

Production:
Jesse Luther Hickman

Contents

Gwathmey Residence, Amagansett, New York

Introduction

For sixteen years we have worked together, often over a common table, always in the same room. The designs are a result of our interaction, which is intense, self-critical, questioning yet always supportive. We share common beliefs and we motivate each other to extend beyond our individual capabilities.

We believe that architecture is generated by the investigation of the specific problem, resulting in a process of ordered evaluations, of analytical priorities and of hierarchical interpretations, all relating to site, orientation, program, circulation, spatial sequence, structure and technology.

By responding to these issues, form is derived as a factual and logical manifestation, rather than an idiosyncratic preconception. Form must be inherently responsive to the constraints of the problem. We believe that form, manifested by implication, can be as or more meaningful than form as fact.

An important confrontation in our work relates to the line of interpretation and meaning between abstraction and representation. If there is a correlation with painting and sculpture, our work appears to rest solidly in the cubist frame of reference, as opposed to either the nonrepresentational or the representational.

There is a conscious reevaluation of architectural language and a genuine concern for the understanding and communication of ideas and meaning in our architecture.

It is our belief that modern architecture has not been able to solve the large scale or urban problem. It has not developed a convincing vernacular language that can create not just the unique or singular "object," but the broader range of buildings and contexts, while simultaneously supporting existing fabrics, scales, systems and constructs. The problem of simple abstraction is the denial of historical reference, precedent, hierarchical coding, multiple rather than singular quotations, and anthropomorphic references. On the other hand, historical misinterpretations and misquotations resulting in cartoon images rather than a true new reality are as suspect and unfulfilling as insistence upon abstraction. We feel that historical reference is important as precedent, not style; as redefining model, not misrepresenting symbol; as understanding organizational principle, not misrepresenting order; as a method of decoding the implications, articulations and hierarchies of ornament, not as justification for decorative appliqué.

Architecture is not skin-deep. To detach the bones (structure) from the skin (facade) is the beginning of formal irresolutions which deny the basic principles of the composite overlay—plan, section, facade—that ultimately produce the building.

We are pursuing an ethic of rational interpretation that can deal with both contextual and noncontextual problems. Our new work is clearly less minimal and unadorned, employing a more complex, extended and enriched language. There is a continued interest in perceptual implication, speculation and interpretation through the formal manipulation of volumetric space and form, made comprehensive by geometry, transparency, and spatial and facade layering.

In summary, how a building is constructed, its ability to endure, and the logic of its details are critical considerations. The language is abstract in the sense that it allows the buildings to be synthesized and reactive to natural and/or contextual stimulants rather than preconceived as total forms with predictable memories.

Design is the final transformation of choice to art. We choose every day. Design is including or excluding—not as accommodation but as meaning. It is about understanding a problem, analyzing the constraints, selecting options, and creating the object that provokes an aesthetic response and engenders an idea.

Charles Gwathmey and Robert Siegel

Index of Buildings and Projects

Date/Project	Project Team			
1964 **Miller Residence** ● *Fire Island, New York* *Page 24*				
1965 **Herlinger-Bristol Ltd** ● **Showrooms and Offices** *New York, New York* *Page 26*				
1965 **Gwathmey Residence and Studio** ■ *Amagansett, New York* *Page 28*				
1966 **Straus Residence** ■ *Purchase, New York* *Page 32*				
1967 **Sedacca Residence** ■ *East Hampton, New York* *Page 34*				
1967 **Goldberg Residence** ■ *Manchester, Connecticut* *Page 36*				
1968 **Cooper Residence** ■ *Orleans, Massachusetts* *Page 38*				
1968 **Steel Residence I** ▲ *Bridgehampton, New York* *Page 40*	Thomas Pritchard, James Swan, Timothy Wood, Christopher Chimera			
1968 **Steel Residence II** ▲ *Bridgehampton, New York* *Page 42*	Thomas Pritchard, James Swan, Timothy Wood, Christopher Chimera			
1969 **Dunaway Apartment** ▲ *New York, New York* *Page 44*	James Swan, Thomas Pritchard, Timothy Wood			

1968
Service Buildings & Heating Plant
State University College at Purchase ▲
Purchase, New York
Page 46

Durwood Herron, Timothy Wood

  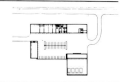

1969
Brooklyn Friends School ▲
Brooklyn, New York

Andrew Petit, Timothy Wood, Stephen Potters

1969
Dormitory, Dining and Student Union Facility
State University College at Purchase ▲
Purchase, New York
Page 47

Andrew Petit, James Swan, Timothy Wood, Stephen Potters, Thomas Pritchard, Durwood Herron

1969
Gwathmey Siegel Architects Offices
New York, New York
Page 50

1970
Eskilson Residence
Roxbury, Connecticut (project)
Page 51

Timothy Wood, James Swan

1970
Whig Hall
Princeton University
Princeton, New Jersey
Page 52

Timothy Wood, James Swan, Stephen Potters

1970
Tolan Residence
Amagansett, New York
Page 58

Timothy Wood

1971
New York Apartment
New York, New York
Page 60

Timothy Wood, Stephen Potters

1971
Cogan Residence
East Hampton, New York
Page 62

Timothy Wood

1971
Elia-Bash Residence
Califon, New Jersey
Page 68

Timothy Wood

11

1972
Cohn Residence
Amagansett, New York
Page 70

Timothy Wood, Marvin Mitchell

1972
Whitney Road Housing
Perinton, New York
Page 72

Marvin Mitchell, John Choi, Timothy Wood, Susan Green

1973
Gwathmey Barn
Greenwich, Connecticut
Page 76

Timothy Wood, Stephen Potters

1973
Pearl's Restaurant
New York, New York
Page 78

John Chimera

1973
Sagner Residence
West Orange, New Jersey (project)
Page 80

Ivan Zaknic, John Chimera

1973
Geffen Residence
Malibu, California (project)
Page 82

1973
St. Casimir Housing
Yonkers, New York (project)
Page 84

Ivan Zaknic, Peter Szilagyi, Marvin Mitchell

1974
Buettner Residence
Sloatsburg, New York

Peter Szilagyi

1974
Transammonia Corporation Offices
New York, New York
Page 88

John Chimera, Peter Szilagyi

1974
Charof Residence
Montauk, New York
Page 90

Ivan Zaknic, Peter Szilagyi

12

1974
Four Seasons Restaurant
Negoya, Japan (project)
Page 92

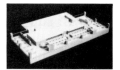

1974
Kislevitz Residence
Westhampton, New York
Page 94

Peter Szilagyi, John Chimera, Ivan Zaknic

1974
Vidal Sassoon
Salon
La Costa, California
Page 100

Tsun-Kin Tam, Gustav Rosenlof

1974
Vidal Sassoon
Salon
New York, New York
Page 102

Tsun-Kin Tam, Gustav Rosenlof

1974
Vidal Sassoon
Salon
Chicago, Illinois
Page 104

Tsun-Kin Tam, Gustav Rosenlof

1974
Vidal Sassoon
Salon
Beverly Hills, California
Page 106

Tsun-Kin Tam, Gustav Rosenlof, Jose Coriano

1974
Vidal Sassoon
Corporate Offices
Los Angeles, California
Page 108

Tsun-Kin Tam, David Murphy

1975
Student Apartment Housing
State University College at Purchase
Purchase, New York
Page 110

Marvin Mitchell, Tsun-Kin Tam, Gustav Rosenlof, Peter Szilagyi

1975
Nassau County Art Center
Roslyn, New York (project)
Page 112

1975
One Times Square
Office Building
New York, New York (project)
Page 114

Peter Szilagyi, Tsun-Kin Tam, Gustav Rosenlof, Ivan Zaknic

 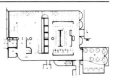

1976
Haupt Residence
Amagansett, New York
Page 138

Peter Szilagyi, Margaret Jann, Gustav Rosenlof

1976
Weitz Residence
Quogue, New York
Page 142

Peter Szilagyi, Gustav Rosenlof, Margaret Jann, Edward Walsh

1976
Thomas & Betts Corporation
Office Building
Raritan, New Jersey
Page 146

Richard Gould, David Murphy, Marvin Mitchell

1976
Benenson Residence
Rye, New York
Page 150

Peter Szilagyi, Eleanor Klein, Edward Walsh

1976
Swirl, Inc.
Showrooms and Offices
New York, New York
Page 152

Gustav Rosenlof

  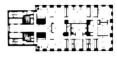

1976
Hyatt Hotel & Casino
Aruba, Antilles (project)
Page 154

Tsun-Kin Tam, Gustav Rosenlof, Andrew Minchun, Ivan Zaknic, Marvin Mitchell

1976
Swid Apartment
New York, New York
Page 156

Peter Szilagyi, Jose Coriano, Margaret Jann

1977
Poster Originals, Ltd.
New York, New York
Page 158

Peter Szilagyi

1977
Garey Shirtmakers
Showrooms and Offices
New York, New York
Page 159

John Colamarino

 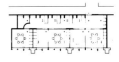

1977
Crowley Residence
Greenwich, Connecticut

Peter Szilagyi, George Wu, Ivan Zaknic

1977
Geffen Apartment
New York, New York
Page 160

Jose Coriano

1977
Belkin Memorial Room
Yeshiva University
New York, New York
Page 162

John Colamarino, Marvin Mitchell

1977
Taft Residence
Cincinnati, Ohio
Page 164

Gustav Rosenlof, George Wu, Karen Jacobson

1977
Northgate Housing
Roosevelt Island, New York (project)
Page 170

Jacob Alspector, Edward Walsh, Michael Monsky, Vincent Mulcahey, Steven Harris

1977
Lincoln Center for the Performing Arts
Administrative Offices
New York, New York
Page 174

Tsun-Kin Tam, Jose Coriano, Vincent Mulcahey

  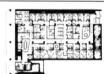

1977
FDM Productions
Offices
New York, New York
Page 176

David Murphy, Edward Walsh, Jose Coriano

16

1977
AT&T
Office Building
Parsippany, New Jersey
Page 178

Richard Gould, Mark Simon, Rotwein & Blake Associated Architects, P.A. (Associate Architects)

1977
The Evans Partnership
Office Building & Offices
Parsippany, New Jersey
Page 180

Richard Gould, Jose Coriano, David Murphy, Rotwein & Blake Associated Architects, P.A. (Associate Architects)

1977
The Evans Partnership
Offices
New York, New York
Page 183

Gustav Rosenlof, Tsun-Kin Tam, David Murphy, Ivan Zaknic

1978
Amax Petroleum Corporation
Office Building
Houston, Texas

George Wu

1978
Knoll International
Showroom and Office Building
Boston, Massachusetts
Page 184

Jacob Alspector, Nick Toecheff, David Murphy, David Hingston, John Colamarino

---

1978
Sycamore Place
Elderly Housing
Columbus, Indiana
Page 188

Jacob Alspector, William Garbus, Dean Marchetto, Lynn Bensel, Glen Fries, Joseph Ruocco

---

1978
Pence Street
Family Housing
Columbus, Indiana
Page 190

Jacob Alspector, Jose Coriano, Margaret Fitzpatrick, William Garbus, Lynn Bensel, Dirk Kramer, Dean Marchetto, Joseph Ruocco, Irene Torroella

---

1978
Shezan Restaurant
New York, New York
Page 192

David Murphy, Margaret Jann

1978
Giorgio Armani, Inc.
Showrooms and Offices
New York, New York

Joel Bargmann, Jose Coriano

1979
Library and Science Building
Westover School
Middlebury, Connecticut
Page 194

Jacob Alspector, Paul Aferiat, David Knowlton, Thomas Whitrock, Howard Goldstein, Richard Gould, Richard Clarke

---

1979
Hines Residence
Martha's Vineyard, Massachusetts (project)

Gustav Rosenlof, Jose Coriano

1979
Triangle Pacific Corporation
Office Building
Dallas, Texas
Page 200

Jacob Alspector, Gustav Rosenlof, Glen Fries, Karen Jacobson, Bruce Nagel

---

1979
Knoll International
Desk and Credenza System
Page 202

Gustav Rosenlof, John Petrarca

1979
de Menil Residence
Houston, Texas
Page 204

Bruce Nagel, Daniel Rowen, Michael Monsky, Victoria Hage

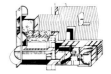

1979
de Menil Residence
East Hampton, New York
Page 208

Bruce Nagel, Daniel Rowen, Paul Aferiat, John Meder, Thomas Phifer, Frank Lupo, David Steinman, Barry McCormick, Henry Ayon

1979
Block Residence
Wilmington, North Carolina (project)
Page 222

Bruce Nagel, Daniel Rowen

1979
Einstein Moomjy
Showroom
New York, New York
Page 223

Joel Bargmann, Jose Coriano, David King

1979
Greenwich Savings Bank
New York, New York
Page 224

Joel Bargmann, Paul Aferiat, David King, Glen Fries, Jose Coriano

1979
Reliance Group Holdings, Inc.
Offices
New York, New York
Page 226

Joel Bargmann, David Knowlton, David Steinman, Joseph Ruocco, Paul Aferiat, Jose Coriano, Richard Clarke, Frank Lupo, Gustav Rosenlof, Jeffrey Feingold

1979
Morton L. Janklow & Associates
Offices
New York, New York
Page 230

Richard Gould, Joseph Ruocco

  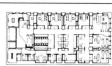

18

1979
Lincoln Center for the Performing Arts
Concourse
New York, New York
Page 232

Gustav Rosenlof, David King, Jacob Alspector

1979
Viereck Residence
Amagansett, New York
Page 234

Bruce Nagel, Daniel Rowen, Paul Aferiat

1979
Ally & Gargano, Inc.
Offices
New York, New York
Page 236

Gustav Rosenlof, William Garbus, Barry McCormick, Richard Gould, Fuensanta Nieto, Robert Anderson, Victoria Hage

1980
First City Bank
Bank and Office Building
Houston, Texas
Page 238

Joel Bargmann, Mark Simon, Victoria Hage, Robert Anderson, Urban Architecture, Inc. (Associate Architects)

1981
The Evans Partnership
Office Building
Montvale, New Jersey
Page 240

Richard Gould, Rotwein & Blake
Associated Architects, P.A. (Associate
Architects)

  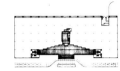

1981
Wick Alumni Center
University of Nebraska
Lincoln, Nebraska
Page 242

Bruce Nagel, Thomas Phifer, David
Steinman, Barry McCormick, Jo Merriman,
David Fukui, Fuensanta Nieto, Thomas
Whitrock, Paul Aferiat, Richard Clarke,
Frank Lupo

 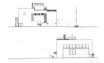 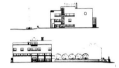

1981
Summit Hotel
New York, New York (project)

Thomas Phifer, Daniel Rowen, Earl
Swisher, Howard Goldstein, Thomas
Whitrock, Joseph Ruocco

1981
Arango Apartment
New York, New York
Page 246

Jose Coriano, Frank Lupo

1981
Westport Public Library
Westport, Connecticut
Page 250

Bruce Nagel, Dirk Kramer, Reed Morrison,
Johannes Kastner, Irene Torroella,
Margaret Fitzpatrick, Steven Forman,
Daniel Rowen, John Petrarca, Bruce
Donnally, Renny Logan

1981
de Menil Residence
Santa Monica, California
Page 254

Bruce Nagel, John Meder, Karen Renick

1981
Gimelstob Residence
New Vernon, New Jersey
Page 256

Gustav Rosenlof, David Knowlton, Barry
Silberstang, Dirk Kramer, Millan Galland

1981
Speculative Office Building
New York, New York (project)

Joel Bargmann, Richard Clarke

 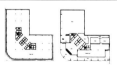

1981
de Menil Residence
New York, New York (project)

Bruce Nagel, John Petrarca, John Meder

1982
Gwathmey Siegel & Associates Architects
Offices
New York, New York
Page 260

William Garbus, Dean Marchetto

1982
Steinberg Apartment
New York, New York

Bruce Nagel, John Petrarca, John Meder

1982
Liberty National Bank
Bank and Office Building
Hobbs, New Mexico (project)

Jacob Alspector, Daniel Rowen

1982
Guggenheim Museum
Renovation and Addition
New York, New York
Page 264

Paul Aferiat, Steven Forman, Alexandra Villegas, Irene Torroella

1982
Nassau Park
Office Building
West Windsor, New Jersey

Jacob Alspector, Dirk Kramer, Margaret Fitzpatrick, Barry Silberstang, Ivan Zaknic, Earl Swisher, Elisabeth Post

1982
IBM Product Center
Prototype
Page 268

Jacob Alspector, Steven Forman, Dirk Kramer, Irene Torroella

1982
IBM Product Center
Albany, New York
Page 269

Jacob Alspector, Steven Forman, Margaret Fitzpatrick

20

1982
The Evans Partnership
Office Building
Rutherford, New Jersey
Page 270

Joel Bargmann, Joseph Ruocco, Howard Goldstein, Bruce Donnally, Christopher Egan

1982
The Evans Partnership
Office Building
Paramus, New Jersey
Page 271

Joel Bargmann, Thomas Phifer, Earl Swisher, Christopher Egan, Joseph Ruocco

 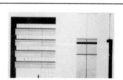

1982
The Evans Partnership
Office Building
Parsippany, New Jersey
Page 272

Thomas Phifer, Daniel Rowen, Reed Morrison, Dirk Kramer, Irene Torroella, Tim Greer, Peter Guggenheimer

1982
Beverly Hills Civic Center
Competition
Beverly Hills, California
Page 274

Jacob Alspector, Thomas Phifer, Daniel Rowen, Gustav Rosenlof, Margaret Fitzpatrick, Steven Forman, Frank Lupo, Dirk Kramer, Alexandra Villegas, Howard Goldstein, Earl Swisher, Irene Torroella, David Steinman

1982
de Menil Table Series
ICF
Page 276

Millan Galland

1982
Tapestry
V'Soske
Page 277

1983
Spielberg Apartment
New York, New York

Jose Coriano, Reese Owens

1983
International Design Center
Showroom Buildings
Long Island City, New York

Bruce Nagel, Bruce Donnally, Stephen
Lepp, P.C. Architects & Planners
(Associate Architects)

1983
The Evans Partnership
Office Building
Piscataway, New Jersey
Page 278

Thomas Phifer, Daniel Rowen, Dirk
Kramer

1983
Museum of the Moving Image
Astoria, New York
Page 280

Jacob Alspector, Tim Greer, Jude LeBlanc,
Jay Measley

1983
New York Public Library
Yorkville Branch
New York, New York

Jacob Alspector, Johannes Kastner

1983
Garey Residence
Kent, Connecticut

Bruce Nagel, Frank Lupo

1984
Gymnasium Addition and Renovation
Dartmouth College
Hanover, New Hampshire

Jacob Alspector, Reese Owens, Joseph
Ruocco

1984
Administration and Classroom Building
New York State College of Agriculture
and Life Science
Cornell University
Ithaca, New York

Bruce Nagel, Daniel Rowen, Thomas
Levering, Jude LeBlanc

Buildings and Projects

Miller Residence
Fire Island, New York

1

The site was a typical 75-foot by 100-foot linear subdivision, surrounded by existing structures. Oblique views of the ocean were possible from a height 10 feet above grade. By raising the habitable space, two objectives were accomplished; views to the ocean and a sense of privacy unattainable in an on-grade parti.

In plan, the articulated bedroom, bath and kitchen volumes flank a central, open space. Four decks extend from this space with outdoor stairs off three of them and access to storage under the fourth. The structure appears to be primarily solid, reading as a "shingled fortress." Each of the closed volumes has a shed roof, affording a clerestory window over the central volume, and natural ventilation through a wood louver system on the outside walls. These spaces are finished in rough-sawn pine, and open directly onto the central horizontal volume extended by the four decks and the views beyond. It is essentially a pavilion articulated by the shingle solids of the

2

surrounding volumes and voids between. The
building is simultaneously protected and
open, retaining a sense of seclusion and
self-containment.

3

4

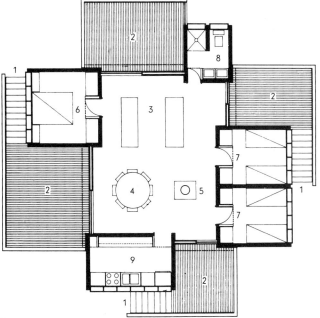

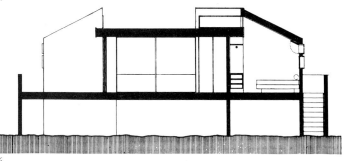

5

6

Herlinger-Bristol Ltd.
Showrooms and Offices
New York, New York

Herlinger-Bristol Limited incorporated the merging of two firms, a textile design firm and a textile manufacturing firm. The location was an existing Broadway loft building with an oblique floor plan of 6,000 square feet.

The program required a reception area, two showrooms, a design/weaving room, offices for the president and vice-president, and production, accounting and sales areas. The fabric designs are conceived and woven in the weaving room, then sent to the factory for production.

The plan configuration was generated by a need for public circulation and access to the showrooms, weaving room and offices. These spaces contain major transparent openings to the circulation space, which admit natural light to the center of the floor while allowing reference to the outside walls of the building. The circulation space is further articulated by a low curved wall in the center, enclosing the production area, an open space furnished with custom-designed work stations.

The materials are maple flooring, painted gypsum-board walls, acoustical tile ceiling and lacquer cabinetwork.

1

1.Entry/reception gallery 2.Reception gallery
3.Showroom 4.Production work area
5.Weaving room 6.Plan

2

3

4

5

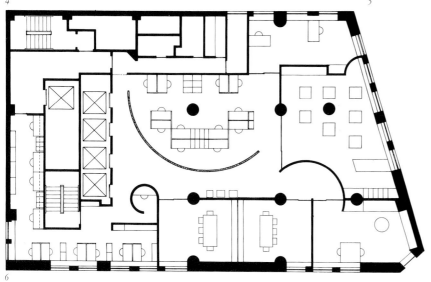

6

Gwathmey Residence and Studio
Amagansett, New York

At the time of design, the one-acre flat field was surrounded by undeveloped adjacent sites. Future construction was anticipated, however, and has since occurred. Access and views over the dunes to the ocean are from the south. The program was to initially provide a living/dining space, kitchen, master bedroom/studio, two guest bedrooms and a workroom. A year after completion a second structure was added, accommodating a guest room and full studio.

Within the limited budget, a design parti and vernacular were developed that set precedents for later work. The house is 1,200 square feet and 30,000 cubic feet, describing a composition of geometric and volumetric assemblages.

By organizing the building vertically, programmatic and site constraints were inherently resolved through section as well as plan manipulation. The guest rooms, workroom and covered terrace occupy the ground floor, the living/dining room, kitchen and deck occupy the second floor, with the master bedroom/studio on the third-floor balcony overlooking the double-height living space. Raising the public spaces one level above grade not only capitalized on the extensive views, but established a living/ground relationship that was unique to rural house architecture. By placing the continuously occupied portion of the habitable house on a base of intermittent functions, the parlor floor was reinterrupted and a sense of privacy was established.

With the addition of the studio building, the site/object relationship was extended and enriched. The second structure's section was derived from the house, but by siting it at a 45-degree angle to the initial structure a perceptual formal dynamic was created. A second perception was also established by the juxtaposition of the building to ground relationships: whereas the house clearly is ground anchored, the studio seems precarious and appears almost in movement. The sense of duality, expectation and change adds another dimension to the overall composition.

Both buildings, whose geometric forms are manipulated in response to site, orientation, program and structure, are fundamentally primary and minimal. They appear to be carved from a solid, rather than the result of

1

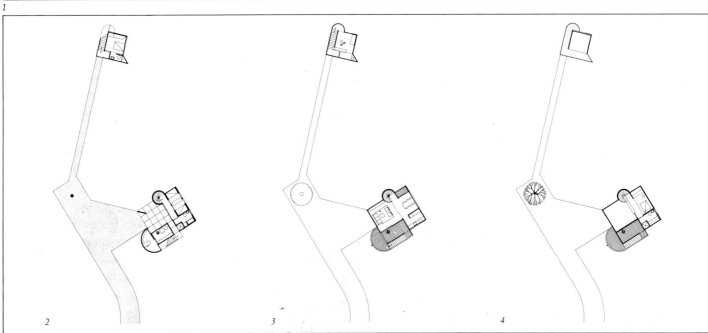

2   3   4

an additive assemblage. The dynamics of form are enriched by exploiting and revealing the intersection, either by erosion or by the inclusion of natural light, or by both. The buildings are wood frame with cedar siding on both the interior and exterior, establishing a primary referential container from which secondary and tertiary elements are articulated. Transparency, perceptual and literal extension, and volumetric interpenetration give this small building a unique sense of scale and presence.

1. Studio and residence from northwest
2. Ground floor plan 3. Second floor plan
4. Third floor plan 5. North facade 6. Studio and residence from southwest 7. South facade
8. Section A 9. Section B

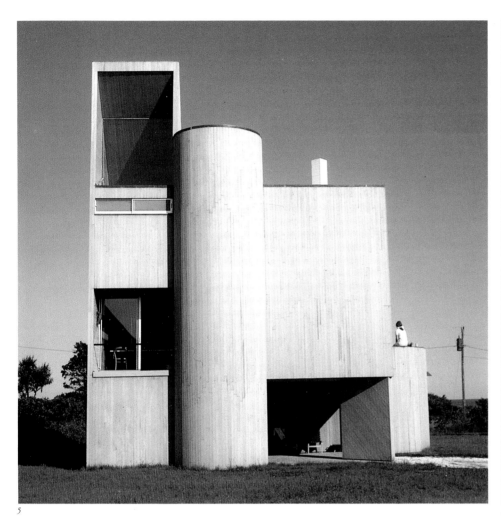

5

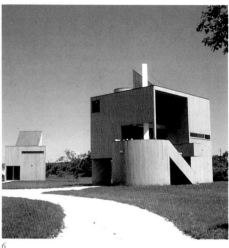

6

7

29

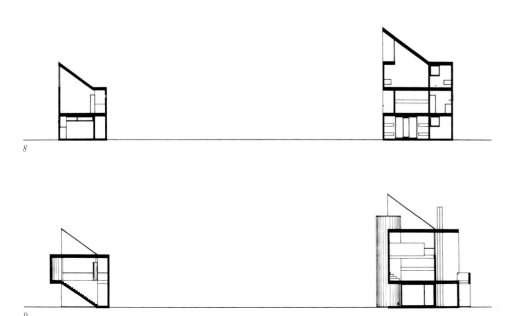

8

9

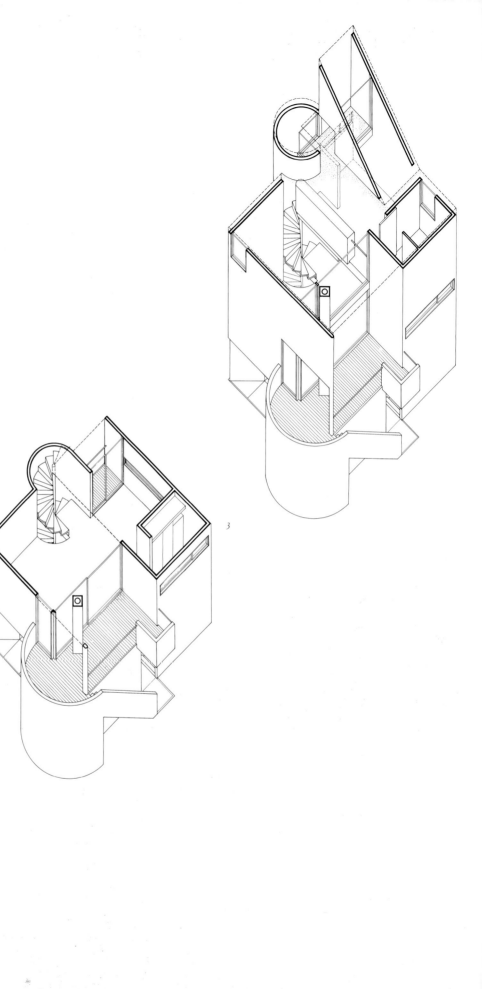

3

2

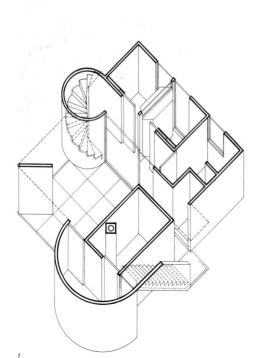

1

1.Ground floor axonometric 2.Second floor
axonometric 3.Third floor axonometric
4.Living room 5.View of deck from balcony
6.View of living/dining room and master
bedroom balcony 7.Ceiling detail 8.East
facade 9.West facade 10.South facade

4

5

6

7

31

8

9

10

The problem was to design a residence on a large wooded site which did not offer preferable views or topographical variation. The client was a couple with two children. Local zoning ordinances required that a new structure enclose a minimum volume of 30,000 cubic feet and be designed in the colonial style with pitched roofs. These constraints provoked a reinterpretation of a known vernacular idiom.

The program specified a living room, dining room and kitchen which would be organized on the ground floor, and a master bedroom, dressing-room suite and two children's rooms which would be disposed on the second floor. This traditional vertical organization was manipulated volumetrically, allowing for the transformation of the standard center-hall plan X type.

Both the plan and sections were articulated by the two diagonal roof planes which transverse the entire structure and are revealed in elevation and from both the second and ground floor spaces.

Since the site has no specific views, the variation in the fenestration reveals the ground, the middles of trees, the tops of trees and the sky, through openings which also articulate the intersection of forms and the formal disposition of spaces.

The major materials are stucco, exterior and interior, slate floors on the ground, oak floors on the second floor, oak cabinetwork and terne-metal standing seam roofs.

1

2

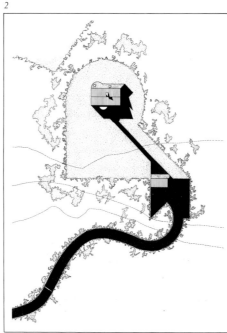

3

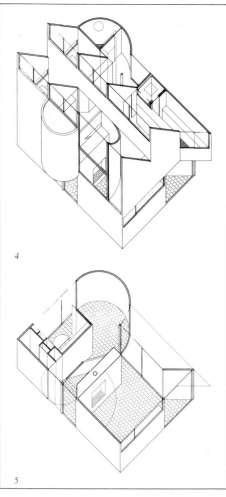

4

5

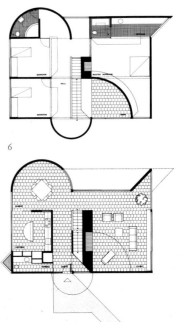

6

7

1.East facade 2.South facade 3.Site plan
4.Second floor axonometric 5.Ground floor
axonometric 6.Second floor plan 7.Ground
floor plan 8.North facade 9.Living room
10.Dining room and gallery space 11.Living
room 12.Section A 13.Section B

8

9

10

33

11

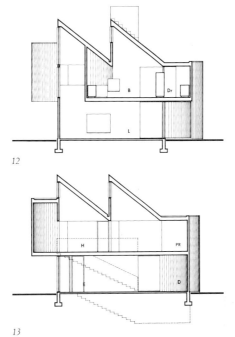

13

12

Sedacca Residence
East Hampton, New York

The problem was to design a vacation house on a two-acre wooded, sloping site. The client was a graphic designer. The program required a major living/dining space, a kitchen, a master-bedroom/studio suite and a separate guest bedroom, plus a storage structure. In addition it called for a view to the bay from the second level.

The parti was derived from the constraints of a modest budget, a buildable site proximate to the road, and a desire for maximum privacy. The storage structure defines the area and the transition from the parking place to the entry walk. The walk leads directly toward an erosion on the curved volume of the primarily solid front facade. Upon entry, the major two-story living/dining space opens to an outdoor terrace extension, modulated by the chimney element engaged by the two-story glass facade. The space is airy and transparent, enclosed on two sides by the kitchen and guest suite on the ground floor and the master-bedroom suite and studio on the second level.

The plan is elemental; a rectangle with a semicircular extension. The volume becomes more complex, involving the manipulation of section, transparency, extension and the juxtaposition of solid/void relationships. The articulation of the chimney element, the spiral stair, the built-in cabinetwork and furniture enrich and complete the composition and articulate its parts.

1.Ground floor axonometric 2.Second floor axonometric 3.Ground floor plan 4.Second floor plan 5.Section A 6.Section B 7.Section C 8.West facade 9.Southeast facade 10.Living/dining space toward entry 11.Living/dining space from entry 12.Studio space and bedroom at second floor

34

5   6   7

8   9

10   11   12

Goldberg Residence
Manchester, Connecticut

1

The problem was to design a residence on a four-acre, wooded, sloping site with a major view northwest across the valley to Hartford. The client was a family with three children. Access was from the west and bottom of the site, with the drive meandering vertically through the woods.

The parti was generated by the client's desire to have a horizontal organization, accommodating entry, garage/storage, living/dining space, kitchen and terrace on the main level, locating the master-bedroom suite and study one half-level up, and the children's bedrooms and playroom one half-level down from the main level. This organization not only separates the living spaces from the sleeping spaces, but separates the parents from the children by a full level; at the same time it exploits the views and integrates the topography.

The section manipulation allows for south to penetrate the major spaces while preference to views across the valley. grass terrace extends the living level

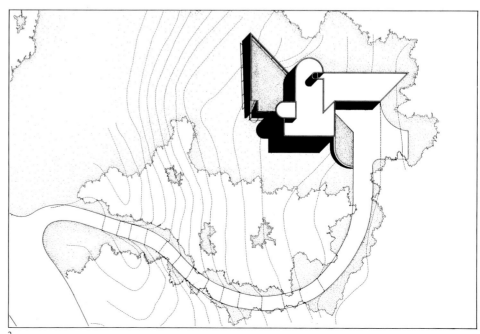

2

both literally and perceptually, establishing "new ground" overviewing natural ground, defining the useable area yet participating in the extended site and views. The terrace wall guarantees privacy from the road and anchors the house to the site.

1.West facade 2.Site plan 3.Stair with view to study and terrace 4.Living/dining space 5.View of living/dining space from terrace 6.Axonometric 7.Basement and first floor plan 8.Second and third floor plan

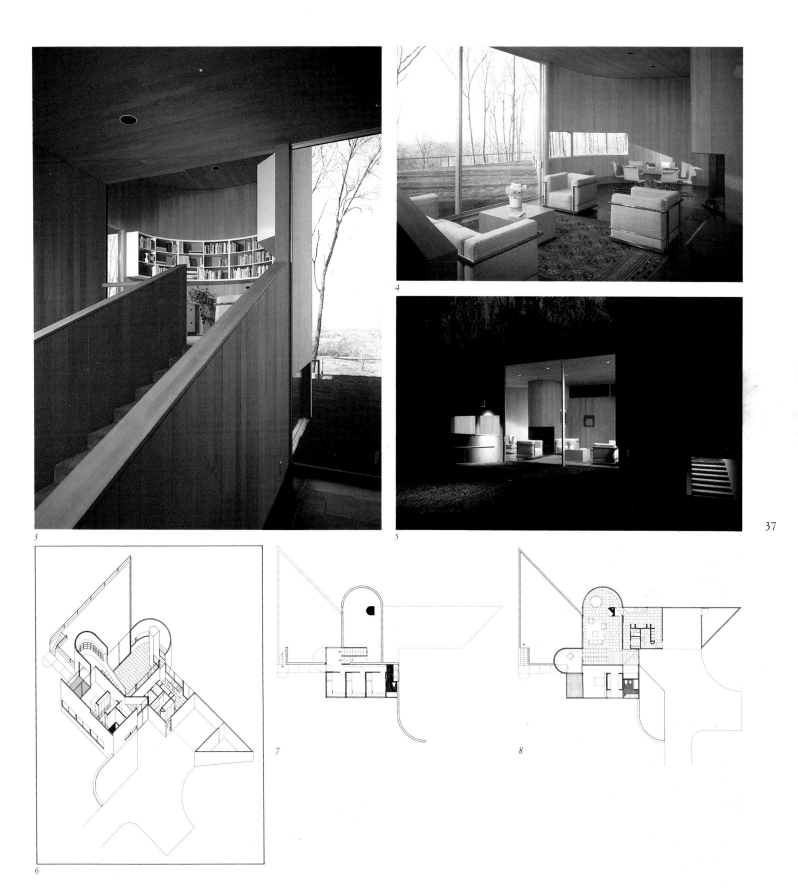

3

4

5

6

7

8

Cooper Residence
Orleans, Massachusetts

The problem was to design a residence on a peninsula with panoramic views of both the bay and ocean beyond. The client was a family with four daughters. The building site was limited to a knoll with access from the north. There was a programmatic requirement to separate the parents' master-bedroom suite from the children's bedrooms and to build a separate garage and boat storage structure.

The organization is similar to the Gwathmey Residence in that the public spaces—living room, dining room and kitchen—separate the two private spaces vertically. The entry is by a ramp/bridge from the parking area and garage into the public or middle level of the building. The master bedroom is a balcony overlooking the double-height living space and terrace, and is extended by a semicircular deck over the dining space below. The children's rooms are dormitory-like and adjacent to a major playroom, all opening to grade at the lower level.

The formal manipulation of transparency, extension and volumetric interrelationships are referential, yet more complex than in the Gwathmey Residence. The nautical quality is more evident because of the site, the access, and the sense of leaving the land and being surrounded by water.

1

2

1.*Southeast facade* 2.*West facade* 3.*Ground floor axonometric* 4.*Second floor axonometric* 5.*Third floor axonometric* 6.*Site plan* 7.*View of living space from balcony* 8.*View of deck and dining area*

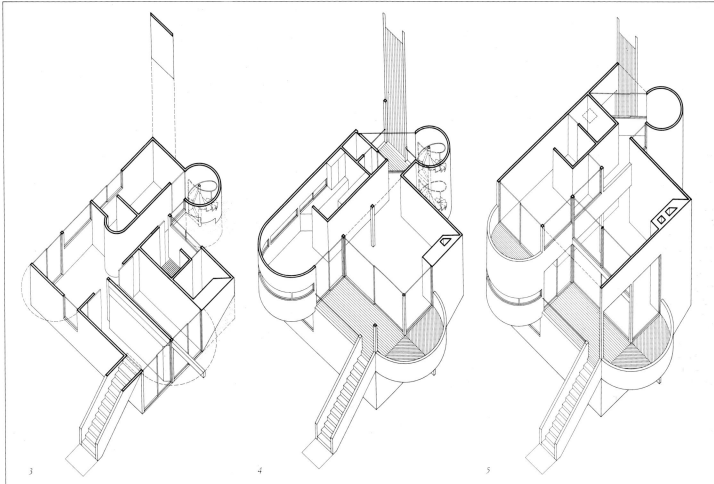

3   4   5

39

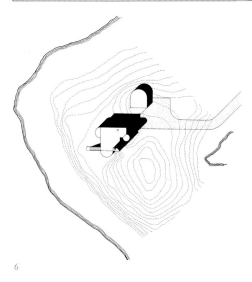

6

7

8

The problem was to design a residence for a
retired couple on a three-acre ocean/dune
site, to be shared by another Gwathmey
Siegel residence built for one of the couple's
children and his family. The beach and ocean
is due south with the access road on the
north.

The program required an indoor pool and
related facilities, living/dining space, kitchen,
two guest bedrooms, master-bedroom suite
and garage.

The organization was generated by the
vertical layering of a major central space. The
pool, one half-level below entry and grade,
the living/dining space and the study are all
interconnected, literally and visually, by a
center stair, chimney element and balcony
overviews.

The garage and guest bedrooms occupy the
ground floor and the kitchen and
master-bedroom suite share the second level
with the living/dining space, which opens to
an outdoor deck facing the ocean on the
south facade.

The parti, though many times larger, is
similar to that of the Sedacca Residence in
that it combines the solid rectangular and
semicircular plan elements, presenting a
"solid" front and an "open" back; however,
it is more complex and intensified in the
section/volumetric manipulation and the plan
intersections and erosions.

It also refers, on the south facade, to the
Gwathmey Residence, in that the major roof
overhang completes the primary rectilinear
form. The roof overhang also becomes an
architectonic brise-soleil which
simultaneously extends the living spaces
visually and shades the southern glass
expanse from the summer sun.

40

1

2

3

4   5

6   7

1.Residences I and II from west 2.Northeast facade 3.South facade 4.North section
5.South section 6.East section 7.West section
8.View east from deck toward residence 2

9.Pool space with view to dining balcony
10.Site plan 11.Sectional axonometric
12.Ground floor plan 13.Second floor plan
14.Third floor plan

8

9

10

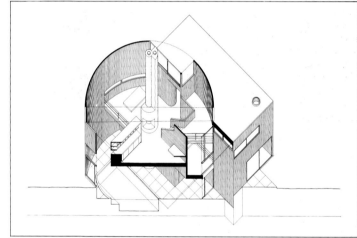

11

41

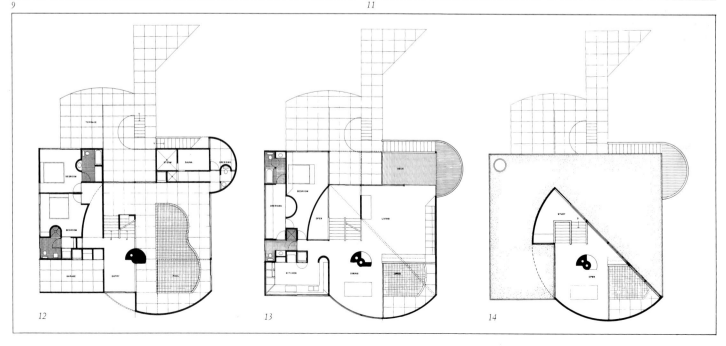

12

13

14

Steel Residence II
Bridgehampton, New York

The problem was to design a residence for a family with three children on the same three-acre ocean/dune site where another Gwathmey Siegel residence, designed for the parents of the owner, already existed.

The parti was generated by the desire to accommodate the family bedrooms on the ground level, with the living/dining and kitchen spaces on the second level and a guest suite on the third level. Thus the ground floor, which also includes a garage/storage room, a maid's room and a playroom, is dense and horizontal. The only vertical extension is the stair and the one-and-a-half-story playroom, which is overviewed from the kitchen above. The second level is composed of a major two-story living/dining space which is modulated by a fireplace chimney element and a bar/hi-fi storage cabinet. This space is extended by a two-story deck which is connected to the dune by a bridge. The guest suite on the third level partially overviews the living/dining space and opens to a roof deck over the kitchen below.

The functional organization was overlaid with a formal geometric plan construct of two equal intersecting circles. These circles were subsequently eroded in plan and section to articulate and order the spatial hierarchies. As with the earlier Gwathmey Siegel residence, the front is "solid," the back is "void." The use of the integrated brise-soleil and the resultant structure presents primary volumetric readings with major exterior erosions.

Both of the Bridgehampton buildings were

42

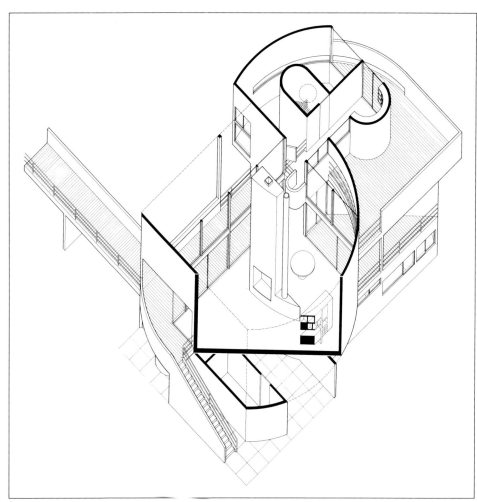

1

manifestations of formal geometric investigations overlaid with programmatic requirements. The result was a compromise in that there is not the clarity or the control that existed in the earlier houses. However, the lesson learned was that the composite structuring of the smaller primary buildings could not be directly extendable into larger programs without a new construct, a denser and more complex system of privacy, and secondary and tertiary architectural hierarchies.

1.Sectional axonometric 2.Northeast facade
3.Ground floor plan 4.Second floor plan
5.Third floor plan 6.Southwest facade 7.East
section 8.West section 9.North section

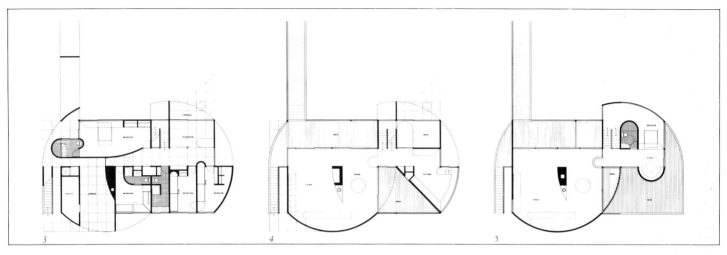

3   4   5

6

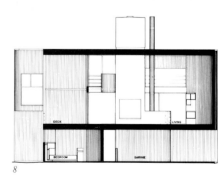

7   8

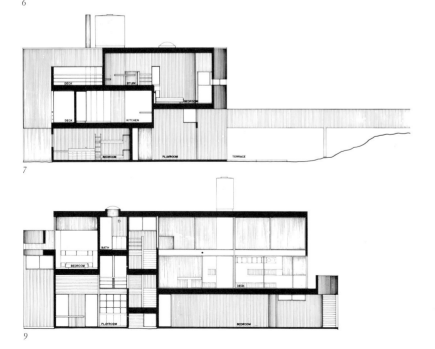

9

Dunaway Apartment
New York, New York

The problem was to design an apartment on the twentieth floor of an existing 1930s building. The floor was originally two apartments, forming a maze of small rooms with varying ceiling heights and random exposed structure. The views east over Central Park, south to the Manhattan skyline and west to the New Jersey Palisades are extensive and provoked the widening of all major window openings.

The intention was to create a "pavilion in the sky" where there would be a sense of isolation, privacy, serenity, permanence and sanctuary—elusive qualities in a city dwelling. One enters a gallery which opens to the living/dining space and the views beyond. Off the gallery is a guest room, a library, a maid's room, a kitchen and a bar/hi-fi room, all of which are distributed linearly front-to-back. Off the living/dining space is the master-bedroom suite which includes a dressing room and extensive bathroom and terrace. This space, separated by a mirrored sliding door, is meant to be a literal as well as an illusory extension of the main space. A black slate floor, white walls and ceilings, and black and white lacquer cabinetwork intensify the surreal and narrative "place creation."

2

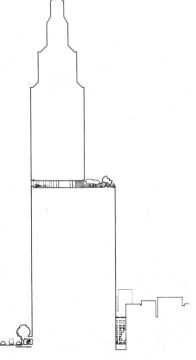

1

3

*1.Section 2.Living/dining space 3.Master
bedroom 4.Axonometric 5.Bathroom
6.Dining area with view toward bedroom*

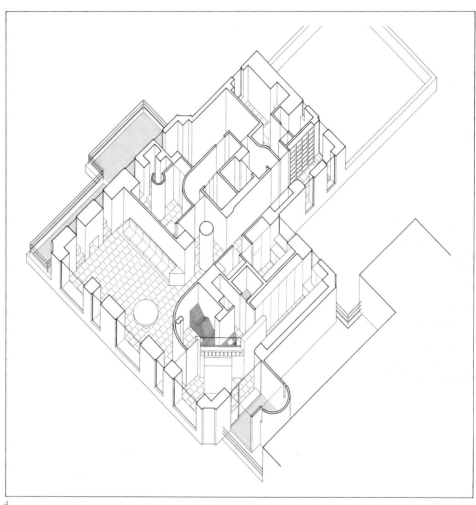

4

5

6

1

The problem was to design a service-group complex for a major new state university. The site was wooded and steeply sloping, with an adjacent access road.

The design was an economical solution which accommodated the strict programmatic requirements on a difficult site. The warehouse, office and workshop building acts as the road reference and site-retaining structure, thus enabling the center service court to be flat. The maintenance garage and supervisor's office acts as the control point and exit building to the campus. The boiler plant structure steps down the hill, enabling the stacked organization of storage stalls on the court side, with offices, electrical meter rooms and storage on the boiler room side at the lower level, maintaining the required

26-foot ceiling height in the boiler room proper.

The exterior walls are block and campus-standard brick, and are separated from the structure by a continuous skylight. This not only provides fresh air, a natural and uninterrupted light source and a freeing of vertical wall surfaces, but it exploits the connection between steel frame roof construction and masonry vertical wall construction as a formal resolution. It also allows for flexible interior planning and helps to create a clear system for ordering the required ceiling height variation within each building.

1.Northwest facade 2.View of service court
3.Site plan and ground floor plan

2

3

The problem was to design the first student dormitory for a major new state university. The master plan and academic buildings were already designed. The parameters were the sloping site, the choice of brick as an exterior material, the glazing system of anodized bronze aluminum, the three-story height limitation on campus elevation and the rigid programmatic and budget requirements of the New York State Dormitory Authority. The residential complex houses 800 students, faculty advisors and a faculty master. The dining facility seats 400 and, with multiple sittings, can provide food service for the residential complex as well as for commuter students. To enrich the living environment, academic and student activity areas are integrated into both facilities.

The U-shaped building complex encloses a major outdoor space which is open-ended to the south, providing a transition between the natural environment of the meadow and the formal discipline of the campus plan.

The two main gateways to the complex are from the commuter student parking lot and from the south end of the academic campus. This entry elevation is a berm, one level above natural grade, which makes it possible for the building to step down a full floor as the grade lowers, and for the horizontal roof height to remain constant while the building changes from three to four stories. The berm also allows for the major existing trees to be retained.

The dormitory organizes student accommodations into eight groups, with four main entrance points off the berm elevation which houses the lobby, a seminar room and a common room. Each floor unit of 20 includes several types of rooms: four-, six- and eight-person suites, corridor doubles and singles and a public floor lounge. Circulation on each level is restricted to the zone between stairs and entry points. A continuous enclosed horizontal corridor is provided at the lower level to facilitate service and to allow indoor circulation throughout the complex during inclement weather.

The dining facility is entered from the berm walk and is serviced on the lower level. Student activity spaces occupy the entrance level and second floor and surround the upper portion of the main dining space. Food is served on the lower level, which opens out to the meadow. Dining spaces can accommodate 15, 50, 100 and 200 persons.

1.Dining hall and student activities center from the courtyard 2.Dormitory wing from the courtyard 3.Pedestrian entry gate

1

2

3

47

1.Lower level plan 2.Entrance level plan
3.Second level plan 4.Third level plan 5.View
looking north 6.View looking east 7.Site plan
8.Axonometric 9.Exterior stair to courtyard
10.Detail of typical dormitory entry
11.Lounge space in dining hall 12.Entry space
in dining hall 13.View of dining hall from
entry balcony

48

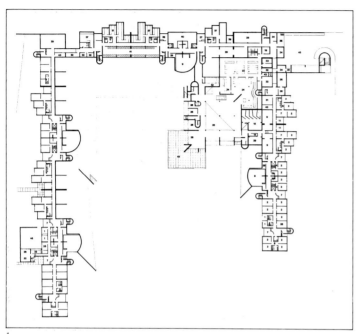

1

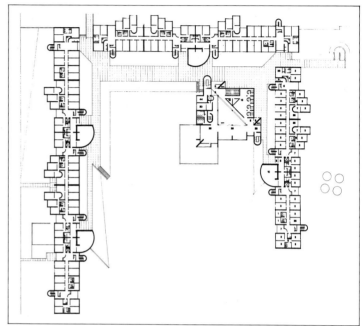

2

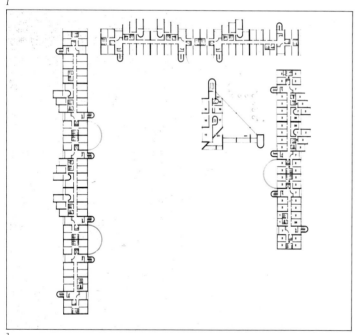

3

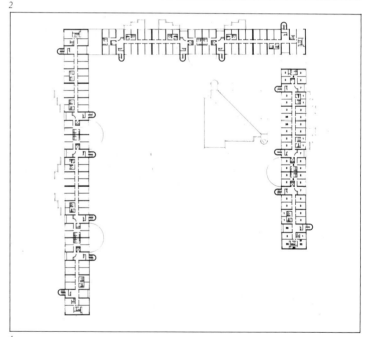

4

5

6

This object building serves as the referential structure in the complex; it is organized vertically and horizontally and modulated volumetrically, in a different scale than, but similar to, the residences.

The construction of the entire complex utilized an oversized clay modular wall unit which, within a single width (8 or 12 inches), satisfied all structural, finish and weathering requirements. A precast concrete-floor deck spans bearing walls 24 feet apart which accommodate two student rooms. Window openings are spanned with a precast brick lintel and glazed with an aluminum window system. Stair systems are standardized precast units extending from floor to landing. Interior in-fill walls, between structural walls, are gypsum board. The major technical objective was to employ prefabricated, factory produced products, thereby reducing the need for field labor and affording a continuous, nonoverlapping construction sequence.

This parti is based upon the reinterpreted model of the large-scale cloister or urban/rural square with a dominant architectural object in its center. It could also be read as frame (dormitory) and object (dining facility), as in the case of Whig Hall, or as the transformation of the medieval walled town, secure and enclosing.

7

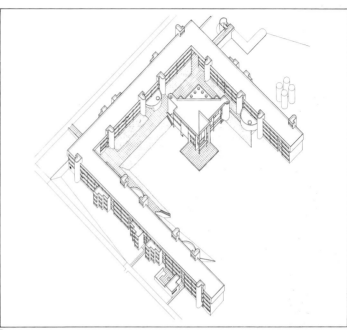

8

9

10

11

49

12

13

Gwathmey Siegel Architects
Offices
New York, New York

This small duplex studio on the seventh floor of Carnegie Hall was not altered in any major way. The existing interior container was simply repainted and the cabinetwork elements strategically placed, describing new versus existing and functional versus literal space. The double-height volume accommodated the reception and waiting area, two drafting stations behind a low exhibition dividing cabinet and a stair up to the second level balcony loft. This space accommodated the conference room, drafting space and other support areas.

This studio/atelier satisfied the needs of Gwathmey Siegel for a period of seven years and represented the second phase of the practice.

1.Entry/reception area 2.Reception area from drafting balcony 3.Detail of drafting space 4.Plan

1

2

3

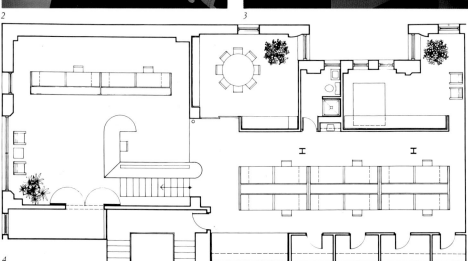

4

Eskilson Residence
Roxbury, Connecticut

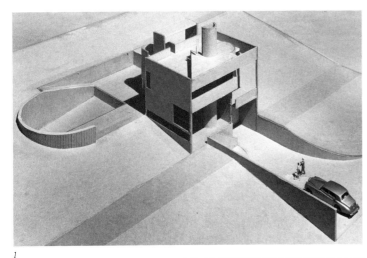

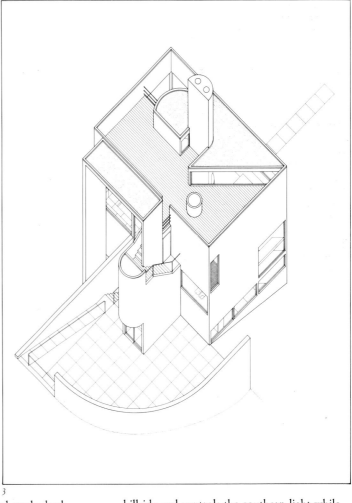

The problem was to design a residence on a 10-acre, steeply sloping wooded site, with a continuously rising hillside to the south and an access road and panoramic views over the valley to the north.

The garage/storage, entry, and two guest rooms are located on the lower level on the north facade. The second level, with grade access to the south opening to a wall-retained pool and terrace, is occupied by the living/dining room and kitchen, while the third level accommodates the master-bedroom suite and study, both balcony spaces overlooking the double-height living space.

This was a pivotal design in that, for the first time, even though the program was not extensive, the primary container, or referential cube, was modulated vertically and horizontally by secondary articulate forms and volumes serving as pertinent architectural elements in the composition. The site/building interlocking stair and articulated brise-soleil establishes a second scale to the hillside and controls the southern light while shifting the architectural gesture of orientation from the front to the back. In other words, the view is still to the north but the articulation and primary reading of the building is to the south—the pedestrian and private side of the house and site.

1.Northeast view of model 2.Southeast view of model 3.Axonometric 4.Ground floor plan 5.Second floor plan 6.Third floor plan

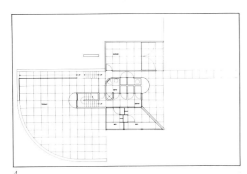

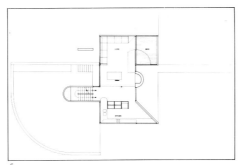

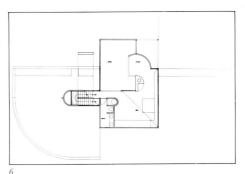

Whig Hall
Princeton University
Princeton, New Jersey

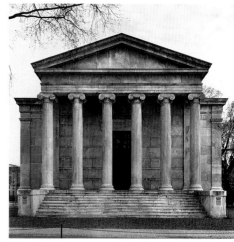

1

2

3

4

Nassau Hall and the twin neoclassical temple structures, Clio Hall and Whig Hall, form an axial composition defining Cannon Green in the center of the Princeton campus. Whig Hall, with the exception of the exterior walls, was destroyed by fire and required the total reconstruction of its interior. The Whig Debating Society was still to be its primary user, but the restructured building would also be open to the public.

The new program specified 10,000 square feet of space to replace the 7,000 square feet of the original structure. The building was to include Whig offices, a conference room, work room, information center, lounge, student president's office, a flexible meeting room with multi-media capabilities which could seat up to 250 people for debates, lectures, movies, receptions and meals, two seminar rooms, and a lounge space, the James Madison Room.

The three major problems were to maintain the privacy and integrity of the Whig facilities while making the remaining spaces accessible to the rest of the university, to reconstitute the structural integrity of the existing shell, and to retain the pertinent historical precedents of the building.

A solution was reached by analyzing these three constraints, while addressing existing campus site and building precedents, existing campus pedestrian circulation systems and priorities, and the new code requirements of a fireproof and air-conditioned building. The initial strategy of retaining the existing shell and building a new structure within that framework supported the university's traditional context and respected the neoclassical type.

First a new structural system that was independent yet wall bracing was designed. After demolition, new full-height columns, with their integral shear heads, were lowered from the top and anchored to new foundations, which were separated from the existing walls to avoid overloading and undermining the existing foundation. Once the columns were in place, the new roof slab was poured, integral with a reinforced concrete tension ring around the entire cornice and a pretension concrete beam on the south wall, thus stabilizing and enclosing the entire shell. The south wall panel was removed and the entire construction was completed in the enclosed structure. The result is a neoclassical temple embracing and revealing a twentieth-century, free-plan object building.

The classic temple elements of base, stair, portico, columns, cornice and pediment enclosing a single space determined the reference and the design parti. In plan and facade, the integrity and revelation of the single space or volume whose corners were inviolate was primary. Whether by implication or fact, this strategy reinforced the idea of the free plan and the resulting forms and spaces. The dialogue between classic temple references and the new object intervention restates the clarity of the original precedents, reestablishes the primacy of the frame, and reinterprets both objects in

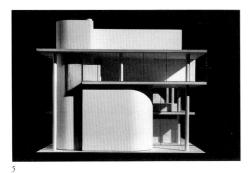

5   6   7

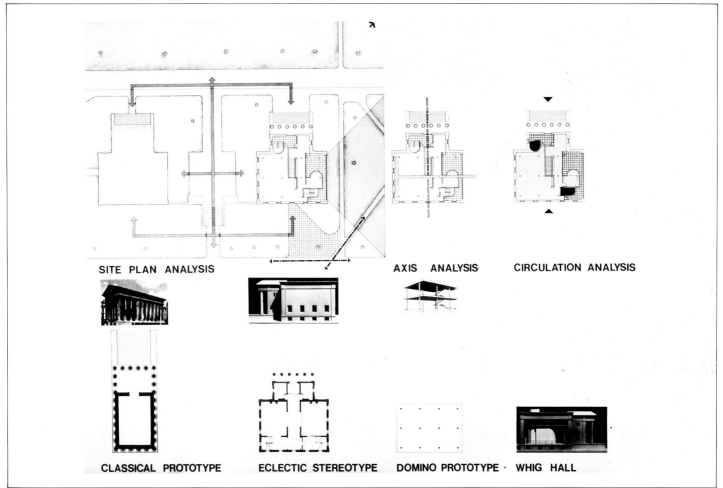

SITE PLAN ANALYSIS   AXIS ANALYSIS   CIRCULATION ANALYSIS

CLASSICAL PROTOTYPE   ECLECTIC STEREOTYPE   DOMINO PROTOTYPE · WHIG HALL

8

53

juxtaposition to, but in support of, the whole.

1.Rear facades of Clio Hall left, and Whig Hall right 2.Whig Hall front facade 3.Facade opposite Clio Hall 4.New facade 5.6.7.Views of model 8.Diagrams 9.Site plan 10.Ground floor plan

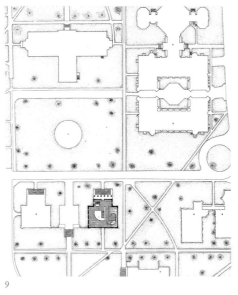

9

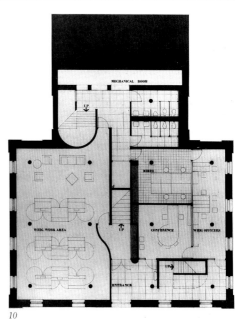

10

1   2   3

54

4

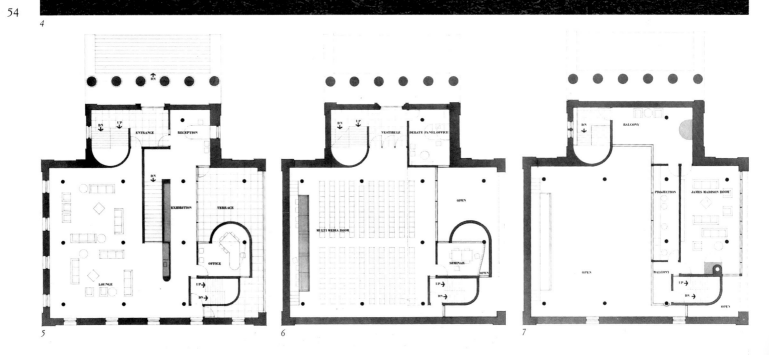

5   6   7

1.New column inserted through existing structure 2.New structure inserted 3.East Wall removed panel 4.Northeast facade

5.First floor plan 6.Second floor plan 7.Third floor plan 8.View of terrace to campus 9.Entry exhibition space 10.East facade

11.Multi-use space and projection room 12.New east facade 13.Stair tower detail 14.View of multi-use space from speaker's platform

8

9

10

11

12

13

14

1

2

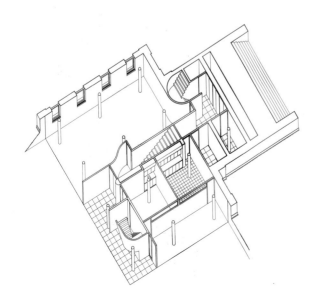

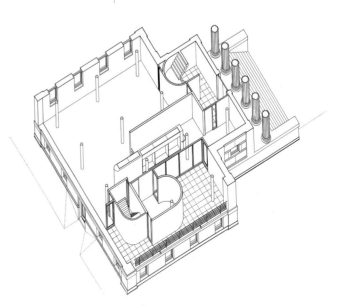

5

6

1.*Soffit detail* 2.*Detail of office* 3.*Stair detail*
4.*Stair detail* 5.*Ground floor axonometric*   6.*First floor axonometric* 7.*Second floor*
axonometric* 8.*Third floor axonometric*

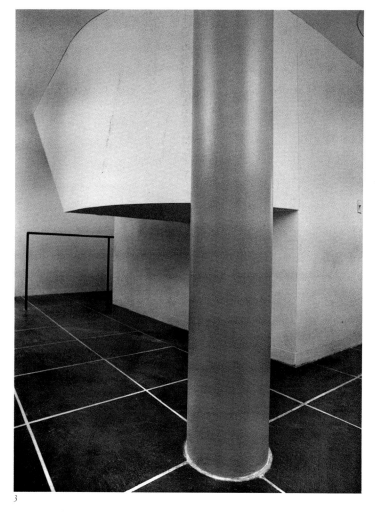

3

4

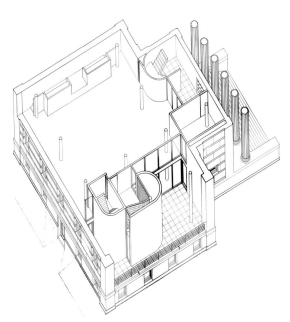

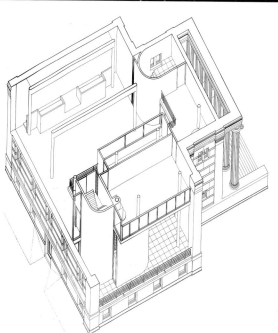

7

8

Tolan Residence
Amagansett, New York

The problem was to design a residence on a one-acre flat field. To the south the site had a natural gully filled with indigenous growth, and on the adjacent site to the east was the Gwathmey Residence and Studio.

The program required a single living/dining/kitchen space, a master bedroom, three guest rooms, a game room and a tennis court. The location of the tennis court was fixed by zoning regulations, thus a 60-foot by 120-foot area was dictated. The strong presence of the two adjacent Gwathmey buildings made necessary an appropriate site organization and building composition that would simultaneously reinforce object identity while preserving programmatic intentions and privacy.

The parti was determined by accommodating the tennis court as integral to the building and site organization and by zoning the house into two distinct, connected, yet articulate elements—the guest house and the main house. The main house is located on the western area of the site, anchoring the southwest corner of the tennis court. The master bedroom is located on the lower level, separated from the guest bedrooms by the main entry, which also connects to the court. The living/dining/kitchen space occupies the second level and opens to a major horizontal deck over the guest room/playroom area below, with overviews of the tennis court to the north and the ocean to the south. At the east end of the deck, a spiral outdoor stair reconnects down to the tennis court and the playroom, while on the west end another outdoor stair provides access to the roof above the kitchen/dining space. This area is private and affords panoramic views of the ocean through the upper clerestory window of the living space.

The east side of the tennis court is bounded by a 12-foot high, 120-foot long wall, terminated by a small guest house/storage structure (unbuilt) which completes the composition. This wall becomes the landscape referential plane for the three object buildings (Tolan, Gwathmey Residence and Studio). They are grouped around a common compass point, from which each radiates outward, presenting a sequence of oblique views to the others. In the composition, each object reinforces the other, creating a perceptual dialogue while maintaining individual privacy and views.

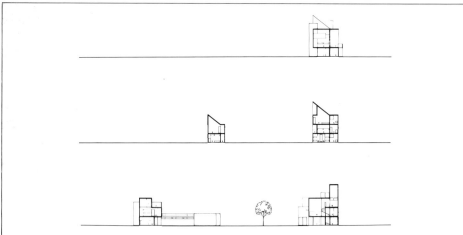

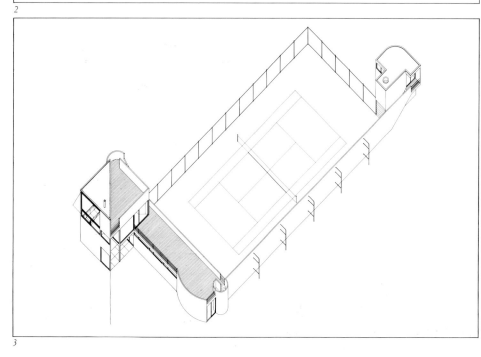

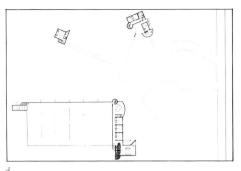

4

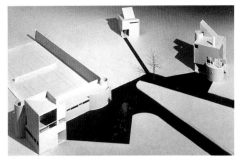

5

1.South facade 2.Sections 3.Axonometric
4.Ground floor plan 5.Model of the ensemble
with Gwathmey residence and Studio
6.Southeast facade 7.View of Tolan Residence
with Gwathmey Studio in foreground 8.View
of north facade from tennis court 9.View of
deck toward living/dining/kitchen space
10.Living/dining space 11.View of living
space from upper roof deck 12.Southeast
facade

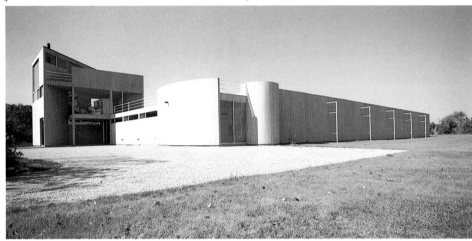

6

7

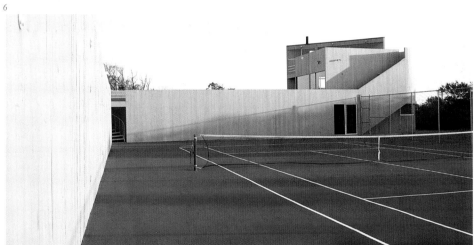

8

9

59

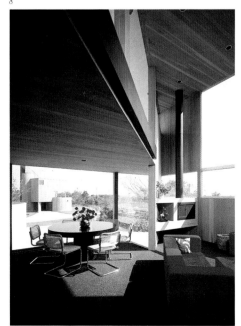

10

11

12

1

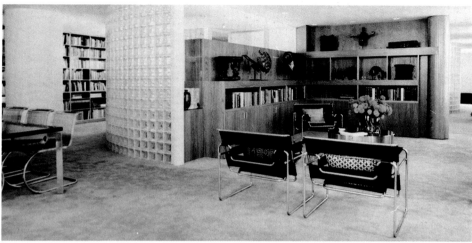

2

3

4

The problem was to renovate a vintage 1920s apartment which had one window facing Central Park and west and others facing north to similar buildings across the street. The existing space was divided into two defined zones, living and service, connected by an opening and corridor that could not be enlarged. Other fixed elements were structural columns, a fireplace wall and the building plumbing lines.

The program was complex in that it provided separate study/offices for a writer couple, storage for an extensive book collection, and exhibition space for an excellent African sculpture collection, in addition to a living/dining space, eat-in kitchen, master-bedroom suite and a private guest room.

The parti was similar to the Whig Hall parti in that the existing container or frame was modulated by the intervention of a complex new "object," which accommodated both studies, master bathroom and dressing room, while articulating the dining, living, gallery and book storage spaces. The kitchen and guest bedroom occupy the service zone, with the existing connection positioned on-axis to the entry and adjacent to the dining space. The use of glass block, oak cabinetwork, interior clerestory windows and sliding mirror pocket-doors reinforces the transformation of a formerly drab, horizontal, cellular interior into a complex, dual-scaled, modulated pavilion, serving as house, office and gallery.

1.Entrance foyer 2.View of living/dining room 3.Study 4.Bedroom 5.Axonometric

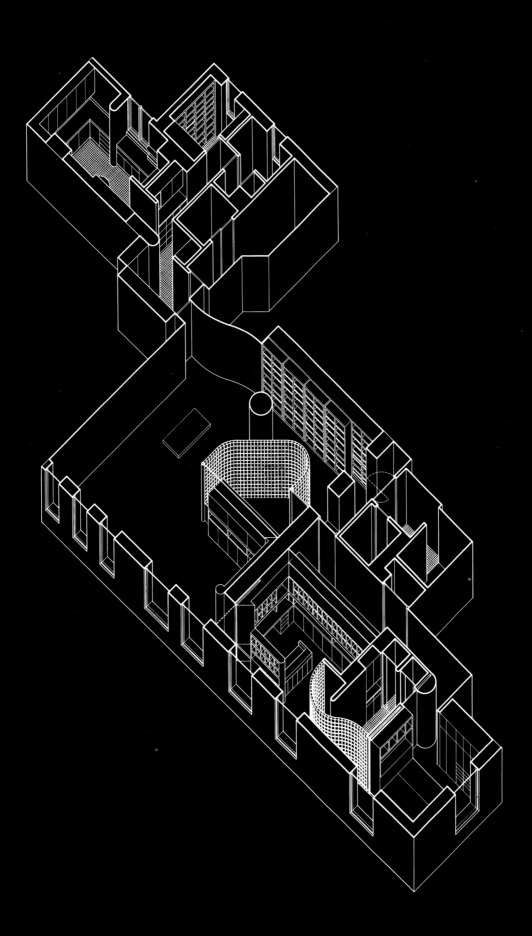

Cogan Residence
East Hampton, New York

The problem was to design a year-round residence on a five-acre gently sloping site, with an access point to the east, an adjacent residence to the north, and a pond to the south and west with dunes and ocean beyond.

This was the largest program since the Steel Residences, and the opportunity came at a pivotal point after the design of the Eskilson Residence and Whig Hall. The program required a separate children's zone incorporating three bedrooms and a playroom, a large living/dining space, a kitchen, a master-bedroom suite which included a sitting room and study, a separate guest suite, covered parking, outdoor storage and a swimming pool.

The major element of the building is the large rectangular frame, penetrated horizontally and vertically by a composite, sculptural secondary building which modulates and extends the primary volume form. To take advantage of the panoramic views and to establish an architectural presence on a majestic site within the two-part construct, the living/dining and kitchen areas and master bedroom were elevated to the second level. The lower level accommodates the parking and service core (dumbwaiter and stair), the two-and-a-half-story entry porch, the foyer, the children's bedrooms, and the playroom which is located a half-level below grade. This zone establishes the base of the building, which is basically solid and cellular, and on which a pavilion has been placed. In a sense, the roof of the base becomes the new datum for the major public space, whose roof is supported by a columnar structure penetrating through the base building and articulating the upper volume.

The lower level is zoned by the entry, which separates the car and service areas from the children's area. The entry permits direct access to the pool terrace, changing rooms and service spaces, and is the point of origin for the ramp. The half-level landings and the linear circulation inherent in the ramp space develop the multiple and sequential spatial and view experiences through the house. The first leg parallels the children's bedrooms, which are articulated as outdoor entries with their doors and frosted-glass interior clerestory windows. This sense of walking past the exterior of a building is accentuated by the linear skylight two-and-a-half stories over the children's corridor and by the use of cedar siding inside as well as out. There is an expectation of going to the roof. The first landing arrives at the master bedroom, a modulated one- and two-story high space. The second landing, above the entry and

62

1

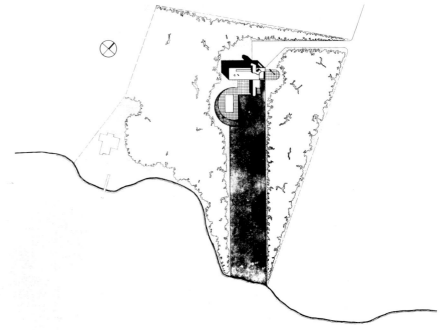

2

looking down through the entry portico, is the living/dining and kitchen level with a large deck and outdoor stair extension. This one-and-a-half-story space is modulated vertically by one-story high fixed glass windows, shaded by an optional canvas awning system, a transom, and a row of louver windows at the top section of the transparent, pavilionesque south facade. The third landing has the study and a balcony over the master bedroom, with its own internal stair reconnecting it privately to the latter space. The guest suite is reached separately by the spiral stair and has its own roof deck with views to the waters beyond.

1.Aerial view from north 2.Site plan 3.South facade under construction 4.View of south facade across pond 5.Southeast facade 6.West facade 7.Southwest facade 8.Detail of north facade

3

4

5

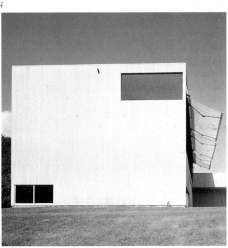

6

7

8

1.North facade 2.Northeast facade 3.Ramp
from entry 4.Railing detail at top of ramp
5.Third floor axonometric 6.Second floor
axonometric 7.Ground floor axonometric
8.Cross sections looking west 9.East facade
10.Master bedroom detail

1

2

3

4

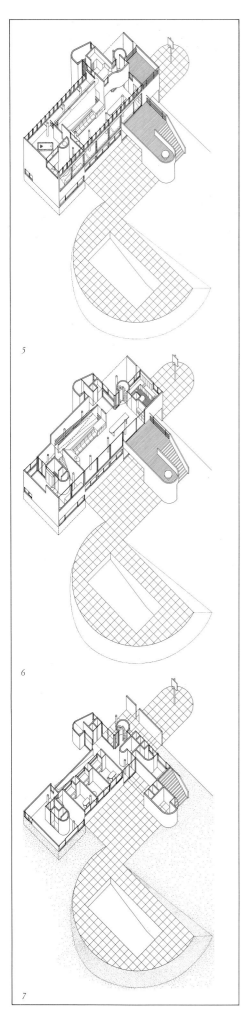

5

6

7

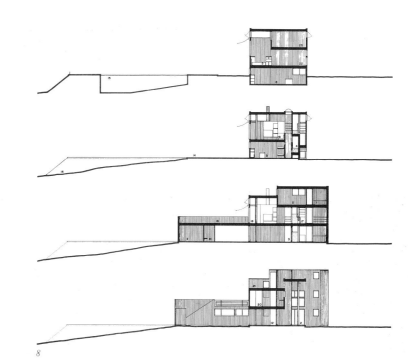

8

9

65

10

66

1

2

3

4

The problem was to design a residence on a steeply sloping wooded site, with panoramic views and access to the southwest.

The program was unique in that it had to accommodate an organ and a grand piano, as well as living/dining area, kitchen, master bedroom, two guest rooms, and a garage/storage and workshop space.

The parti consolidated the geometric plan origins and the volumetric vertical manipulations, summarizing an investigation of composite small buildings begun with the Gwathmey Residence.

The garage/storage and workshop space establishes the building's base. An outdoor stair from the parking area to the entry and terrace over the garage begins the vertical sequence. The ground floor accommodates the entry, guest bedrooms, and the floor of the organ space, a three-and-a-half-story one-third cylindrical volume, which is the referential space of the building. The second floor accommodates the kitchen and the two-story living/dining and piano space, which is a diagonal balcony overlooking the organ room. The third floor accommodates the master bedroom, an orthogonal balcony overviewing the living/dining and the organ spaces.

The plan is generated from the square with a center column, from which the horizontal plan erosions and radial extensions originate. The closed corner is occupied by the bathrooms and the kitchen, and the stair is an articulated composite volume on the rear side and corner of the primary volume.

68

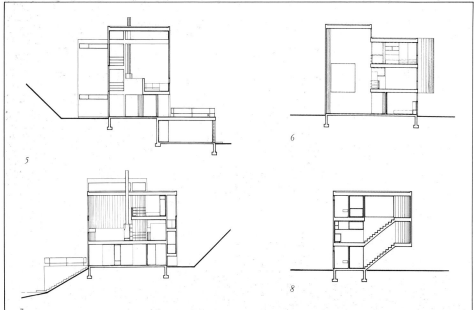

1

2

3

4

5

6

7

8

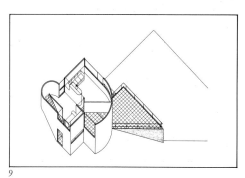

9

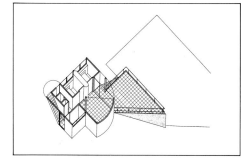

10

1.*Ground floor plan* 2.*First floor plan*
3.*Second floor plan* 4.*Third floor plan*
5.6.7.8.*Sections* 9.*First floor axonometric*
10.*Ground floor axonometric* 11.*Second floor*
axonometric 12.*Site plan* 13.*Northwest view*
of model 14.*Northeast view of model*
15.*South view of model*

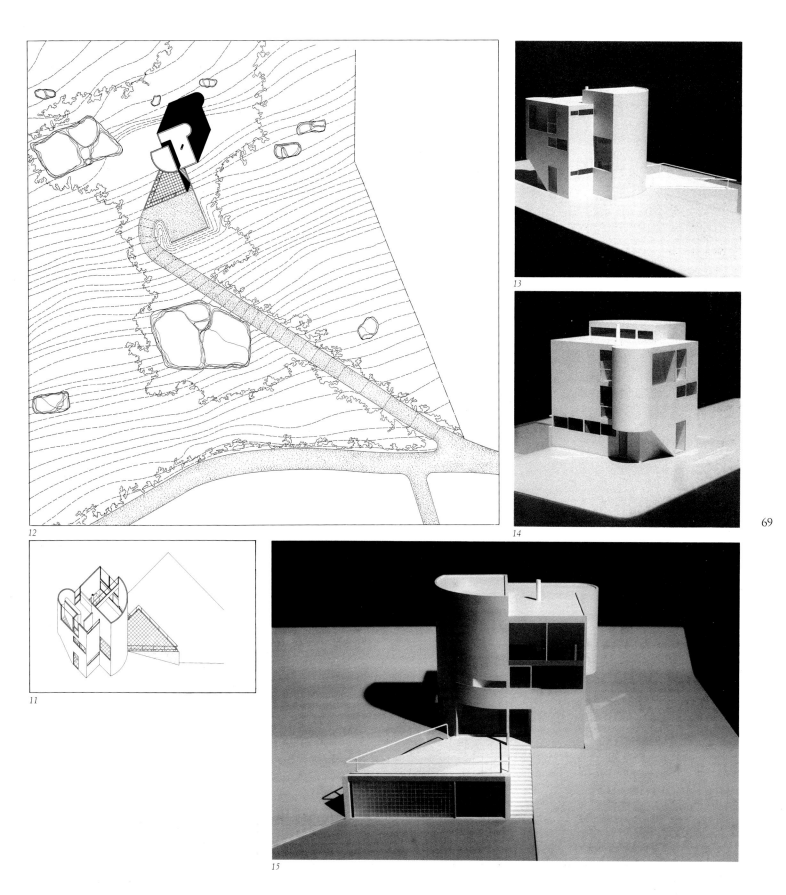

12

13

14

11

15

69

Cohn Residence
Amagansett, New York

1

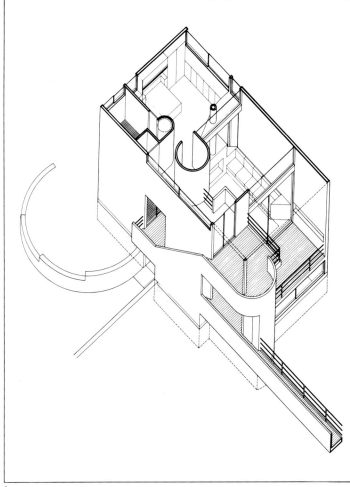

2

3

The problem was to design a residence on an ocean-dune site with view and beach access to the south, a cul-de-sac to the north, and adjacent residences on the east, west and north.

The program was distributed over three levels and organized in a row-house format, with primarily solid side (east/west) walls, a flat, specifically fenestrated, street-facing north facade, and a transparent sun-screened south facade. The ground floor accommodates the entry off the wall-retained auto court, with access to the exterior stair which interconnects decks and a bridge to the beach on the second level, a sun deck on the third level, two children's bedrooms, a playroom and guest bedroom, all a half-level below grade. The second level accommodates the kitchen, with direct exterior access, dining room, and double-height living room which opens to a deck facing the ocean. The third floor accommodates the master-bedroom suite overviewing the living room and a balcony/study with direct access to the sun deck.

The parti zones the vertical organization. The ground floor establishes a base, the second floor establishes a view reorientation and access to the beach, and the third floor establishes the private yet open adult spaces which interlock spatially and hierarchically with the second floor.

The row-house prototype guarantees privacy, views, beach access and section manipulation without compromising programmatic requirements, zoning restrictions and budget.

1.Partial view of south facade from the beach
2.Axonometric 3.Northwest facade 4.South
facade 5.View of living space from deck
6.View of living space from balcony 7.East
elevation 8.North elevation 9.West elevation
10.South elevation

4

5

6

71

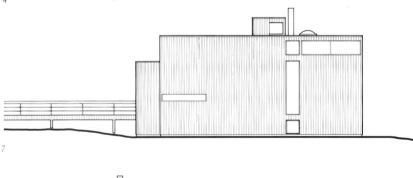

7

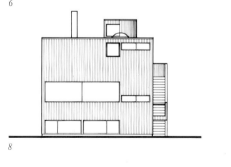

8

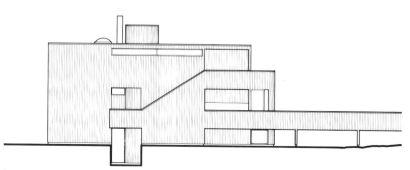

9

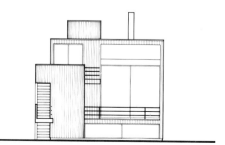

10

Whitney Road Housing
Perinton, New York

1

2

3

The problem was to design a low-rise, low-cost, 560-unit residential community on a 43-acre site which was bounded on two sides by Whitney Road and Fairport Nine Mile Road. The site sloped toward the center from high points east and west, and down from the north.

Aside from the basic unit design, which helped solve local metropolitan housing needs, the program required housing for elderly persons and families at rentals in line with occupants' incomes; ample recreation areas and a community facility; maximum involvement of the private sector in the planning, construction, ownership and management of the housing; and sound planning concepts and superior design.

The parti was derived from an analysis of the ideal unit organization, overlaid with a vehicular and pedestrian circulation system. In all units, the service side incorporating entry, kitchen stairs and bathrooms fronts the streets or mews, while the private side, incorporating living, dining and bedrooms

fronts the green spaces. The two vehicular access points at the furthest diagonal corners of the site establish an outside ring road generating four linear culs-de-sac forming the streets of the project.

Due to the sloping site and the culs-de-sac street organization, from the perimeter of the site one is unaware of vehicles and is presented with a building fabric approximating an Italian hill-town rather than a typical suburban housing development. A local ordinance, requiring that a parked vehicle be within one hundred feet of a residence, generated the next planning strategy; that of raising all of the flats or garden apartments one level above grade, parallel to the streets, affording both covered sidewalks and parking for each unit. Townhouse pedestrian mews exist perpendicular to the sidewalks and at articulated intersections. Each two-story townhouse is provided with a semiprivate terrace which opens onto the common green space.

The units for elderly persons are located at the south end of each cul-de-sac, with an incorporated community and laundry facility serving the entire street. Guest parking is provided in the center of this space. The project community center is located at the south corner of this site, adjacent to the retention pond, and the children's planned recreation area is located at the northwest corner of the site. Of the 560 housing units, 120 are for the elderly, with the remainder divided into two-, three- and four-bedroom townhouses, and efficiency and one-bedroom flats, creating an ideal neighborhood population mix.

The pedestrian circulation system was designed so that access to any area of the site is possible without ever crossing the vehicular system.

In summary, there was an attempt to upgrade the Radburn concept in order to accommodate increased automobile usage. Simultaneously, a housing pattern was postulated that would be open to a changing

1.Overall view of model 2.Typical street
facade of flats 3.View of common green
4.View of typical street 5.Aerial view
6.Sections

4

5

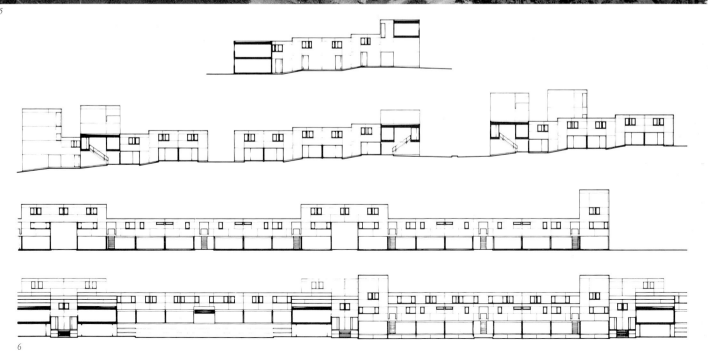

6

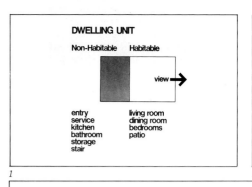

DWELLING UNIT

Non-Habitable | Habitable

view →

entry
service
kitchen
bathroom
storage
stair

living room
dining room
bedrooms
patio

1

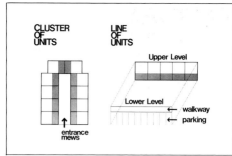

CLUSTER OF UNITS

LINE OF UNITS

Upper Level

Lower Level

← walkway
← parking

entrance mews

1

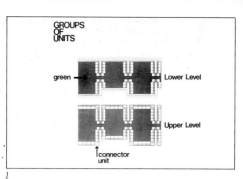

GROUPS OF UNITS

green →

Lower Level

Upper Level

connector unit

1

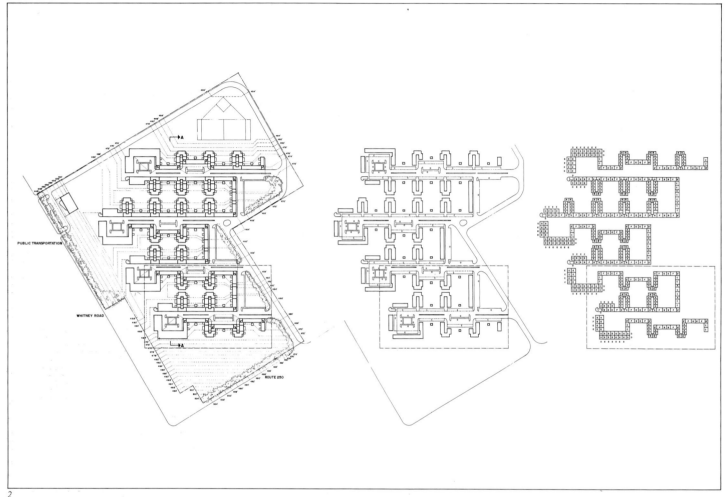

PUBLIC TRANSPORTATION

WHITNEY ROAD

ROUTE 250

74

2

BDRM 88 SF | BDRM 88 SF | BDRM 130 SF | | | | | | BDRM 88 SF

LIVING-DINING 240 SF | TERRACE

CL | CL | D/N | UP | KITCHEN 80 SF

BATH | W/D

2,656 GSF | 1,626 GSF

C 4 BEDROOM TOWNHOUSE
30 UNITS
GROSS AREA· 1282 SF

BDRM 93 SF | UP | DN | CL | CL | BATH | UP | CL | KITCHEN 84 SF

BDRM 93 SF | TERRACE | LIVING-DINING 260 SF | ENTRY

BDRM 93 SF | PR.

2,502 GSF | 1,472 GSF

B 3 BEDROOM TOWNHOUSE
40 UNITS
GROSS AREA· 974 SF

BDRM 88 SF | BDRM 133 SF | TERRACE

CL | CL | DN | UP | BATH | W/D | ENTRY | LIVING-DINING 240 SF | KITCHEN 80 SF

2,446 GSF | 1,416 GSF

A 2 BEDROOM TOWNHOUSE
150 UNITS
GROSS AREA· 852 SF

TERRACE | W/D | BATH | KITCHEN 80 SF | W/D | BATH | PR.

CL | UP | DN | CL | CL | UP

BDRM 155 SF | BDRM 88 SF | BDRM 133 SF | LIVING-DINING 272 SF | ENTRY | BDRM 110 SF | BDRM 88 SF | BDRM 133 SF

3,300 GSF | 2,446 GSF | 1,470 GSF | 2,600 GSF

G 3 BEDROOM TRIPLEX
28 UNITS
GROSS AREA· 1216 SF

G 3 BEDROOM DUPLEX
24 UNITS
GROSS AREA· 1070 SF

BDRM 133 SF | BDRM 105 SF | LIVING-DINING 270 SF

CL | CL | CL | BATH | KITCHEN 64 SF

F 2 BEDROOM SIMPLEX
52 UNITS
GROSS AREA· 765 SF

BDRM 133 SF | LIVING-DINING 207 SF | CL

CL | BATH | CL | KITCHEN 64 SF | ENTRY

E 1 BEDROOM SIMPLEX
204 UNITS
GROSS AREA· 557 SF

STUDIO 297 SF | CL

CL | BATH | KITCHEN 80 SF | CL

D 0 BEDROOM SIMPLEX
36 UNITS
GROSS AREA· 416 SF

3

3

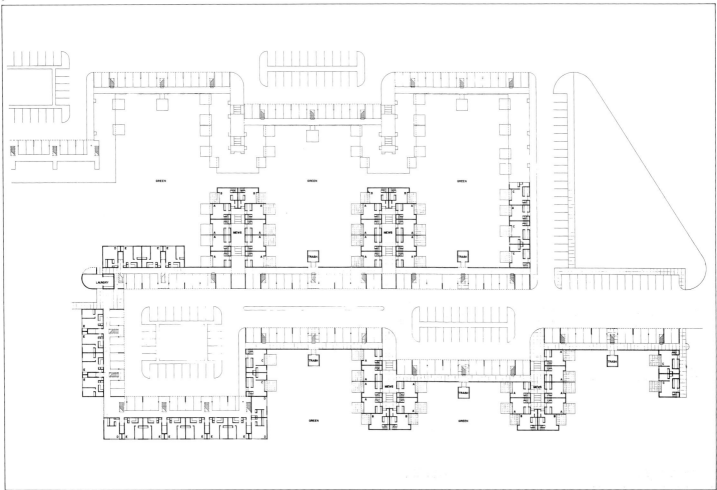

4

sequence of readings as one passed through the different kinds of spaces developed by grid formation, the vehicular system and the green spaces. A scalar relation to the suburban context was maintained, while the overall pattern was more urban than Radburn's. This sense of urbanity derived not only from the stoa-like perimeter walkways, but also from the pedestrian mews and clusters which extended the layering of the scheme. The design provided three spatial experiences: the urbanity of the street, the labyrinthine quality of the mews and the pastoral continuity of the open green spaces, consolidating into a single multifaceted building and site organization.

1.Site plan, diagrams 2.Unit plans 3.View of typical townhouse units from street 4.Lower level partial plan 5.View through arcaded walkway

5

Gwathmey Barn
Greenwich, Connecticut

The problem was to renovate an existing barn shell for a family residence. The redesign dealt primarily with the existing interior volumes. There was a conscious attempt to diminish the scale visually on the exterior while magnifying the scale and volumetric interplay on the interior. Existing were a 30-foot by 42-foot by 30-foot high main volume at the upper entrance grade, with an adjacent 30-foot by 15-foot by 20-foot high volume at lower grade, connected to a 30-foot by 42-foot by 7.5-foot high volume. The formal organization was based upon referencing the new spaces to the center line of the upper ridge by making service and circulation spaces to one side and living spaces to the other, thus creating tension through related asymmetry.

A photomural covering the entire end wall of the double-height playroom is a strong visual reference tying together the upper and lower zones, while concurrently extending the main volume through its conceptual end-wall, thus transforming the playroom, interior, and conceptually-exterior volume.

The nature of the upper-level volume allowed for loft-like planning which reinforces the visual references of the superstructure and permits overviews to the main space while reinforcing the integrity with the new intervention. The master bedroom and study levels were designed to be a separate building or a composite object within the main volume.

1

2

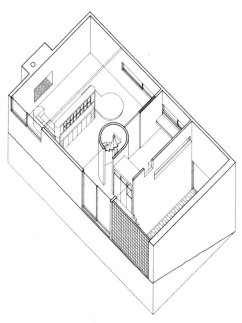

3

The cabinetwork system is separate yet integrated into the building and is consolidated into specialized multi-use configurations which modulate and serve the space. The cabinetwork and the flooring are white oak, the interior walls and ceiling are double-layered gypsum board, painted throughout, and the lower-level floor is brick.

4

1.Northeast facade 2.Living/dining space
3.Axonometric 4.View looking down into
living room 5.View from dining room toward
kitchen and entry 6.View of playroom toward
stair 7.Southwest facade 8.9.Sections
10.View of playroom from stair 11.View of
playroom through glass-block wall
12.Children's bedroom

5

6

7

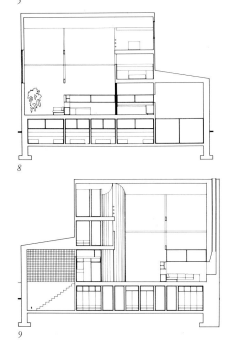

8

9

10

11

12

Pearl's Restaurant
New York, New York

1

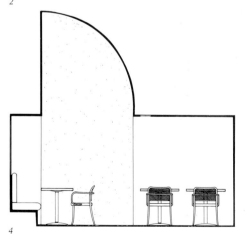

2

3

4

The problem was to design a well-known Chinese restaurant, and install it into an existing storefront space 14 feet wide and 100 feet deep. Capacity to serve 75 to 100 customers was necessary.

The design intention was to establish a facade, a promenade and a place. The facade directly reflects the interior volume and appears to have been slipped, as a container, into the existing masonry-framed opening. The facade is projected as a white stucco square with a setback glass-block panel, under a quarter-circle glass window, with mirror extending through both on the east wall to the outside face. On the west side is

the vestibule, which opens into the space immediately adjacent to the glass-block panel, intimating the spatial sequence and a memory of the facade.

The space is a linear section that presents an illusion of an expanded scale and dimension. The use of mirror as a primary material, on the upper walls and behind the banquettes, both extends the space by transforming the quarter circle into a semicircular barrel vault, and creates an illusionary environment. The result is a sense of reductive spatial harmony with ambiguous extension, where the primary role of the space is to accentuate the people and the food.

1.Existing facade 2.New facade 3.View from
the entry 4.Cross section 5.Detail of entrance 6.Axonometric 7.Ground floor plan
8.Basement floor plan

5

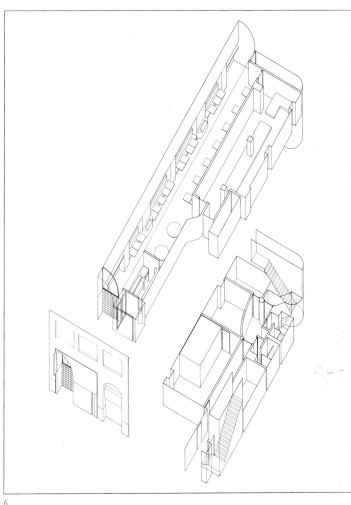

6

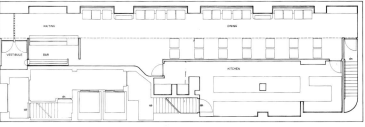

7

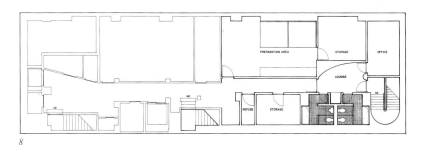

8

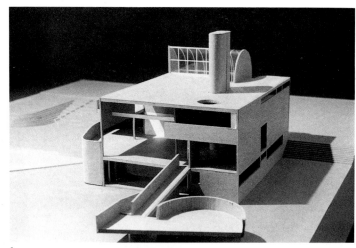

1

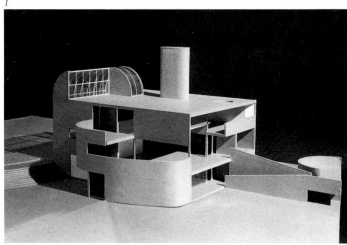

2

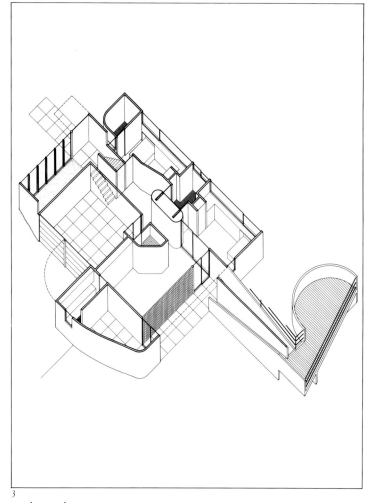

3

80

The problem was to design a residence on a narrow, linear, sloping site situated on a promontory with horizon views of the Manhattan skyline to the south, an access road paralleling the entire length of the site to the north, and existing adjacent residences to the east and west.

The program required a large living/sitting room, dining room, kitchen, master bedroom, study, family room and two guest bedrooms. The program was disposed on three levels with the entry and integrated greenhouse on the half-level. The garage, family room, laundry/storage room, and two guest bedrooms are accommodated one half-level below entry on grade with a terrace extension off the family room. The living/sitting and dining/kitchen spaces are placed one half-level above entry grade, with a ramp extension to a deck/gazebo on the edge of the palisades that also reconnects to the lower level. The third level accommodates the master-bedroom suite and study with overviews to the double-height living space and deck, orienting to the views south. The introduction of the greenhouse as an integral and referential space and the front-to-back plan organization intensified the strategy of spatial layering, internal transparencies, and multiple interior facades that became more prevalent in later projects.

1.Southeast view of model 2.South view of
model 3.Ground floor axonometric 4.Second
floor axonometric 5.Third floor axonometric

6.Northwest view of model 7.Section A
8.Section B

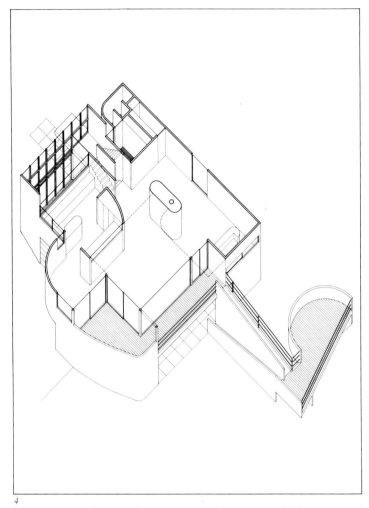

4

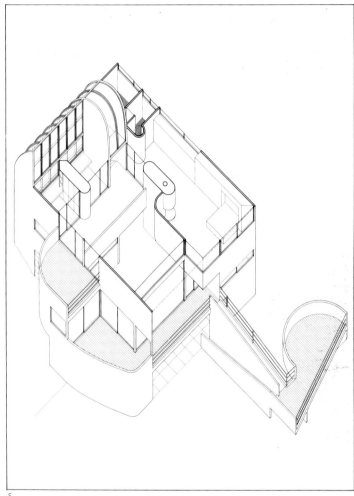

5

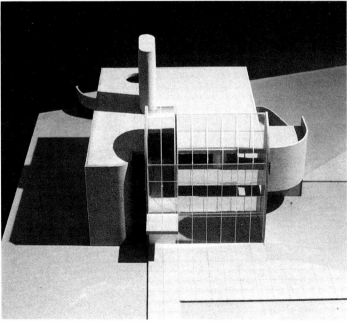

6

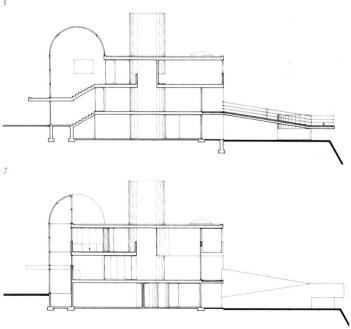

7

8

Geffen Residence
Malibu, California

The problem was to design a large residence on a strip site in Malibu Beach, California. The narrow rectangular site was delineated by the Pacific Coast Highway on the north, two existing residences on the east and west within five feet of the property lines, and the beach on the south.

The program was to accommodate a living room, dining room, kitchen, master-bedroom suite, game room, three-car garage, swimming pool, as well as changing rooms, outdoor terraces and three guest rooms.

The two priorities were to ensure privacy from the highway and the neighbors, and to establish a unique presence on the beach. The parti disposed the program into three zones; the front building, the court, and the rear building. The front building contains the entry and garage on the ground floor, the guest rooms on the second floor, and a roof terrace. It is connected to the rear building by a ramp space, acting as an architectural promenade, which serves as a primary referential space in the composition and parallels the pool/court.

The rear building, which is a half-level above grade, contains the foyer, living room, dining room, kitchen and terrace on the first level, and the master-bedroom suite and study on the second level. The entire south facade, which faces the ocean, is framed by a brise-soleil which integrates the terrace and the interior spaces while framing the views to the ocean.

This parti represents a hybrid type, combining the row house and the court house. Its historical precedents are found in the suburban and maritime villas of the Roman world, where the entire site is rendered as building and the zoning of public and private spaces is both horizontal and vertical.

82

1

2

3

1.Southwest view of model 2.Northeast view
of model 3.Plan view of model 4.Pacific
Coast Highway 5.Street level plan
6.Living/court level plan 7.Master bedroom
plan 8.Roof plan 9.Section A 10.Section B

4

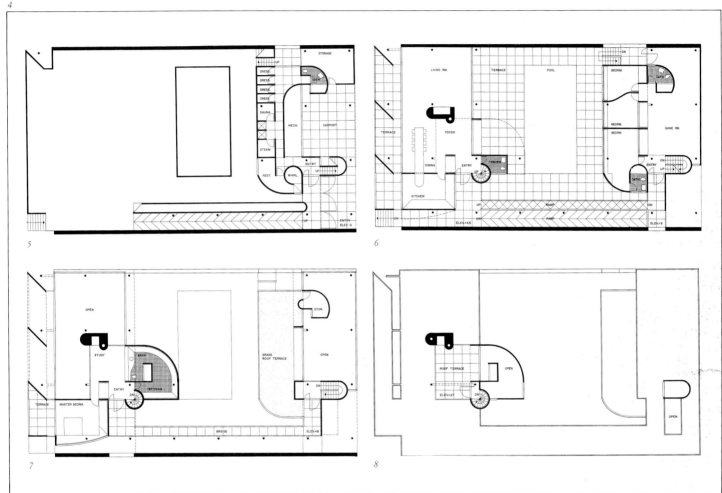

5

6

7

8

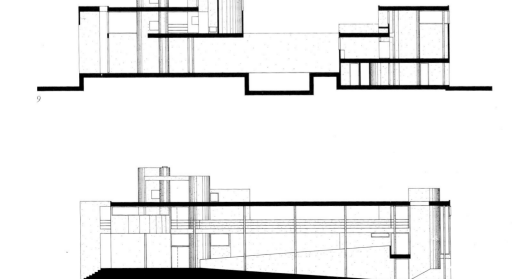

9

10

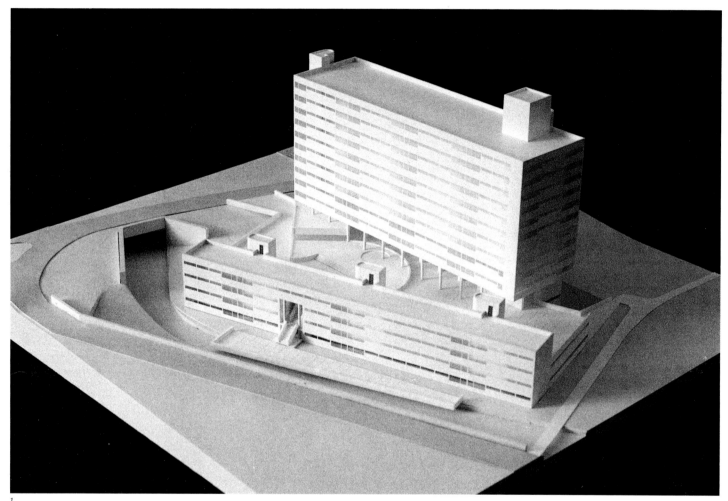

84

1

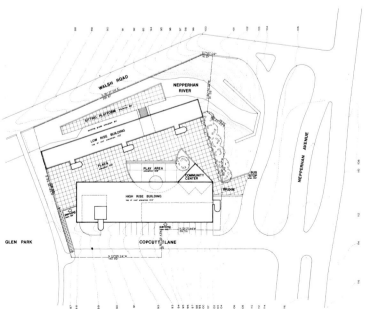

2

The problem was to design two hundred dwelling units with covered parking, a community facility, and convenience retail shops. The site was a one and three-tenths acre area in Yonkers, New York, of which only eight-tenths of one acre was suitable for building. It was bounded on the north by a major avenue, on the west by an access road, on the south by a park, and on the east by a canal.

The natural topography allowed for a pedestrian plaza, retail, community center and building entrance points to be at the same grade as Nepperhan Avenue. Coppcutt Street sloped down toward the park and became a natural service ramp which fed two under-plaza parking levels and a loading dock.

The plaza, which is entered from the north by a bridge or from the south by a ramp, is architecturally defined by a low-rise building which is four stories high from grade and two stories from the plaza, and by a mid-rise building which is twelve stories high from the plaza and whose two-story arcade becomes the volumetric spatial reflection of the low-rise mass. The plaza has a major visual extension to the north by acting as a balcony to the park, and a physical extension to the east by penetrating the low-rise building with a controlled terrace platform at one canal level. It also has views west through large openings in the arcade. The arcade affords covered access to the community center, the retail spaces and the building lobby, while also serving as a major covered sitting space for the plaza.

The land on the east side of Walsh Street slopes upward at a severe angle to the aqueduct, creating, in conjunction with the mid-rise element, a major space definer which is modulated by the plaza, the low-rise building, the canal and the road.

Apartments orient east and west with the exception of the end units on the north facade of the mid-rise building. The mid-rise element is programed for one- and two-bedroom units, but is designed to permit flexibility, allowing conversion of any one and two combination into an efficiency or three-bedroom unit. The low-rise element is programed for three-bedroom units.

In summary, the physical adjacencies which were fixed (park, river, aqueduct, street) provided the positive amenities for high-density housing, yet also demanded a defined and controlled urban space.

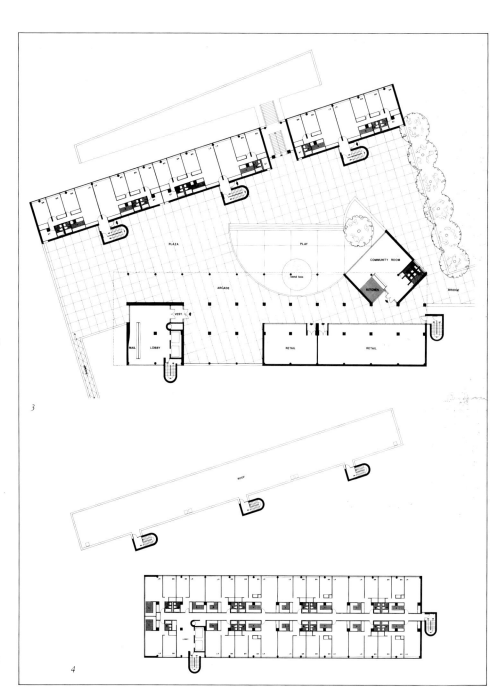

85

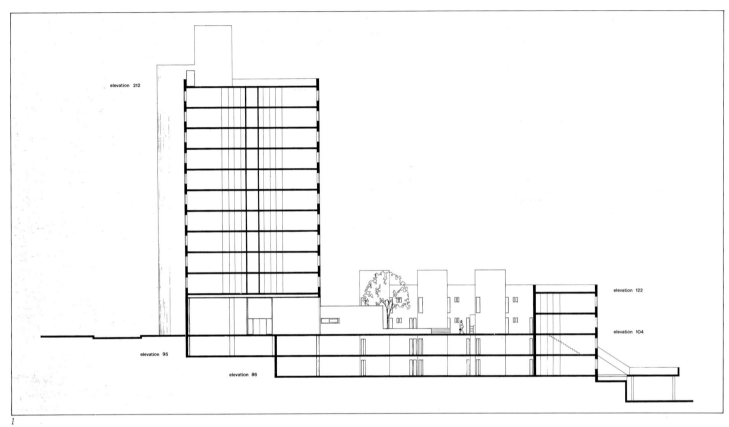

elevation 212

elevation 122

elevation 104

elevation 95

elevation 86

1

2

1.*Cross section*   2.*South view of model*
3.*West view of model*   4.*North view of model*

3

4

Transammonia Corporation
Offices
New York, New York

1

The problem was to design new corporate offices in an existing 10,000-square-foot space with a regular column grid and the core on one side of the rectilinear plan.

The program was dense, requiring a reception/waiting space, 26 closed offices, a president's office, a vice-president's office, three conference rooms, an open staff area, and related storage and support space. The strategy, which became somewhat prototypical for later projects, was to articulate the circulation space as the primary referential zone, in this case by separating the shared open work areas in the center from the closed private offices on the perimeter. The columns are articulated and serve to modulate the circulation space, the storage walls, the Michael Graves murals, and the custom-designed oak secretarial work stations. The perimeter offices are articulated by internal clerestory windows and share low storage walls with integral up-lighting.

The use of clear glass, frosted glass, wire glass and glass block defines specific spaces, affords borrowed natural light, and preserves privacy where required. The overall sense of the environment is one of density, spaciousness and clarity.

2

3

1.View of reception area 2.View of circulation space with Michael Graves mural 3.View of circulation space 4.President's office 5.Main conference room 6.Circulation space with typical secretary station 7.Detail of open work area 8.Detail of work station 9.Plan

4

5

6

7

8

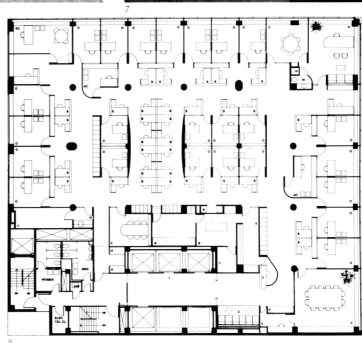
9

The problem was to design a small house on a wooded site with distant ocean views to the south and an access road on the north. The program was typical, requiring a living/dining space, kitchen, master bedroom, two small guest bedrooms and deck space. The problem was extended in order to study the solution as a prototypical design which could be replicated with minor variations for a $50,000 construction cost. The organization placed the entry and bedrooms on the ground floor, the two-story living/dining space and the kitchen on the second floor with a deck extension, and a roof deck over the kitchen on the third floor, all interconnected by a single spiral stair. The solution was a volumetric, hierarchical object building which responded to specific requirements and universal references while meeting the established cost goal.

1

3

2

1.West facade 2.View from northeast 3.View
of living/dining space from kitchen 4.Ground
floor axonometric 5.Second floor axonometric
6.Roof deck axonometric 7.Ground floor plan
8.Second floor plan 9.Roof deck plan
10.Section

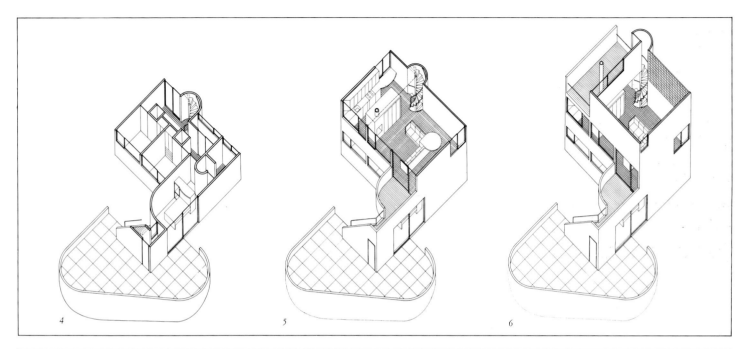

4   5   6

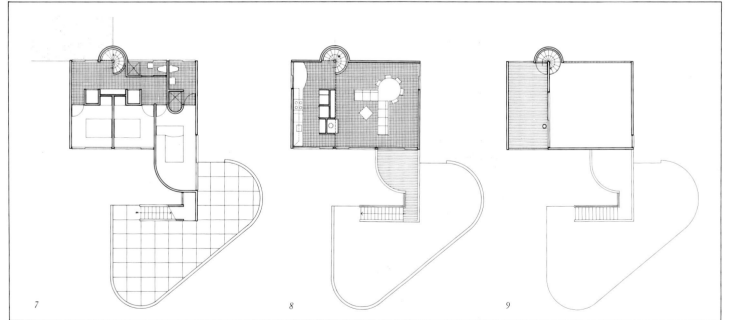

7   8   9

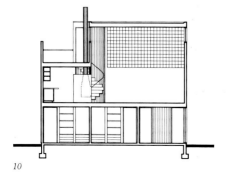

10

Four Seasons Restaurant
Negoya, Japan

The problem was to design a major new restaurant on the top floor of the tallest building in Negoya, Japan.

The space was 10,000 square feet, accessed by an escalator from the floor below and by a service elevator. The existing escalators fixed the point of arrival and the initial orientation. By opening a major skylight over this arrival and departure point, an awareness of being on the top floor of a vertical building with a unique view of the sky was emphasized. From the arrival space, the sequence of options progresses around the central kitchen core, following the perimeter of the building. The bar/lounge is articulated as a separate space that can, when required, open into the dining space. The main room is layered from the perimeter toward the core into three zones, each affording different seating accommodations and views. The perimeter zone consists of flexible tables and chairs; the second zone, facing the perimeter, is continuous banquette seating; and the third zone, raised one-and-a-half feet off the main floor, contains banquette seating perpendicular to the perimeter, with larger articulated seating on each end. The far end of the space is designated for banquet facilities.

The floors are granite, teak and carpet. The walls are teak paneling and the coffered ceilings, which add another spatial articulation, are plaster and stainless steel.

The primary intention was to create a coherent, elegant architectural environment that would be a "great room" while also being intimate. Secondly, there was an attempt to establish a unique space, devoid of the roof-top restaurant stereotype.

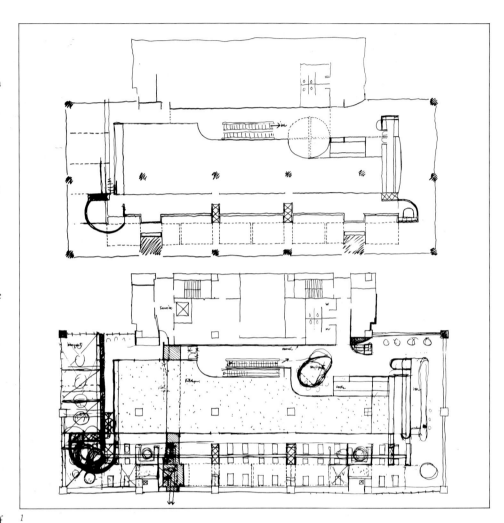

1

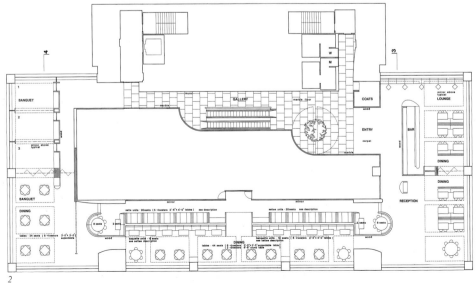

2

1.*Preliminary sketches* 2.*Plan* 3.*View of model* 4.*Axonometric*

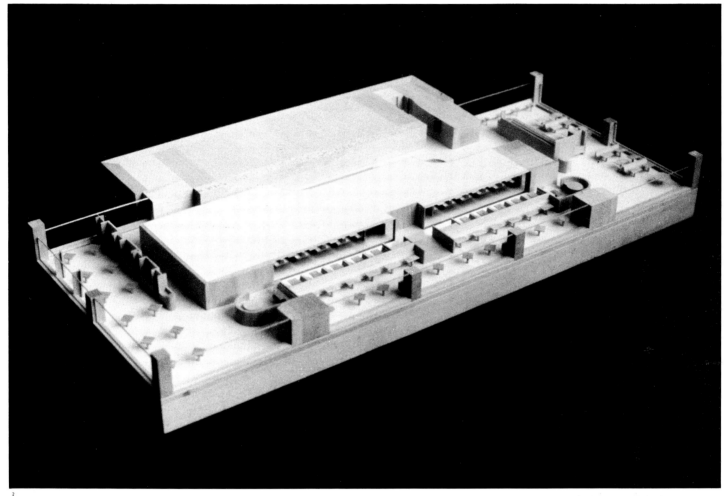

3

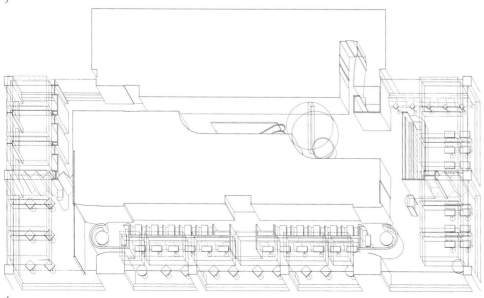

4

1974

Kislevitz Residence
Westhampton, New York

The problem was to completely renovate and add to an existing neo-Spanish residence, an assemblage of four disjunctive yet connected elements on four acres with potential panoramic views of the bay and ocean. The original house offered little response to orientation, light, view or privacy, in the sense of spatial organization or site relationship. The program was to provide accommodations for a family with six children, while guaranteeing a strong sense of privacy for the parents.

The overall strategy was to layer the site through the building and to develop pertinent sequences from the car, through the entry gate, the garden, the building, the lawn, and finally to the water. Thus, the building became a modulating, complex set of spatial experiences, "a volumetric wall," that supported a program and reintensified the entire site/building hierarchy. In this way, the building ceased to be an isolated object and became part of the larger context, with clear topological continuity.

The solution to the building was to maintain the existing exterior volumetric configuration which was defined primarily by the various pitched and shed tile roofs. Within these four separate connected volumes, the intention was to exploit their basic clarity while simultaneously making them spatially continuous and volumetrically interpenetrable.

The building was organized using the center volume as the major referential space, or "great hall." Working from the actual center of the main volume and restructuring a clear vertical and horizontal circulation system not only clarified the spatial organization but offered the essential options inherent in a complex program. The central space is three stories high and is partially capped by a 17-foot, square skylight which extends the volume vertically while affording a view of the ocean from a balcony at the top of the stairs.

This central element also contains the dining room and a library, both with views to the

sound. From the great hall the transformed living room extends to the south and the kitchen/sitting room and breakfast room extend to the north, while two children's bedrooms occupy what had been the connected garage element. On the second level of the central volume, off the circulation balcony, there are two more children's bedrooms, with a view to the sound and access to a bridge/ramp element extending across the lawn to the dock by the water, completing the cross axial, site/building circulation system. Above the kitchen on the second level is the master-bedroom suite with an adjacent outdoor roof deck over the new garage/pool house and a connecting outdoor stair to the pool terrace. On the third level of the central volume is the studio/guest space, an open balcony overviewing the central volume and completing its vertical spatial hierarchy. All of these spaces have views to the water beyond.

In summary, the overall composition is one of additive interior and exterior interventions,

1.*View during demolition* 2.*East facade from entry gate* 3.*Entry gate* 4.*West facade facing bay* 5.*Roof deck* 6.*Great hall*

5

creating a harmonious collection of separate though related spaces and forms, collaging into a reinterpreted manor house with its central hall and extended wings.

6

1.Ground floor plan 2.Second floor plan
3.Third floor plan 4.View of great hall from
entrance 5.Stair to studio/guest room suite

6.View of great hall from balcony 7.View
from great hall up to diagonal stair and
skylight

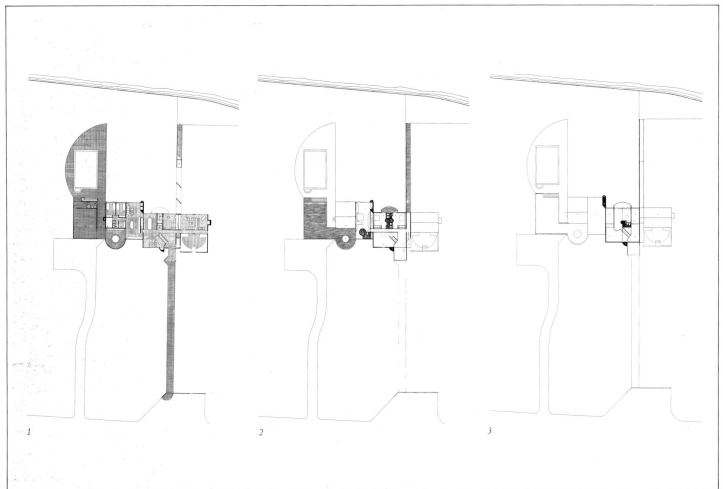

1

2

3

96

4

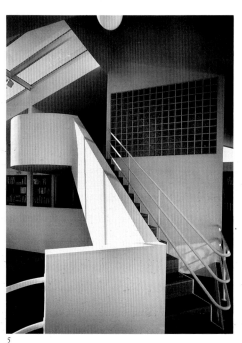

5

6

1

2

3

1.*Living room* 2.*Breakfast room* 3.*Living room* 4.*Master bedroom* 5.*Guest bedroom*

4

5

Vidal Sassoon
Salon
La Costa, California

The problem was to design four new haircutting salons, each located in different parts of the country, with varying configurations and square footages. The challenge was to develop an image of corporate identity through the program and to design replicatable elements that would establish and reinforce a sense of unity and continuity.

The three organizing activities were grouping the traditionally separate cutting stations into continuous linear elements articulated by mirrors and cabinets; developing the entry, reception and sales space as the core of the salon; and selecting a palette of colors and materials to complement both the product and the corporate identity.

The intention of the design was to create an environment of informal restrained elegance, positive anticipation and total participation, combined to promote a sense of well-being and to encourage a strong desire to return.

This was the first and most difficult installation because of its prototypical implications and the triangular configuration of the space. The shopping mall interior façade was treated as a totally transparent plane, with the exception of a rear-screen slide projection element that added content and a continuously changing graphic for the pedestrian user and passerby.

The cutting areas for men and women are kept separate, as in all the installations, but are designed to be similar. The washing stations are articulated as a separate element, modulating the front entry space from the working areas of the salon.

The material palette includes dark brown quarry tile floors, dark brown plastic laminate cabinetwork, light gray vinyl walls, polished aluminum pan ceilings, and mirrored walls above the cutting station cabinets.

1

2

1.*Reception and entry* 2.*Entry facade* 3.*View of entry and waiting area toward cutting space* 4.*Washing stations* 5.*Cutting space* 6.*Plan* 7.*Axonometric*

3

4

5

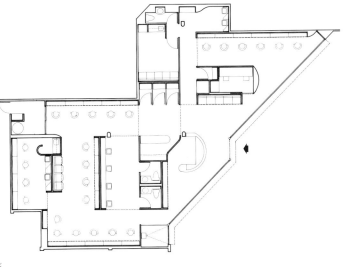

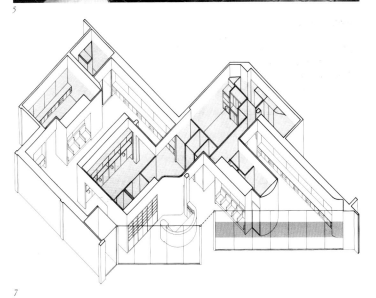

6

7

Vidal Sassoon
Salon
New York, New York

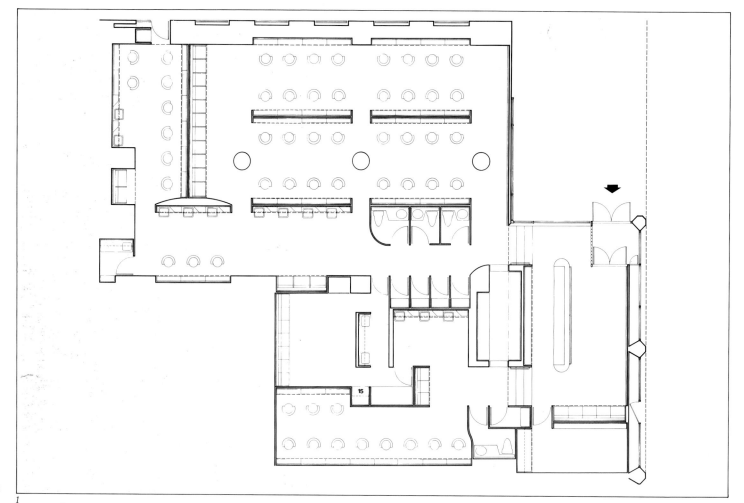

1

102

Located off the sunken plaza of the General Motors Building on Fifth Avenue, this is the largest installation.

The plan organization works from the entry/reception/display space, with a common coat-check area behind the desk bridging the men's area on the north and the women's area on the south.

The plaza facade incorporates the transparent area of the entry space with changing graphic show windows which are designed to be read clearly from the sidewalk 60 feet away.

1.Plan 2.View of reception area 3.Washing station 4.Cutting station 5.Drying station 6.Detail

3

4

5

6

Vidal Sassoon
Salon
Chicago, Illinois

This installation is on the third floor of a shopping mall in the Watertower Place complex on North Michigan Avenue.
The facade in this case had to conform to the mall criteria and was designed using travertine for the required solid areas, glass block to screen the men's cutting area and clear glass to front the entry/reception/waiting and product display area.
Of the first three salons, Chicago most successfully consolidated and unified all of the intended goals—from materials through cabinetwork—and created the desired density, quality and image.

1

2

3

1.Reception and waiting area 2.Exterior
facade 3.Mirrored interior corner detail
4.Drying stations 5.Cutting stations 6.Plan

4

5

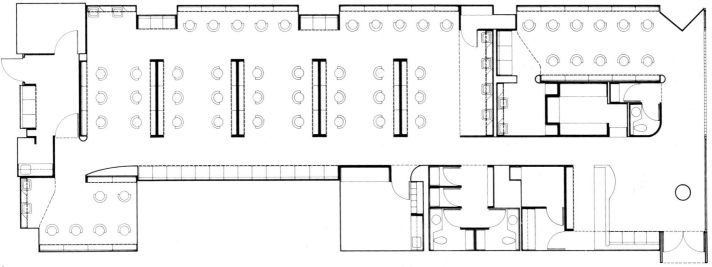

6

Vidal Sassoon
Salon
Beverly Hills, California

1

The final design in this series was the flagship salon, located in a discrete building on Rodeo Drive, the only direct street-front unit. The facade, in this case, was designed to summarize the entire Sassoon image and marketing strategy. It is singularly architectural and reflects the spatial organization of the interior. The two-story glass element accommodates the waiting sofa behind and opposite the reception and product desk, with the stairs up to the women's salon revealing the primary public volume of the project. The single-story glass entry doors with glass-block panel set over the lit transom graphically complete the facadal composition. On a shopping street with the visual and chaotic intensity of Rodeo Drive, the stainless steel, glass-block and glass Sassoon front sparkles in its elegant simplicity and architectural clarity.

The color palette was adjusted for this installation to be less specific and more universal. The dark brown quarry tile was replaced by travertine and the dark brown plastic laminate cabinets were replaced with white oak, thus elevating the color and material palette to one of more endurance and elegance. The access galleries to both the men's and women's cutting areas are unique. The long north wall in both is floor-to-ceiling mirror with a two-foot slot at eye level for changing photographs of varying hair styles. The ceilings are reflective polished aluminum and the floors are travertine. The sense of positive expectation is made manifest by the surreal illusions in this space, illustrating the desirably fine line between reality and fantasy.

2

1.*Entry facade* 2.*Gallery/circulation space*
3.*Cutting stations* 4.*Washing station with*
gallery beyond 5.*Second floor plan* 6.*Ground*
floor plan

3

4

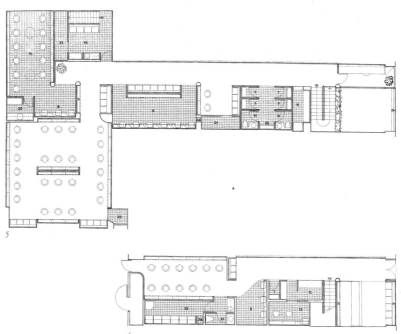

5

6

Vidal Sassoon
Corporate Offices
Los Angeles, California

The problem was to design the executive offices and support space on a 10,000-square-foot floor of an existing office building. The program incorporated the president's office and conference room, two vice-president's offices, controller's office, manager's office, two conference rooms, presentation theater, laboratory and staff room. The solution was an expansive "pavilion in the sky," with perceptual illusions and extensions that establish a total sense of calm. The materials include slat floors in the public spaces, oak cabinetwork, verte antique marble, glass block, and mirror.

3

1

2

1.Reception 2.Reception and waiting 3.Plan
4.President's office 5.Conference room
6.Vice-president's office

4

5

6

**Student Apartment Housing
State University College at Purchase**
Purchase, New York

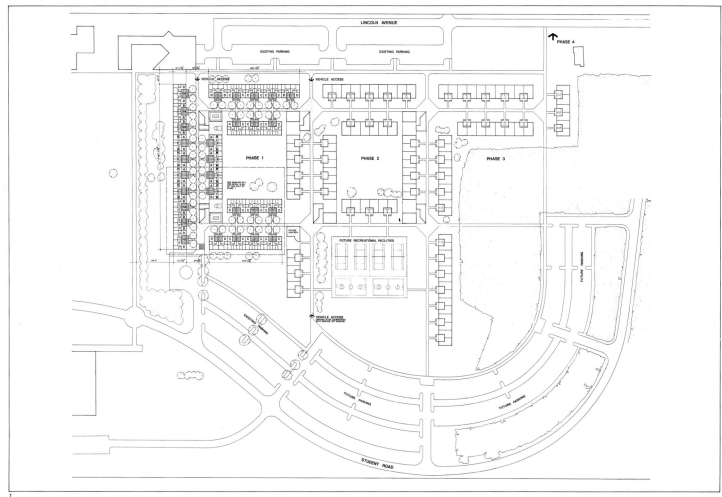

1

The design was the result of an invited competition, designated by the New York State Dormitory Authority, between architect/builder teams. The site was opposite Gwathmey Siegel's existing dormitory on the north side of the mall. The master plan required a design to accommodate 1,200 beds, with the first of three construction phases to accommodate 400 beds.

The constraints were numerous, including budget limitations, existing campus utilities, Type 5A construction, campus aesthetic guidelines, as well as the specific site, which was bounded on the east by the existing student parking areas defined by the master plan, on the west by outdoor planned recreational spaces, on the south by the existing sloping mall with its mature trees, and on the north by the existing wooded preserve.

Once again, as in the other housing projects, the analysis overlaid the ideal unit plan, the pedestrian circulation system, and the special facilities. In this case, the outdoor spaces were formed by the organization and combination of apartment units which were designed to have an active/public side and a quiet/private side. The two basic apartment types are a six-bed (two doubles, two singles) duplex unit and a four-bed (one double, two singles) stacked flat unit. each with a living/dining room and kitchen.

The pedestrian tree-lined mews serve as the circulation system to all points of entry. They were designed as a series of active, well-lit linear spaces, able to accommodate trash pick-up, bicycles, and emergency fire apparatus. Corners were produced by the intersections of these mews, which establishes the location for community facility structures. The skylit, covered entry porches with their outdoor stairs, trash modules, bike racks, and second-floor balconies modulate and order these linear referential spaces. To further activate and establish the desired unit zoning, all living and dining spaces face the mews, while all bedrooms face the outside perimeter or green court spaces which are inactive, private, and unlit, and which are formed by the building.

To add an exterior reading to the plan organization, the mews facades were constructed of bleached plywood panels, with large windows in the living/dining rooms. The end and back, or outside, walls were constructed of campus brick with small punched windows in the bedrooms. These features served to support the overall campus master plan.

1.Site plan 2.Axonometric 3.Pedestrian street 4.Section through entry court 5.Ground floor plan 6.Typical entry court to four units

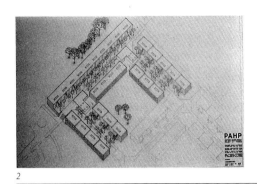

2

3

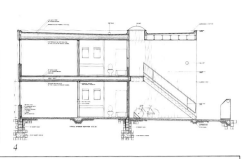

4

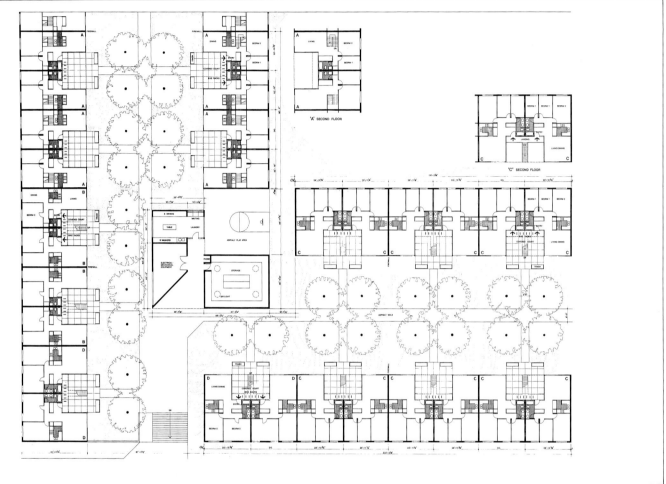

5

6

Nassau Country Art Center
Roslyn, New York

The problem was to convert the Frick Mansion into an art museum.

The building is a dominant object in the landscape. Historically, it has references to Palladio and to the English manor houses of the eighteenth century. It is axial, frontal and symmetrical in its basic organization.

Respect for the land and the historical context of the existing structure determined the architectural parti. The existing terrace, off the main parlor floor, was the inspiration for the design, which is harmonious with the existing building and landscape, yet provides flexible museum space.

By extending the terrace level and making it a roof, under which a multilevel series of exhibition spaces sequentially steps down toward the lake, the existing building's relationship with its surroundings is extended. The roof also serves as a sculpture terrace off the main parlor floor. An amphitheater ends the new construction and reinforces the relationship between the lake and the entire complex.

The existing basement houses the loading dock, storage and packing areas, shops, and locker and mechanical spaces. It is adjacent to the new construction which provides approximately 14,000 square feet of gallery space, with ceiling heights that range from 10.5 feet to 20 feet. Within the exhibit area, a ramp system unifies the various levels and facilitates the moving of art objects.

The new space is designed to permit circulation options and overviews, and to provide containment for individual exhibition spaces that link together while forming a larger framework. One moves from the lower ceiling spaces to the higher ceiling spaces toward the lake, which acts as a reference to the overall volume.

The main public entrance is at the parlor floor of the mansion and utilizes the existing portico. The existing building becomes the symbol of entry to the museum. This floor houses visitor services, the board room, the Carnegie organ and specialized exhibition space, and allows for chamber music and other adjunct uses available to the public. A combination of new interior construction and restoration reinforces the positive existing conditions and provides what is required to reuse the building as a museum.

112

1

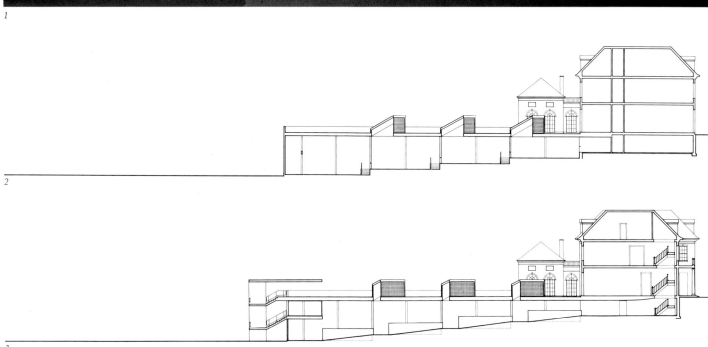

2

3

1.North view of model 2.Longitudinal section A 3.Longitudinal section B 4.Longitudinal section C 5.Aerial view of model 6.View of model 7.Plan

4

5

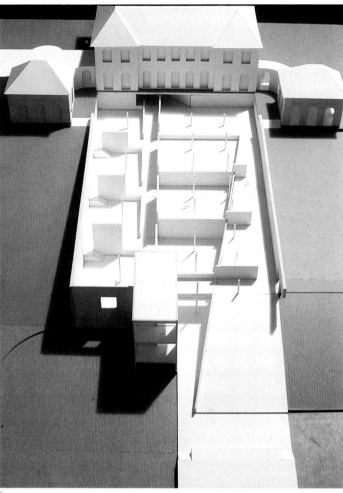

6

113

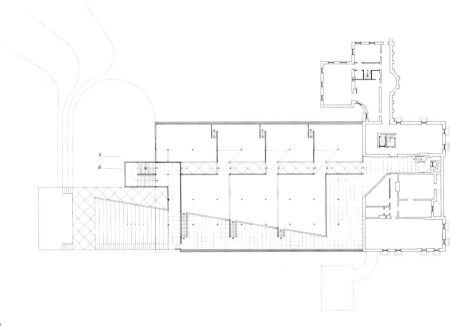

7

The problem was to renovate this famous triangular structure that was originally built in 1904 as The New York Times Building. Located at the intersection of Broadway, Seventh Avenue, and 42nd Street, this building has long been symbolic to New Yorkers and visitors because of its horizontally illuminated news ribbon and its traditional "falling ball" signifying the new year. In 1964 the building was purchased by Allied Chemical and stripped of its deep limestone beaux-arts facades, which were replaced with an insensitive flat marble skin. Because of the triangular plan configuration, the core on the south portion of the structure occupies one-third of the building's area, rendering it totally inefficient as a normal speculative office building.

When the building was sold again in 1974, its new owners sought to reclaim its once architectural image and to create a unique multiuse cooperative commercial building. They incorporated the New York Visitors Center on the ground, second and third floors, rented the existing theater space to tenants and exhibitors, leased the restaurant and small areas of space, at higher costs, to textile and related industries for showrooms and public relations offices.

By enclosing the north roof with clear glass to the upper roof, a major public exhibition space was created in this proposal and the silhouette of the building was changed from a one-step, flat-roofed building to a three-dimensional prism.

For the remainder of the facades, the proposal was to add a new teflon-coated, reflective-glass skin directly to the existing marble, creating an insulating air space and rendering the building a multifaceted optical object, reflecting and participating in the light works of Times Square.

In summary, the intention was to transform a mute, opaque, solid object into a prismatic, reflective, reflecting, graphic symbol that would be useful as an urban image.

114

1

2

1.Original New York Times Building
2.Renovated New York Times Building
3.Northwest view of model 4.Northeast view
of model 5.Section 6.East elevation of model
7.Ground floor plan

3

4

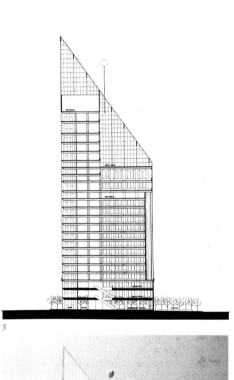

5

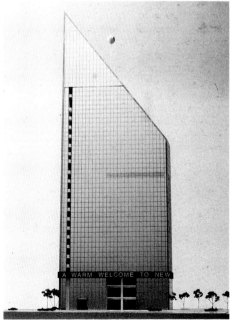

6

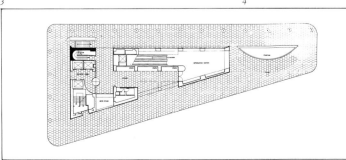

7

Island Walk Cooperative Housing
Reston, Virginia

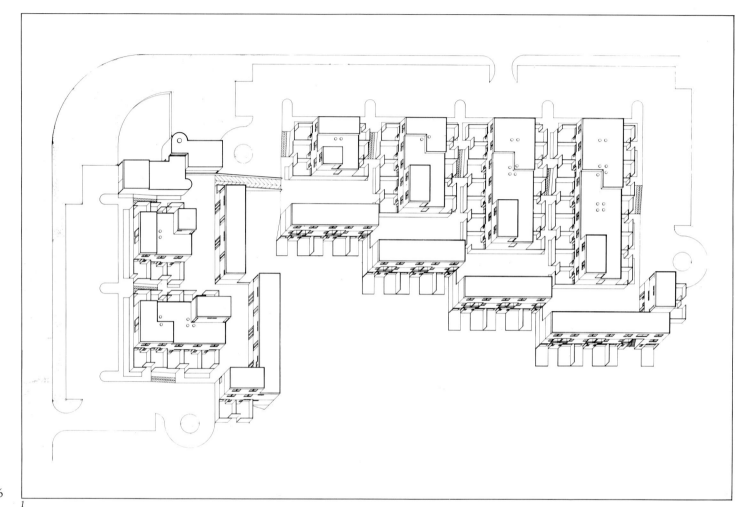

1

The problem was to design the first federally-financed housing project in this upper-middle-class, planned suburban community outside Washington, D.C.

The site was a seven and two-tenths acre gently sloping bowl, bounded on two sides by existing access roads and opening to an existing public park space 10 feet below road grade. The project was programmed to accommodate 102 dwelling units for low-to-moderate income families. By overlaying the site and planning strategy with the unit design, a comprehensive parti was developed.

The distribution of dwelling units on the site clearly defines the public, semiprivate and private realms, relating all open spaces to a particular building or building group.

Parking follows the perimeter road system and sets up the initial site zone. From the parking, a system of pedestrian mews forms a ramp between, and perpendicular to, the outdoor entry courts of the townhouse units. These mews terminate in interconnected, open plazas which serve as controlled recreation spaces and as forecourts to the stacked garden apartment structures which, in turn, front the outdoor public green space. Two major outdoor covered stairs connect the plazas to the green space that is a level below and interconnected with the public pedestrian walk system.

The overall plan configuration is an L, anchored at the corner by the community building, which interlocks the diagonally stepping plaza spaces, creating a sequentially reorienting progression.

The perception of the project from the outside is varying and unique. From the road, the blank silhouette end facades of the back-to-back townhouses and courts present a series of open gateways to the mews, which gives the project a sense of privacy and transition from vehicular to pedestrian scale. Planned tree areas help to make this transition. Because of the sloping site and the L configuration, the reading from the green is one of a rich, village architectural fabric with a composite layering of orthogonal and diagonal planes. In evidence here is the transformation of the typical suburban row-house community.

*1.Axonometric 2.View of model from field
3.Aerial view of model 4.Aerial view of
model 5.Aerial view of model from field*

2

3

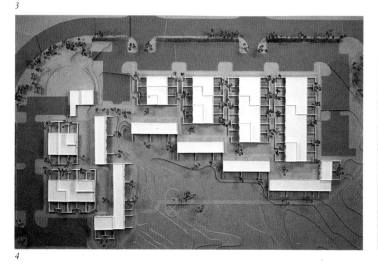

4

5

Bower and Gardner
Law Offices
New York, New York

1

The problem was to design law offices for the partners of a prominent litigation firm in a 12,000-square-foot existing space on Madison Avenue. The plan was square, with a regular column grid. The building core was located in the northeast corner.

The program required space for reception and waiting, seven partners' offices, eight associates' offices, three conference rooms, a lunch room, an accounting department, law library, and file storage space.

As in earlier designs, the strategy used to intensify the circulation space was repeated. In this case, however, the major portion of the Madison Avenue facade is devoted to public circulation and a natural light reference for the library and adjacent glass-block conference rooms. The result is a comprehensible spatial hierarchy with the partners' offices located on the south perimeter wall. The secretaries are separated by a file storage wall with a clerestory window over and across the circulation space.

2

The glass walled associates' offices form the south side of the library and the lunch room core.

1.Reception and waiting area 2.Circulation space and secretary stations 3.View of reception and waiting area toward lobby 4.Law library 5.Detail of secretary station toward associates' office and conference room 6.View of library and perimeter 7.Floor plan

3

4

5

6

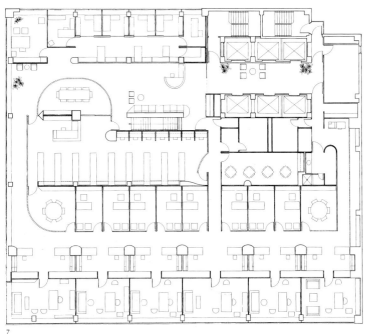

7

The Evans Partnership
Office Building
Prototype

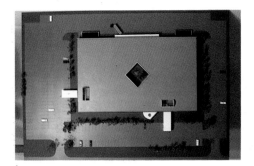

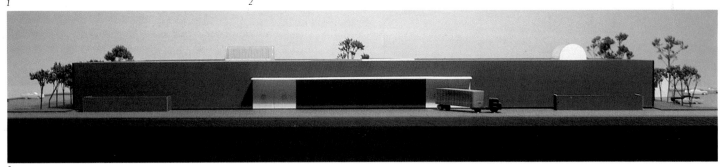

The problem was to analyze the basic properties and potential variants of a typical one-story office/industrial loft building, with an emphasis on economy, flexibility, expansion and multi-use options.

The solution addresses structure, enclosure and special conditions, providing a universal palette with a potential for specific modifications.

The structure is steel-frame, with a 30-foot by 30-foot bay spacing. This module is both economical and plan flexible. The interior space is 18 feet high to the bottom of the steel, affording vertical space option within a single enclosure.

Three sides are enclosed with a general gray glass curtain wall grid, five feet wide by three feet high, allowing transparency or opacity. A gray spandrel glass on a three-foot vertical increment allows options without visual disruption of the primary referential grid. The fourth side was conceived of as the expansion service and/or back wall, the concrete block painted to add a color and graphic option to the whole.

The special conditions such as entries, conference rooms, cafeterias and courts were proposed as additive or reductive elements that would articulate and modulate the general framework, thus introducing the specific and unique interventions necessary to elaborate and vitalize a simple type.

*1.2.3.Views of model 4.Ground floor plan
5.View of model 6.North elevation 7.West
elevation 8.South elevation 9.East elevation*

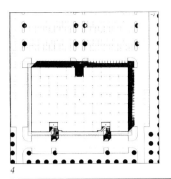

4

5

6

7

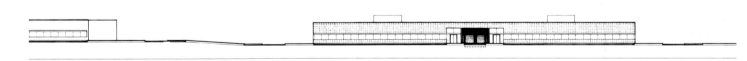

8

9

The Evans Partnership
Office Building
Piscataway, New Jersey

1

3

The problem was to design an 80,000-square-foot, one-story, flexible, multitenant office building on a corner site in an existing office/industrial building park. The solution and plan configuration was generated by an analysis of the site, parking, arrival and entry requirements. By stepping the corners, establishing a court, and zoning the parking on the two back facades, the resulting building establishes the corner, presents unobstructed facades to the road, and allows for multiple entries and graphics. Thus it appears to be a group of smaller elements completing a more complex yet comprehensible whole.

The material vocabulary of two-foot by two-foot travertine tiles, butted gray glass and white porcelain transom panels was selected to establish an architectural presence that appears dense, refined and abstract, devoid of false readings and superfluous extravagance.
The vocabulary also establishes a reference and a rationale for future buildings that could be at once specific yet part of a contextual whole.

1. *View of court from corner* 2. *View of court*
3. *View of entry* 4. *View of rear corner*

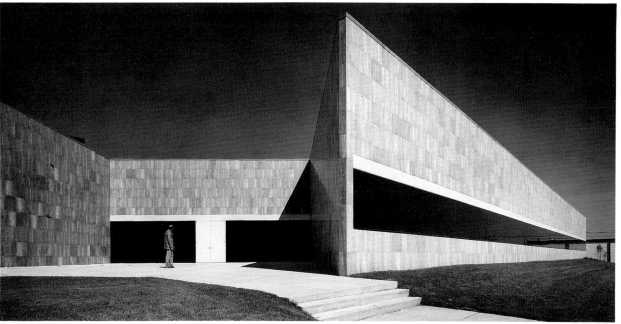

The problem was to renovate an existing 1940s apartment with a north orientation. The client was a fashion designer who occasionally worked at home.

The program required a large living room for entertaining, a dining room, kitchen, master bedroom/dressing room, guest bedroom/study, and studio/work space.

The solution was generated by exploiting an existing stepped-down living room and fixed fireplace wall. The sitting area of the living space is defined by a curved built-in sofa which negotiates the step down from the open entry gallery, which accommodates a grand piano and bar/hi-fi cabinet. The dining room, on the opposite side of the travertine reconfigured chimney wall object, is connected to both the gallery space and stepped-down living room. The public spaces are thus interconnected and open to one another, yet articulated and defined by the change in section and by the referential fireplace wall.

The organization and rendering of the spaces establishes a sense of intimacy, privacy and enclosure while simultaneously offering a sense of unity and extension.

1

2

3

4

1.*Living room* 2.*View of living room and gallery* 3.*View from entry toward living room* 4.*View of dining room toward gallery* 5.*Bedroom* 6.*Study/guest bedroom* 7.*Dining room* 8.*View of living room and dining room* 9.*Axonometric*

5

6

7

8

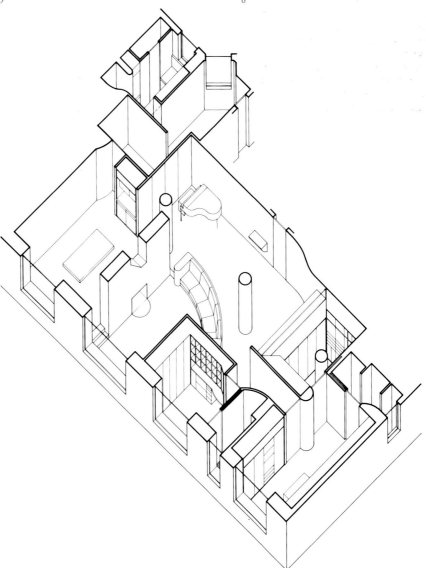

9

**Damson Oil Corporation
Office Building**
Houston, Texas

The problem was to design a 60,000-square-foot speculative office building, including a small proportion of covered parking, on a site adjacent to the Northbelt Freeway.

As in the Evans Partnership Buildings, an analysis of the site, parking, arrival, structure, enclosure and orientation helped to determine the design parameters.

This three-story (20,000 square feet per floor) steel-frame building of 32-foot by 36-foot bays sits a half-level above grade, affording a short ramp which accesses basement parking, and setting the first floor window sills above on-site cars.

The exterior is marble crete, a combination of cement plaster and marble chips which is applied to waterproof gypsum on steel studs.

Essentially it is a form of stucco which, when left its natural gray color, articulated with expansion joints, and molded, is transformed into a dense material which appears very solid.

Orientation was a primary determinant in the rendering of the plan organization of the facades. The freeway/north facade is enclosed in a floor-to-ceiling gray glass curtain wall, which reads as a one-story building, presenting a unique image and scale presence to the highway. The east and west facades are primarily solid, and the south entry facade is coffered with the glass set back three feet from the facade, affording sun control and a pedestrian scale. The entry is articulated by a three-story lobby space, and overviewed by public circulation balconies and private offices.

5

Barber Oil Corporation
Offices
New York, New York

1

The problem was to design corporate offices for an expanding oil shipping company within an existing 12,000-square-foot space with a difficult plan configuration.

The program required a large entry, a reception/waiting space with an adjacent boardroom, four senior executives' offices, ten executives' offices, five associates' offices, twelve secretary stations, two conference rooms, a staff lounge, an accounting department, and a file storage/photocopying room.

The entry is set back from the existing nondescript corridor opposite the elevators and articulated by a logo/kiosk, walnut wood floor, mirrored wall opening through a walnut door and glass wall to the reception/waiting space.

The reception/waiting space is the center of the senior executive boardroom area and the end of the circulation gallery space. The gallery space separates the executives' offices on the perimeter, which are articulated by recessed niches/vestibules, from the secretaries' offices, which are located behind low file walls with up-lighting and in front of the associates' offices.

The walnut cabinetwork, doors and trim, combined with the layered planning, internal transparencies, and intensified public circulation spaces offer a sense of density, permanence and quality to this working environment.

2

3

1.*View of entry vestibule from elevator lobby* 2.*Executive office* 3.*Boardroom* 4.*View of reception and waiting space* 5.*View of gallery and secretary station* 6.*View of circulation gallery* 7.*Floor plan*

4

5

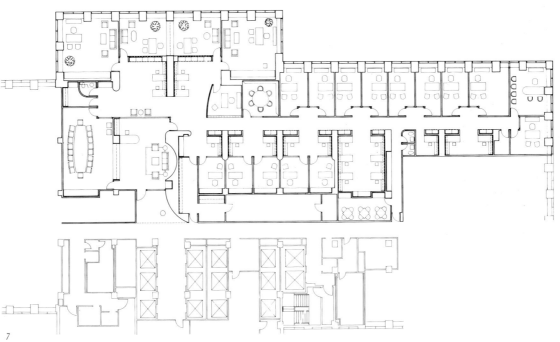

7

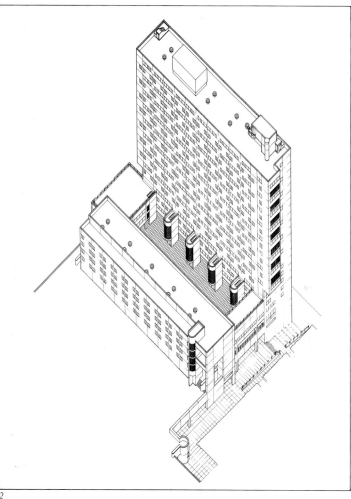

1

2

The problem was to design a housing complex for 750 students which would also include an academic center for interdisciplinary study and research, a student/faculty lounge, a resident dean's apartment, a hotel service for visiting faculty and guests of the university, student activity space, student office space, neighborhood storefront facilities, and a service garage. Topographically, the site is one of the highest natural elevations in Manhattan, located on Morningside Drive between 117th Street and 118th Street on the eastern edge of the campus. The Faculty Club and Judson Hall Dormitory are adjacent structures to the south, the Law School and School of International Affairs and the campus are to the west, neighborhood residential buildings are to the north, and Morningside Park and panoramic views are to the east.
An existing bridge over Amsterdam Avenue and a raised platform, built in the 1950s, extend from the campus to the western edge of the site. The elevation of this platform is

30 feet above Morningside Drive and the entrance elevations to the Faculty Club and Judson Hall, leaving a vast, unpopulated and unused outdoor area on the campus.
The parti was generated through an analysis of ideal housing types, building density, campus circulation, site constraints, and historical college building precedents. The complex is based on the English college in that it is a self-contained unit of housing, academic and activity space, organized around a major outdoor space—in this case an urban cloister—which acts as both the referential "room" for the complex and the primary public outdoor circulation and housing entry space.
The main gate faces the campus and is entered both from the elevated plaza and by a major outdoor stair. The stairway originates from the Morningside Drive level pedestrian mews and connects the Faculty Club entry, the Student Activity level entry, which is a two-story space under the cloister, and the Law School and Judson Hall entries. Over

the entry gate is the mail room and the two-story dean's house. The single security point under the gate is an extension of the low-rise, split-level townhouse building which faces the campus (west) and the cloister (east). A covered outdoor arcade surrounds the open courtyard and provides access to the townhouse entries, the academic center entry on the north end of the court, and the elevator lobby entry on the southwest corner of the court. The stair towers, which are entry points to the third level of the townhouse units, modulate and articulate the pedestrian townhouse scale of the cloister, which is a "rationalist" urban space. The base of the slab is also occupied by split-level townhouse units, which become duplex flats on the west side below the cloister level. On Morningside Drive, the ground floor is reserved for storefront occupancy, a break in the Columbia tradition of elevating buildings on a solid base. Behind the storefronts is the parking garage.
The lounge crosses the south end of the

1.View from Morningside Drive of southeast
facade 2.Axonometric from campus 3.Entry
gate 4.Section 5.Detail of stair and cloister

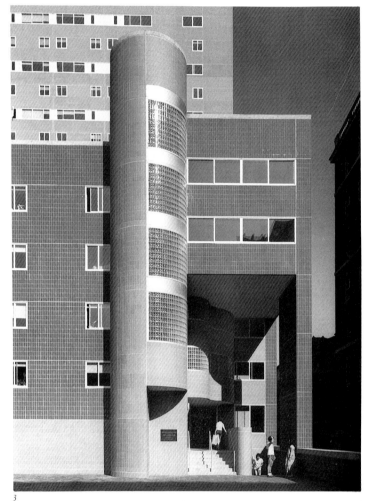

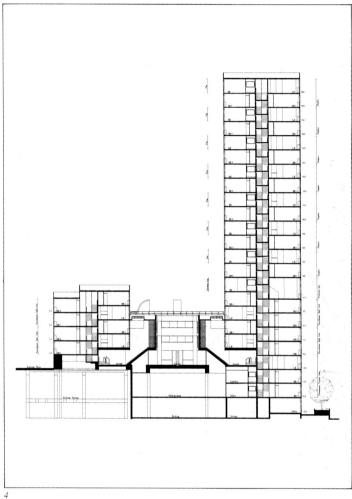

3

4

131

5

cloister one level above ground and is a
two-story linear volume orienting back to the
court. The hotel floor is a one-and-a-half
story space above the townhouses at the base
of the slab and is the transition between the
walk-up and the elevator circulation systems.
The tower consists of 14 skip-stop floors of
duplex and flat units, articulated by
cantilever two-story high floor lounges at the
elevator stops, affording panoramic views
south over Central Park to the lower
Manhattan skyline.

The entire concrete structure is designed as a
section manipulation, giving maximum
privacy, individual identity, and minimum
public circulation space to the complex. The
basic apartment consists of four single rooms
with a shared kitchen, with the dining and
living room on a separate level, thus
establishing a private and a shared level with
two orientations and views.

The complex is sheathed in two colors of tile:
terra-cotta, which articulates the low-rise
elements, and beige-gray, which articulates

the tower and public functions. Aside from
adding a programmatic reading, the two
colors successfully negotiate the campus
material vocabulary, varying from limestone
to brick to precast concrete, while also
addressing the contextual relationship to
Morningside Drive.

1.*Southwest facade* 2.*View of northeast facade* 3.*Detail of southeast corner* 4.*Model of typical section* 5.*Typical tower student lounge* 6.*Typical hotel suite* 7.*Typical* *living/dining/kitchen* 8.*View of cloister* 9.*View of hall and meeting room* 10.*View of lobby from boardroom* 11.*View of cloister* 12.*Detail of typical stair-tower in cloister*

1

132

2

3

4

5

6

7

8

9

10

133

11

12

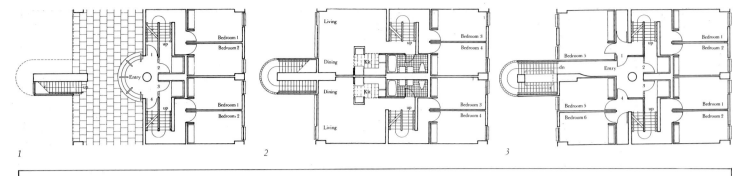

1 2 3

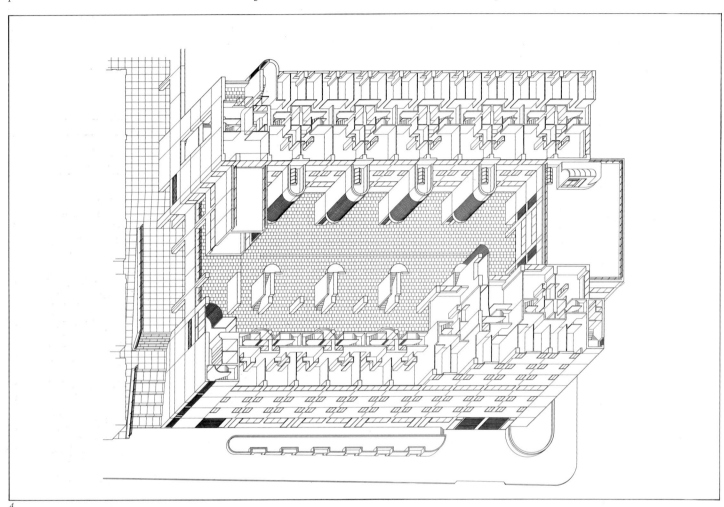

134

4

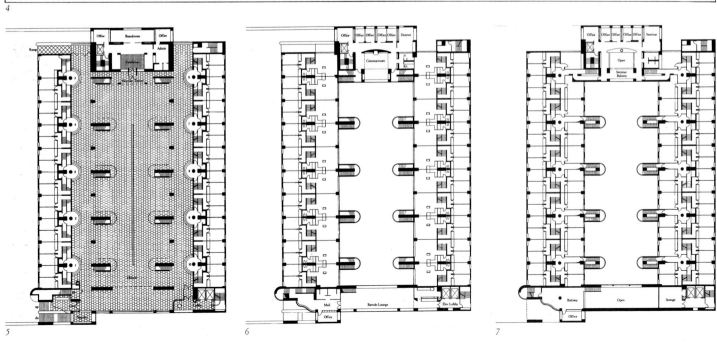

5 6 7

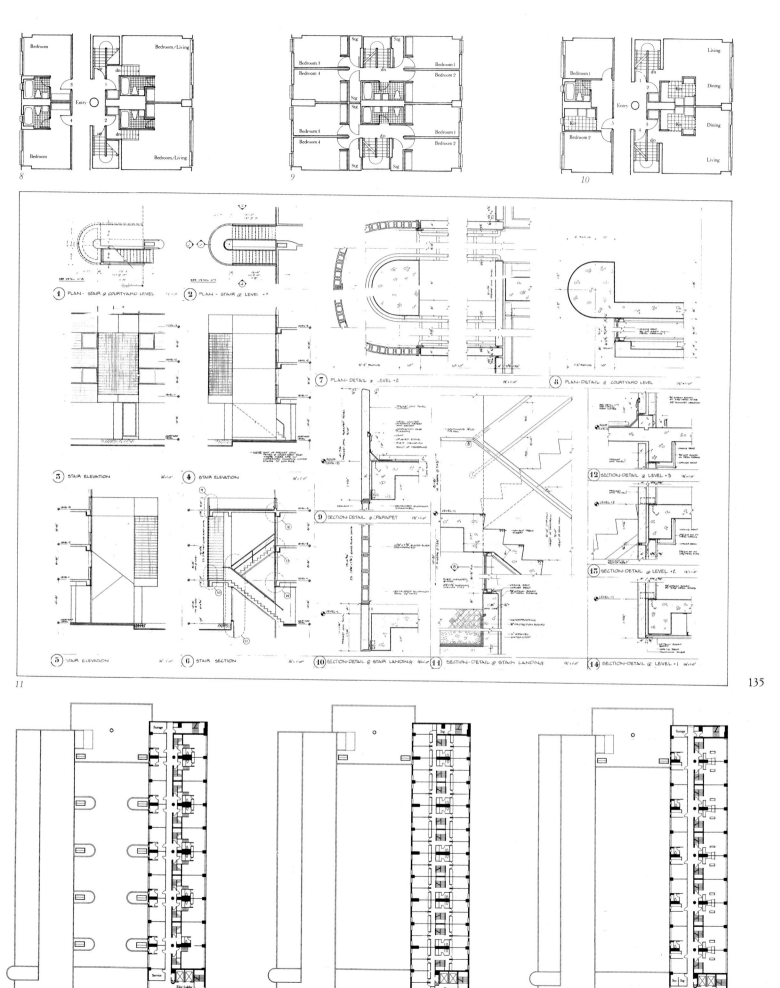

8

9

10

11

135

12

13

14

1.*View of east campus complex from bridge over Amsterdam Avenue* 2.*View from Sulzberger Plaza* 3.*View of cloister looking north toward the Heyman Center for the* Humanities 4.*Stair approach from Morningside Drive* 5.*Entry gate detail* 6.*Entry gate detail* 7.*View from Morningside Park*

1

2

3

136

4

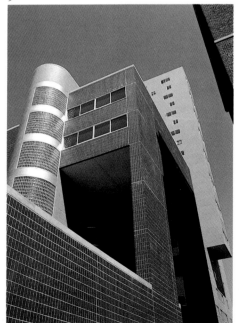

5

6

The problem was to design a residence in the middle dunes on a one-acre tract site, with an access road from the west, ocean/horizon views to the south from one level above grade, and adjacent residences on the north, south and west.

Zoning ordinances required that all living levels in a dune area be at an elevation 14 feet above sea level, which in this case placed the first floor a half-level above grade. A solution which was generated overlaid the program requirements, orientation, and the owner's desire for privacy, while exploiting the southern views.

The garage and entry are located on the north facade at grade. From the entry, the first leg of the stepped ramp runs along the north facade and arrives at the living/dining, kitchen and pool terrace level which extends from the south facade as the major outdoor space. The master-bedroom suite, a one-and-a-half-story volume over the garage with a private deck and outdoor stair down to the pool terrace, is located off the second ramp landing, one level above grade. Off the third ramp landing, one-and-a-half levels above grade, with an overview of the two-story living/dining space, are the study and two guest bedrooms with their balconies facing south and overlooking the pool terrace. The south facade is recessed, with the continuous roof overhang completing the primary rectilinear frame and serving as the architectonic brise-soleil.

1

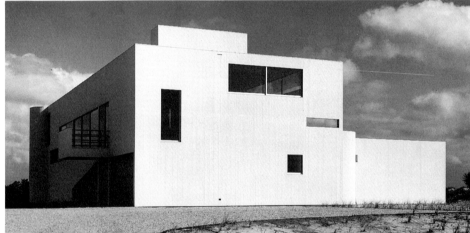

2

138

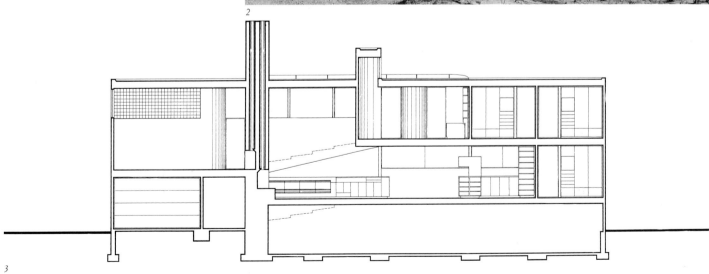

3

The parti is conceptually similar to that of the Cogan Residence, but the interior spatial modulation is more complex. For the first time, the use of color becomes a primary element, adding another layer in the articulation and coding of planes and intersections, reinforcing the primary, secondary and tertiary interrelationships.

1.Southeast facade 2.Northwest facade
3.Section 4.Ground and first floor
axonometric 5.Second and third floor
axonometric 6.Ground and first floor plan
7.Second and third floor plan

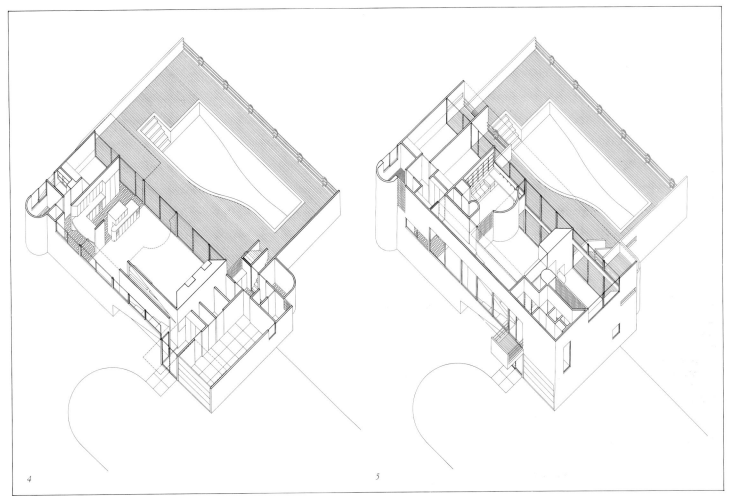

4

5

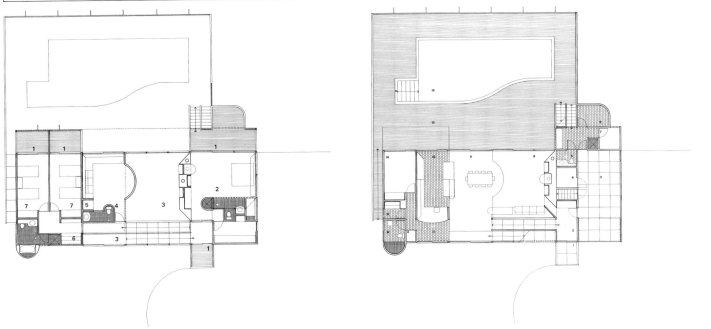

6

7

1.North facade 2.Detail of south facade from
master-bedroom deck 3.Detail of south facade
from deck 4.Entry 5.6.Living room 7.View
of stepped ramp

140

1

4

5

6

Weitz Residence
Quogue, New York

1

3

4

2

143

The problem was to design a residence with a complex program on an ocean dune sloping site, with an access road and views to the bay on the north, access and views to the beach and ocean on the south one level above entry grade, and existing adjacent residences on the east and west.

The program combined a main house which accommodated a living/sitting room, a dining room, kitchen, a master-bedroom suite and two working studies, plus two distinct guest suites with kitchenettes and direct outside access, a carport, a swimming pool, a tennis court and extensive outside deck space. Organizationally, this house is a hybrid of the row house implications and section organization of the Cohn Residence and the integration of two masses around the entry and circulation point of the Tolan Residence. However, in the Weitz Residence the "knuckle" is more complex in that it overlays both inside and outside vertical and horizontal systems, culminating in a bridge extension to the beach from the second level.

The site and building layering are integral at all times, relating to the section manipulation, as well as to orientation and views. The driveway, which is on axis to the carport, is parallel and passes to the tennis court, whose south wall retains the pool terrace at a higher elevation. The entry stair is an integral extension of the pool terrace and connects the second-level outdoor deck space and the bridge to the south, the guest-suite deck and entry to the west, and the kitchen and main entries to the east. On the pool terrace level, the second guest suite orients north and shares the kitchenette with an outdoor service counter and covered dining terrace. This suite can also be reached by the second interior stair via the main kitchen and by a dumbwaiter.

The second level is occupied by a single-height sitting area and adjacent double-height living room, both of which offer access to the south-facing deck. This level also accommodates a kitchen and dining space with views over the pool terrace, tennis

court and bay.

The third level is occupied by the master bedroom, which overlooks the living room and is extended by a south-facing deck which also overviews the living deck below. Interconnected to the master bedroom are two separate studies, one at the top of the main stair facing the ocean, the other at the top of the secondary interconnecting stair, overviewing the living room, the ocean and the bay. An outdoor roof deck over the second floor guest suite connects to the master bath and dressing space and affords 360-degree views while maintaining its privacy.

As in the Haupt Residence, the use of color is extensive, reinforcing and articulating the spatial and planar layering and intensifying the multifaceted internal transparencies.

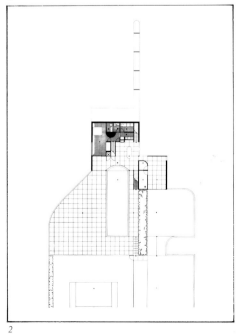

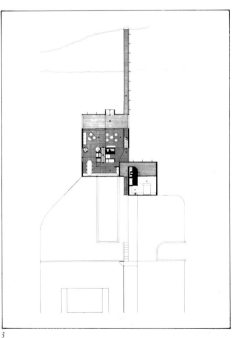

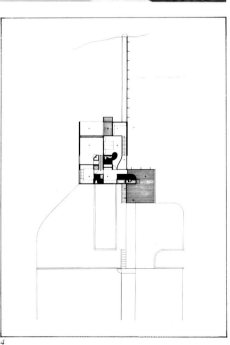

144

1

2

3

4

1.North facade 2.Ground floor plan 3.First floor
plan 4.Second floor plan 5.View from roof
deck 6.East facade 7.View from guest bedroom
deck 8.South facade 9.10.Living room

5

6

7

8

9

10

**Thomas and Betts Corporation
Office Building**
Raritan, New Jersey

1

The problem was to design a
160,000-square-foot, low-cost multifunctional
building for an electrical component design
and manufacturing company. The 12-acre
sloping site had a large flat knoll at its top,
access road on the south, and dense woods
on the east, west and north.

The program required areas for
reception/waiting, corporate offices,
engineering space, research space, a
laboratory and model shop, an employees'
cafeteria and executive dining room (to be
served by a common kitchen), and loading
dock facilities. Separate entries were required
for visitors, for corporate officers and for
employees.

The plan organization is articulated by a
two-story corporate element, a two-story
engineering and research element, a
one-and-a-half-story laboratory element, and
a two-story cafeteria/dining and loading dock
element. These masses are joined by a
300-foot-long, two-story, balconied, skylit
interior "street" which also connects the
three entry points. This circulation spine,
which admits natural light to the center of
the building, was conceived of as the public
referential space, accommodating reception
and waiting, stairs, interior entries to the
various departments and elements, and
service and mechanical spaces.

The steel-frame building construction is
exposed and articulated in the circulation
spine and cafeteria; the prefabricated
steel-supported lightweight concrete panels,
the gray glass and aluminum curtain wall,
and the skylight system are the primary
materials.

The program, site, entry and circulation
systems generated the massing and the clear
and functional plan parti.

146

2

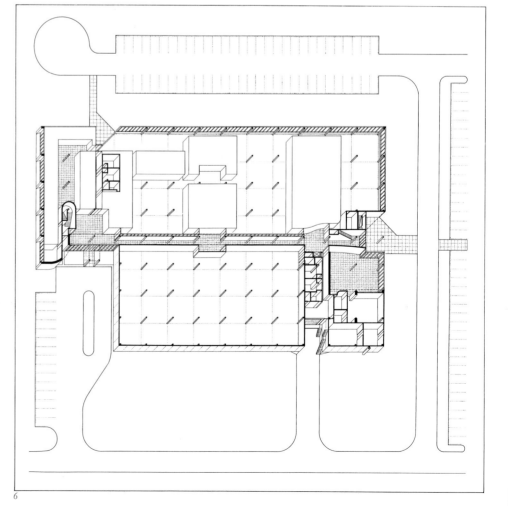

6

1.*Visitor entry* 2.*View from southwest toward entry* 3.*Circulation gallery* 4.*Gallery detail* 5.*View of gallery from balcony above* 6.*Ground floor axonometric* 7.*Second floor axonometric*

3

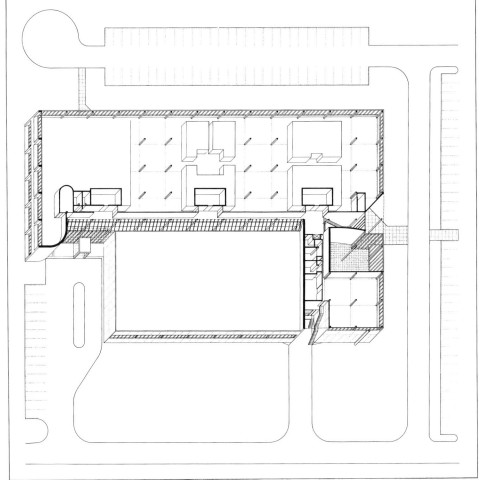

4

7

5

1.*North facade* 2.*Stair detail* 3.*North end
stair* 4.*View of reception and gallery* 5.*View
of gallery from entry*

148
1

2

3

4

5

Benenson Residence
Rye, New York

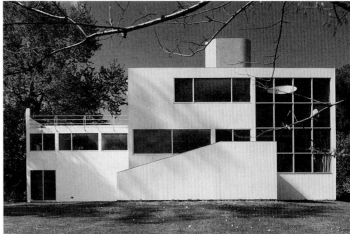

The problem was to design a residence on a two-acre flat site with an access road from the north, views to Long Island Sound to the south, and adjacent existing structures to the north, east and west.

The site conditions were similar to the Haupt Residence with regard to the flood plane and the requirement that the first living level be four feet above grade, and similar to the Tolan and Weitz Residences in terms of the two-part massing, which, in each case, was interconnected vertically and horizontally by the entry and stair. The entry, central stair, and two-car garage are located on grade facing north. The double-height living room and screened porch, the dining room, and kitchen are located on the first half-level. The

two children's bedrooms and guest bedroom are located above the garage on the second half-level. A sitting-room balcony overlooking the living room, the master bedroom overlooking the screened porch, and a dressing room are located on the third half-level. The study and roof deck over the children's bedroom wing are located on the fourth half-level.

The two vertical interlocking and pivotal references are the stair space and the chimney, which contains four fireplaces, one each in the living room, the screened porch, sitting-room balcony and the master bedroom.

The use of color is extensive and renders the volumetric modulation with a cubist intensity.

The screened porch, used for the first time, extends all of the living spaces both functionally and visually, while adding a new dimension to usable outdoor covered space. The Haupt, Weitz, and Benenson Residences, despite their different partis, collectively summarized and consolidated earlier residential investigations.

1.Screened porch 2.South facade 3.South facade 4. Roof level axonometric 5.Second and third level axonometric 6. Ground and first level axonometric 7.Living space 8.Sitting balcony

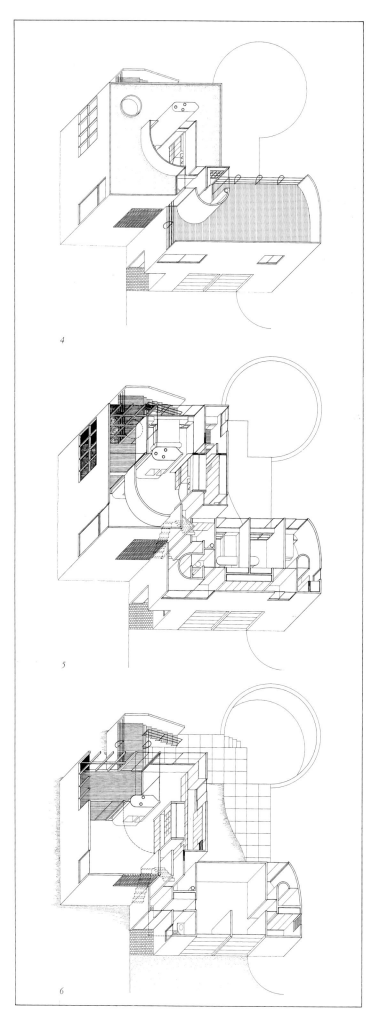

4

5

6

7

8

Swirl, Inc.
Showrooms and Offices
New York, New York

1

2

3

The problem was to design new offices and showroom space for an apparel design firm. The space was a 6,000-square-foot floor in one of the original Rockefeller Center buildings.

The program required a reception/waiting area, two executive offices with a shared conference room, five showrooms, dressing rooms, sales offices, accounting offices and a workroom space.

The square-foot limitation lead to a parti in which the three showroom spaces would also accommodate display and circulation. Two

4

designer showrooms are separated and articulated by large-scale photomurals depicting a current designer-chosen fashion image.

The slate-gray display cabinets are designed as flexible graphic devices, exposed wardrobes, and spatial definers. When combined with beige carpeting, reflective tile ceilings and neutral wall colors, the cabinets accentuate and highlight the hues, fabrics and designs of the apparel, making the object of sale the focus while the environment remains a subtle abstract support reference.

1.View of reception and elevator lobby 2.View
of special showroom 3.Showrooms and
circulation space 4.Detail of special showroom
entry 5.View of showroom toward reception
6.Floor plan

5

153

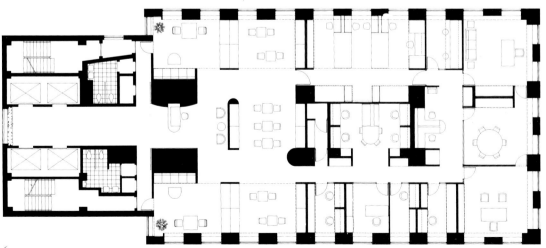

6

The problem was to design a major new hotel and casino on what was the only remaining ocean site on the island. The site is the first to be encountered from the airport and features panoramic views of the beach and ocean. Breezes come from the land side and are generally strong and constant, making building placement critical for screening outdoor terrace spaces.

The program requirements were extensive and helped to generate a design which was site responsive, environmentally accurate and programmatically suitable.

In this proposal the hotel entry and main lobby are elevated a full level above grade to accommodate the service, kitchen and support spaces at grade level. A looped-ramp drive connects the main road to an entry courtyard, defined by the hotel complex on one side and the casino on the other. The open lobby was designed as a three-story-high promenade, which creates balcony and mezzanine space above and terrace related space below. The lobby is axial and open-ended to the ocean on one end and contained by the entry court and casino on the other.

From the lobby level, there is direct access to the showroom, a dinner/entertainment terraced seating space for eight hundred persons, a cocktail lounge and lobby lounge. One level below the lobby at the beach level a terrace room, pool area, pool bar, men's and women's health club, tennis shop and five wind-protected tennis courts are provided. The area between the tennis courts and the beach accommodates 26 cabana units.

On the level above the lobby, the mezzanine accommodates a specialty restaurant and shopping arcade.

Two levels above the lobby is the meeting room and club floor, with access to a major roof terrace over the showroom.

Above the club level, there are nine hotel floors with thirty-one double rooms and two suites per floor, each with balconies and views to the ocean. The top two floors provide 11 large, subdividable duplex units.

154

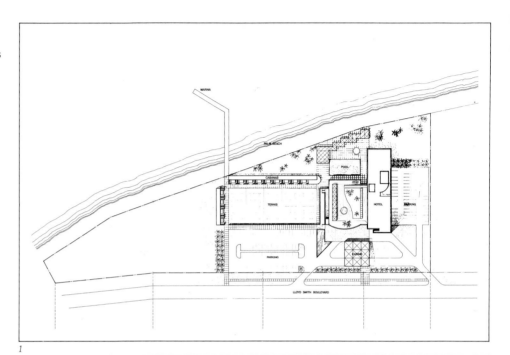

1

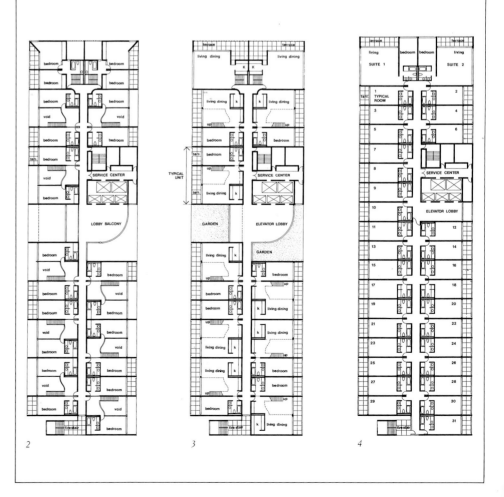

2   3   4

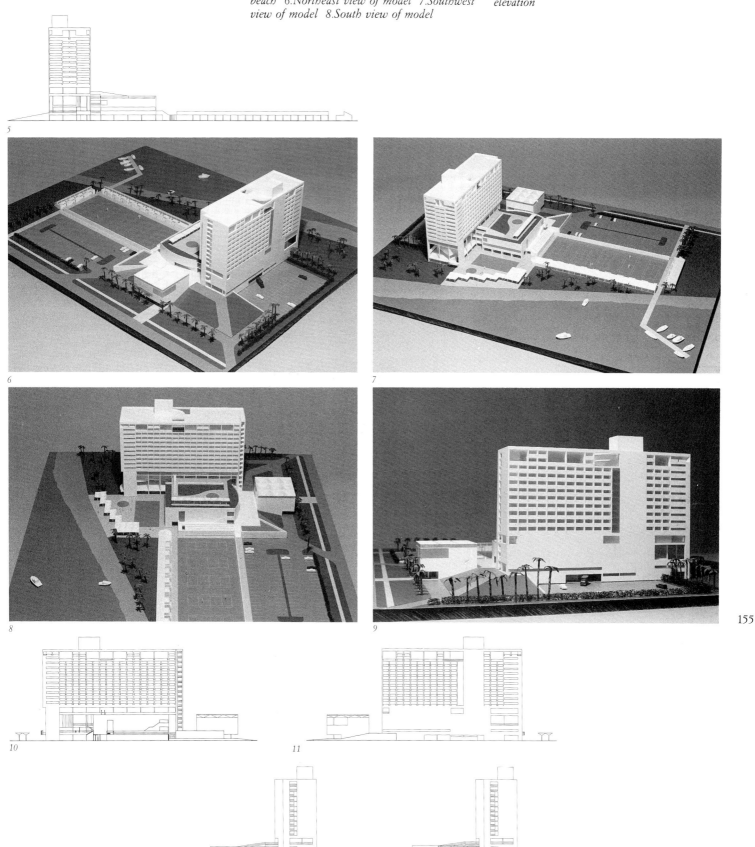

1.Site plan 2.Duplex unit floor plan 3.Lower floor plan 4.Typical floor plan 5.View from beach 6.Northeast view of model 7.Southwest view of model 8.South view of model 9.North view of model 10.South elevation 11.North elevation 12.East elevation 13.West elevation

5

6

7

8

9

155

10

11

12

13

Swid Apartment
New York, New York

The problem was to design an apartment in an existing 3,400-square-foot space for a couple with three children.

The program required large living and dining rooms for extensive entertaining and for a display of contemporary art; it also required a master-bedroom and library suite, three children's rooms, a playroom, a kitchen and breakfast room, and a servant's bedroom suite.

In plan the parti disposed the public rooms, living and dining rooms, off the entry gallery to the south with the private rooms off the widened articulated circulation space/playroom to the north. The kitchen and breakfast room is anchored in the center, simultaneously serving and dividing both zones.

The changes in ceiling heights, the use of floor materials, color and mirrors, and the built-in cabinetwork add a complexity and sense of spatial transformation which support the design's programmatic duality.

1.*View of entry gallery* 2.*Entrance* 3.*View of gallery toward living room* 4.*Living room* 5.*View of dining room from gallery* 6.*Kitchen* 7.*Master bedroom* 8.*View of bedroom suite from hall* 9.*Plan before* 10.*Plan after*

7

6

8

157

9

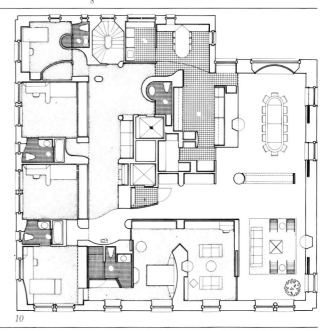

10

1

The problem was to design a gallery with the capacity to display over three hundred American and one thousand European posters within a linear 1,200-square-foot storefront space on Madison Avenue. Sales space, office space, and storage space were also required.

The design was developed from an analysis of creative display and storage techniques. The European poster display is related to the front window and encountered first upon entry. Three large vinyl indexed books, mounted on a sloped shelf in a mirrored niche, accommodate 1,200 posters, editions of which are stored in flat files for immediate retrieval.

The American posters are all wall-hung through the space from floor to ceiling. The lower third of the wall is canted out at the bottom, affording better viewing and the illusion of a larger space.

The walls are light gray, the floor medium-gray carpet, and the cabinets are white plastic laminate. The polished aluminum ceiling extends the space vertically while reflecting the multiplicity of wall-hung poster imagery, thus establishing an intense architectural graphic collage.

1.View of gallery from entry 2.Poster display books toward entry

2

159

The problem was to design an office/ showroom space in an existing narrow rectilinear 2,000-square-foot area with south-facing perimeter windows on one long elevation. The program required three office/showroom spaces, a design studio space, and a special showroom space. The entry, reception/waiting space, three sales work stations, and circulation spine are accommodated in the initial linear zone,

reinforced by a wood floor, polished aluminum ceiling, and gray lacquer cabinetwork. Parallel, yet separated by a transparent and frosted glass paneled wall, are the three office/showroom spaces and the designer's studio, each with natural light and articulated from the initial space by a gray carpet floor, coffered plaster ceiling and oak cabinetwork.

1.*Detail of showroom wall from gallery*
2.*View of showroom and workroom from gallery* 3.*Circulation and work station space*
4.*Sales-showroom* 5.*Floor plan*

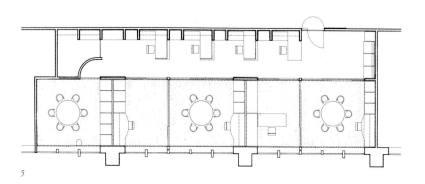

Geffen Apartment
New York, New York

1

2

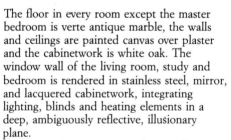

160

The problem was to design a working/living apartment in an existing 1,700-square-foot space on the 17th floor, with panoramic views to the west of Central Park and the Manhattan skyline.

The parti was derived from the design of a continuous pavilion with an extended sense of space, and from the rendering of the window wall as both totally transparent and spatially referential.

The entry gallery widens into a split living/dining space and continues around the core to the study/sitting room. This room, in turn, connects to the bedroom suite, whose floor is one foot higher. The kitchen and service areas are in a separate zone off the dining area.

The floor in every room except the master bedroom is verte antique marble, the walls and ceilings are painted canvas over plaster and the cabinetwork is white oak. The window wall of the living room, study and bedroom is rendered in stainless steel, mirror, and lacquered cabinetwork, integrating lighting, blinds and heating elements in a deep, ambiguously reflective, illusionary plane.

The composite integration of materials, colors, and textural and spatial modulations created a sense of subtle elegance and richness while maintaining the abstract clarity and rigor of earlier projects.

3

1.Den 2.View from gallery toward bedroom
3.Bedroom entry 4.Entry gallery 5.Living
room 6.Dining room 7.Floor plan

4

161

5

6

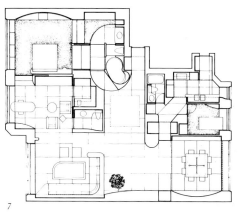

7

Belkin Memorial Room
Yeshiva University
New York, New York

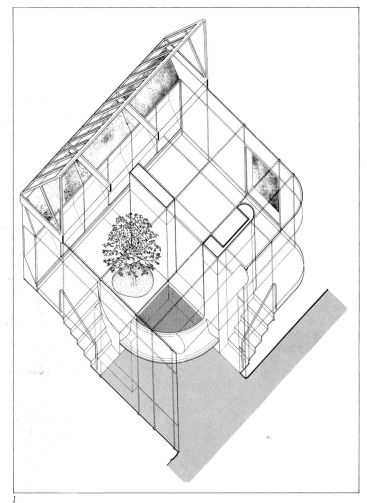

1

The problem was to design a space in recognition of President Belkin's contributions to the university and to education that would be both functional and symbolic. The intention was to create a space of enduring purpose and quiet elegance. An existing space in the university library was transformed materially and extended physically by this new programmatic and physical intervention.

The room had to accommodate space for special meetings, a pool, a tree and a display of memorabilia and audio-visual material recalling the history of President Belkin's life. The plan is square, with horizontal and vertical movement around the center, which is occupied by the pool, integral bench, and tree. The major display cabinet occupies the expanded back wall, which was reconnected to the facade by a new skylight which both naturally lights and extends the space.

The granite floors and oak paneled walls and ceiling establish a new material reference which juxtaposes yet supports the existing brick and concrete interior of the library.

1.Axonometric 2.View from existing library
3.View of pool and display from entry 4.Pool
and bench detail 5.Stair and bench detail
6.Display space

3

4

5

6

Taft Residence
Cincinnati, Ohio

The problem was to design a large residence on a totally private six-acre gently sloping site, with access from the north, horizon views toward the valley and hills to the south, and woods to the east and west. The site had no strong existing architectural features, nor a site construct that was sequential with view and orientation overlays. The parti was a transformed court house derived from an assemblage of forms, responding simultaneously to programmatic and spatial requirements.

The building and site overlay sequence begins with the entry/auto court, defined on the north by a retaining wall and integral greenhouse structure, and on the south by the entry facade, a primarily solid wall with a major opening and two garage doors at the base. Immediately to the west, under the outdoor, covered, axial entry space, is the separate entry to the children's house, a two-story element accommodating a living/dining room and kitchen on the ground floor and two bedrooms and

bathrooms on the second floor.

The garage wing, with two guest rooms and baths on the second floor, is located to the east opposite the children's house, thus forming the gateway from the auto court. The pool terrace is located on the west in front of the children's house with views south, and a grass sculpture court is on the east between the garage and the main house. The entry to the main house is a translucent incident on the axis; inside, the view is extended through the entry hall/gallery to the sitting room, terrace, lawn and beyond. Immediately east of the entry hall is the kitchen and double-height breakfast room. Off the gallery on the west is the stair and the double-height living room, extended on the east by a single-height sitting space with a fireplace/chimney element which separates the dining room. All the public spaces share an outdoor terrace which is integral to the brise-soleil and which forms the lawn edge with its horizontal views beyond.

The second level interconnects the guest

rooms and children's bedrooms to the main house by a gallery space which extends from the entry wall through the brise-soleil.

The gallery is the largest, most complex space in the composition. It reinforces the north/south axis, clarifies orientation, and accommodates a sitting area for the guest rooms, a study overlooking the breakfast room, a stair landing, a sitting balcony and fireplace overlooking the living room, and a double-height screened porch in the brise-soleil. The brise-soleil interconnects via the gallery with the master-bedroom suite, which is separated from the sitting room by the chimney element.

The last major outdoor space is the roof terrace on the third level of the main house, which commands the entire site.

In summary, this house represented a major departure in its compositional and organizational principles. It is asymmetrically tripartite, horizontally sequential and multilayered, and traditionally planned.

Finally, it is a building in scale with its site, one which has the capacity for self-definition; it is at once a village, a series of articulate spaces, and a composite object establishing place.

1.*Aerial view* 2.*View of courtyard from entry* 3.*South facade* 4.*Detail of east facade from pool terrace* 5.*Living room* 6.*Living room stair* 7.*Sitting room/balcony*

4

6

7

1

3

4

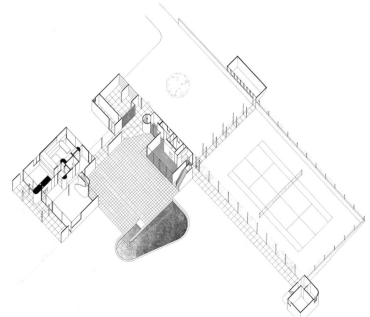

9

10

1.East facade 2.Master bedroom and screen porch 3.Detail of living room corner 4.Southwest facade 5.Breakfast room with view of study above 6.Study 7.View of gallery from sitting area 8.Gallery/sitting area 9.Ground floor axonometric 10.Second floor axonometric 11.Roof axonometric Following page: southeast facade

2

5

6

7

8

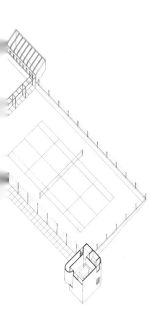

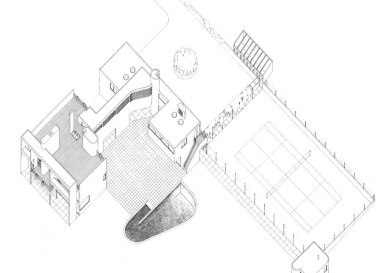

11

The problem was to design one thousand units of housing on the east side of Roosevelt Island facing Manhattan, to be located in front of the existing parking garage and north of the initial built housing.

The site was five acres, and included a large area with existing 80-foot high trees. The project was designed within the FHA guidelines, with extensive programmatic requirements. The existing contextual references were pertinent to the design realization.

Of the one thousand housing units, seven hundred were to be market rate, consisting of studios, one- to four-bedroom flats and three- to four-bedroom duplexes; one hundred were Section 8 Elderly, consisting of one- and two-bedroom flats; and two hundred were

Section 8 Family, consisting of one- to four-bedroom flats. Also included in the requirements were a daycare center, community centers, an intermediate public school, and a 1,500-car parking structure, doubling in size the existing one.

The site plan was organized about a major outdoor space, Northtown Plaza, defined on the east by a parking garage, a dense, articulated six-story high concrete structure with shopping and commercial space at its base, on the north and south by the two L-shaped Section 8 Family Structures, and on the west by the H-shaped Market Rate structure. The plaza was an extension and modulation of Main Street, rendered as an informal referential outdoor room and maintaining all of the existing trees.

All the buildings were designed with covered arcades at their bases. These arcades accommodate entries, lobbies, and community facilities, and laundry room facilities and roof terraces are at the twelfth floor level.

The daycare center is located at the base of the South Family Structure, opening to a playground, which is defined by the Elderly Structure to the south and the river wall to the west, with a pedestrian path paralleling the East River and extending the length of the island.

The proposed construction is exposed slab reinforced poured concrete with polychrome brick infill walls. The use of color is programmatic: charcoal gray for the bases and vertical circulation elements, rose for the

170

1

2

3

spandrels, and red for the remaining walls. The massing, the site construct, the integrated and varying outdoor spaces, the polychrome graphic articulation, and the sympathetic scale establish a coherent urban fabric with the required amenities, while simultaneously supporting the original town plan and creating an identifiable neighborhood.

1. *View of model from west* 2. *View of site from garage* 3. *View of Main Street from north* 4. *Aerial view of model* 5. *Aerial view of model* 6. *Site plan*

4

5

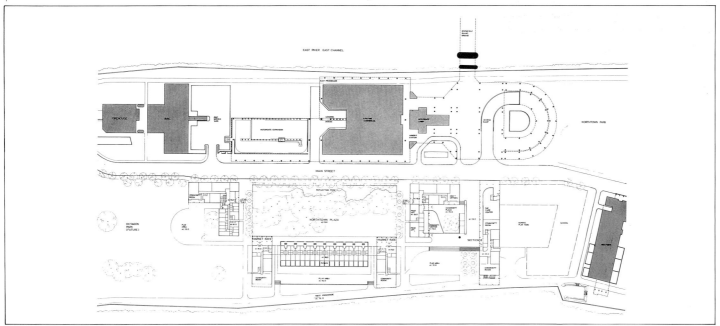

6

BASEMENT PLAN
BUILDING A
(BUILDING B OPPOSITE HAND)

BUILDING A   GROUND FLOOR PLAN

GROUND FLOOR PLAN   BUILDING B

PLAN   FLOORS 3-12   BUILDING B
(BUILDING A OPPOSITE HAND)

BUILDING A   SECOND FLOOR PLAN

SECOND FLOOR PLAN   BUILDING B

TOWER PLAN   13-21   BUILDING B
(BUILDING A OPPOSITE HAND)

1

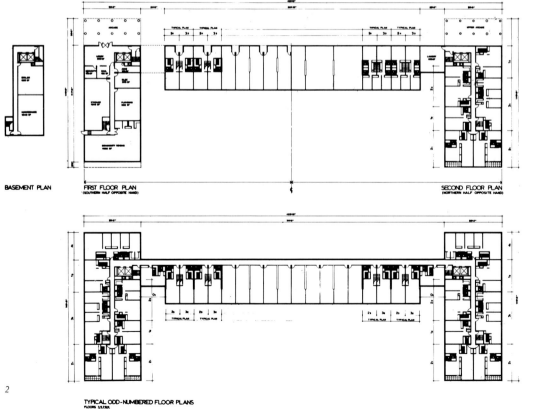

BASEMENT PLAN

FIRST FLOOR PLAN
(SOUTHERN HALF OPPOSITE HAND)

SECOND FLOOR PLAN
(NORTHERN HALF OPPOSITE HAND)

2

TYPICAL ODD-NUMBERED FLOOR PLANS
FLOORS 3,5,7,9,11

1.Section 236 plans 2.Market rate plans
3.Detail of exterior wall 4.West elevation
study 5.Market rate unit plans

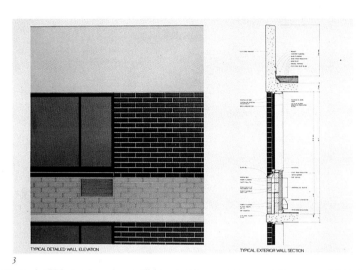

TYPICAL DETAILED WALL ELEVATION

TYPICAL EXTERIOR WALL SECTION

3

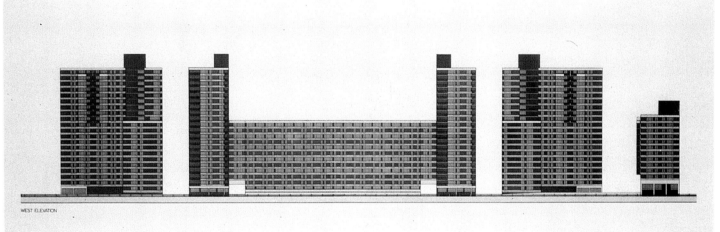

WEST ELEVATION

4

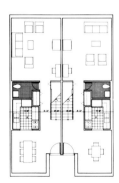 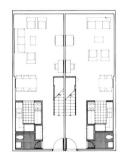 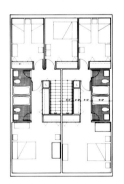

 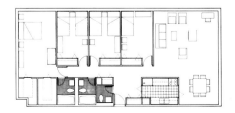

5

1

2

3

The problem was to design new offices and support space in an existing 12,000-square-foot basement area under the performing arts theater sculpture plaza. The space was devoid of natural light, and entry was from a single point under the pedestrian bridge on 65th Street, three feet above the finished floor elevation.

The entry/reception/waiting space is connected to the main internal gallery circulation spine by a stepped ramp. Off the 12-foot high gallery, displaying Lincoln Center posters and modulated by columns four feet in diameter, the entries to the various office spaces are articulated by a dropped ceiling, change in floor material, and graphics. At each end of the "street" are two conference rooms enclosed by glass-block walls, offering unique material and spatial articulation.

In principle, the central referential circulation space is similar in approach to the Thomas and Betts Corporation Offices.

1.Entry 2.Reception 3.Circulation gallery
4.Conference room 5.View of gallery at
conference room 6.Waiting area 7.Floor plan

4

5

6

175

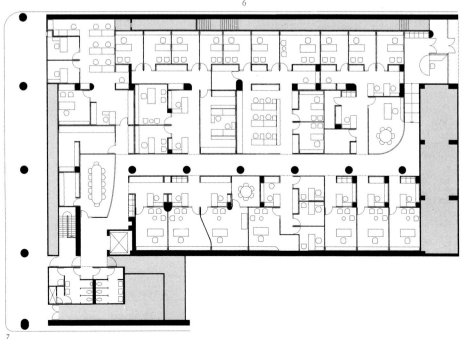

7

1

176

The problem was to design new offices in an
existing 1,200-square-foot space which wraps
around two sides of a building core. The
orientation is to the north and west.
The program required a waiting/reception
space, which was located in the public
elevator lobby. Entry to the working space is
from the public corridor into the secretarial
area, which is immediately adjacent to the
two executive offices and the conference
room. Two offices, three work carrels, a
kitchen and service space are located on the
narrow leg of the L configuration.
The material palette of gray quarry tile floors
and brushed aluminum ceilings in the
circulation space, carpet floors and plaster
ceilings in the offices, as well as the oak
cabinetwork and use of color throughout
establishes a spatial hierarchy and an intimate
working environment that transforms the
office norm.

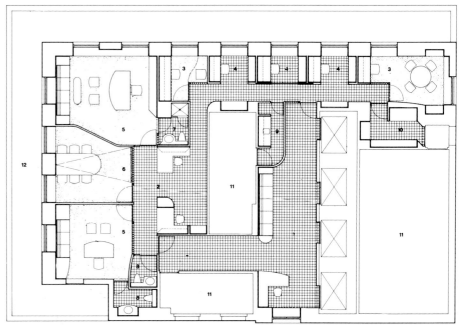

2

3

1.Reception and waiting area 2.Floor plan
3.Secretarial area 4.Executive office
5.6.Conference room 7.Work carrel

4

177

5

6

7

AT&T
Office Building
Parsippany, New Jersey

1

3

The problem was to design a 300,000-square-foot office building in an existing office park with a parking requirement for one thousand cars.

This was the first opportunity to elaborate on the Evans Partnership prototype investigation by employing a defined program within an existing site constraint and context.

The design was generated by the following program requirements: multiple building entries controlled by a single security point, a maximum area of perimeter wall, and capacity to accommodate a greater number of tenants in the future.

Since this was to be the largest building in the park, the exterior materials and plan configurations were critical. There are three 100,000-square-foot floors surrounding a

grass courtyard, which is the primary entry/referential space and the generator of additional perimeter. This space, which includes a covered arcade, terminates in a three-story lobby. The lobby accepts the two side entries with their articulated monumental stairs and balconies, while also resolving the two side entries and single security point.

The exterior walls form a gray grid glass curtain wall with travertine base, stair, and entry walls, rendering the building as a one-story abstraction that both reflects and absorbs. All volumetric erosions, as well as the exterior walls of the courtyard, are travertine and gray glass, revealing the juxtaposed graphics and scale transformation from the exterior.

4

1.Northeast facade 2.Northeast facade
3.Detail of north facade 4.Detail of north
facade 5.Typical east/west entry 6.View from
court to entry 7.View of court 8.View of
court 9.Site plan 10.Ground floor plan

5

6

7

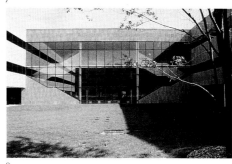

8

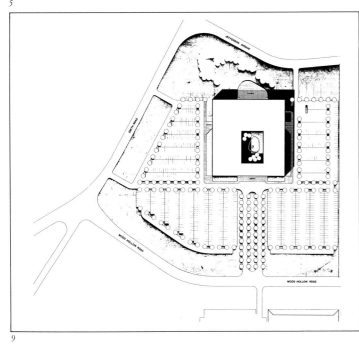

9

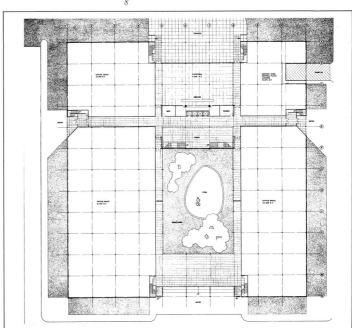

10

179

1

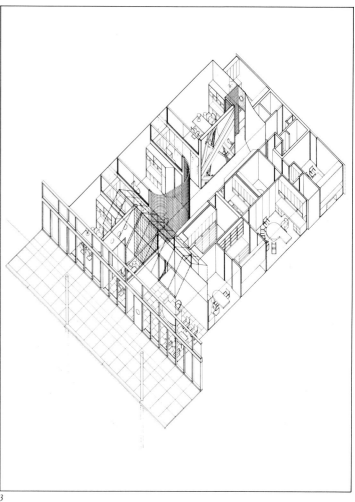

2

3

180

The problem was to design a 60,000-square-foot office building on a linear, narrow site which required a storm drainage retention pond.

The parti evolved, as in other similar projects, primarily through the site constraints. Required parking was located on the east and west ends of the site, accessing the building through two porticos at the end of a continuous covered arcade, paralleling a reflecting pool and adjoining the integrally landscaped retention basin.

The site and building are thus composite; overlay begins at the road, progresses through the retention basin, the pool, the arcade, and through the building to the north facade parallel to the highway. The arcade not only serves as the public entry space and parking connector, but acts as a sunscreen for the floor-to-ceiling glass on the south facade.

The travertine walls, gray glass, and white porcelain transom continue the material theme of the earlier Evans building while reflecting the image of the AT&T Building which is located across the road.

The second phase of this project was to design the Evans Partnership offices in a 7,000-square-foot rectilinear space within the building.

The major design decision was to maintain the 15-foot-high ceiling datum of the arcade in the skylit entry, the conference room, the main circulation and executive secretary space, and the three executive offices. The management and service spaces were organized under nine-foot high ceilings adjacent to the main circulation space.

The vertical layering established on the facade by the nine-foot high glass, the one-and-a-half-foot high transom, and the four-and-a-half-foot high glass, is reinforced by the oak framing and cabinetwork system, color modulations, transparencies, reflections, and glass-block infills, transforming the interior perceptual environment into a continuously expanding spatial hierarchy.

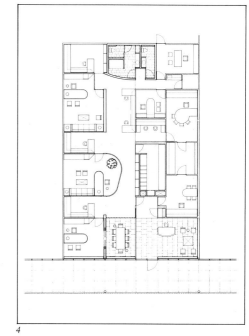

4

1.View of south arcade with reflecting pool
2.Entrance arcade 3.Axonometric 4.Plan

5.Executive office 6.Executive office 7.Entry
arcade 8.Reception and waiting area
9.Executive office

5

6

7

8

9

1.Conference room 2.Executive office 3.North
elevation 4.Gallery 5.Gallery detail

1

2

3

4

5

The Evans Partnership
Offices
New York, New York

1

2

3

4

The problem was to design the company's executive offices in a 2,500-square-foot L-shaped space, with its fixed entry location at the extreme corner of the configuration. The entry sequence around the glass-block walled conference room is rendered by a black glass gallery wall which is interrupted at its corner and stands opposite the entry door. A 45-degree floor-to-ceiling mirror reflects the waiting and reception space beyond, which is adjacent to the president's corner office, the controller's office and two executive offices.

The palette of materials and colors includes verte antique marble floors in the circulation space, oak cabinetwork, black glass, and variously shaded off-white walls and ceilings, which render the space texturally opulent and perceptually sedate.

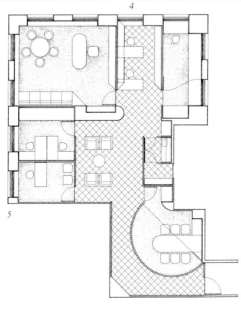

5

1. View of gallery from entry 2. Waiting area
3. Secretarial area 4. Conference room 5. Floor plan

**Knoll International
Showroom and Office Building**
Boston, Massachusetts

1

The problem was to design a showroom office building on a 28-foot by 85-foot urban, contextual site on Newbury Street.

The program required a 7,500-square-foot furniture textile showroom, 2,500 square feet of storage space and 7,500 square feet of rentable office space.

The historical references to Boston's urban fabric included the stoop, the bay window, and the pedestrian commercial/residential scale, and were critical factors in determining the design parti.

The showrooms occupy the first three stories and the basement of the six-story building. The extended showroom window, which is integrated into the three-story erosion, faces the sidewalk and features a terrace on the second floor. This window establishes entry and showroom identity and reinterprets the stoop, bay window and parlor floor, while also creating a referential pedestrian scale.

The vertical glass-block stair enclosing element, articulating the circulation and service core, supports the street scale while integrating the lower and upper three office floors of the building.

The facade is simultaneously an object and a wall; it supports existing contextual images while rendering a morphological structure in which new elements are integrated.

The showroom space is designed as a flexible loft with exposed concrete columns on the long wall opposite the core wall. It is zoned front-to-back by the stair, which internally connects the three showroom floors.

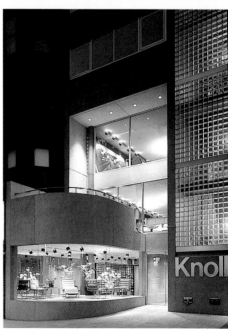

2

1.Newbury Street facade 2.Detail of facade
3.View of terrace from second floor showroom
4.Ground floor showroom space 5.Stair detail
6.Third floor showroom

3

4

5

6

1 2 3 4

5

6

1.Ground floor plan 2.Second floor plan
3.Third floor plan 4.Fourth floor plan
5.Ground floor showroom at rear 6.Stair
detail 7.Axonometric

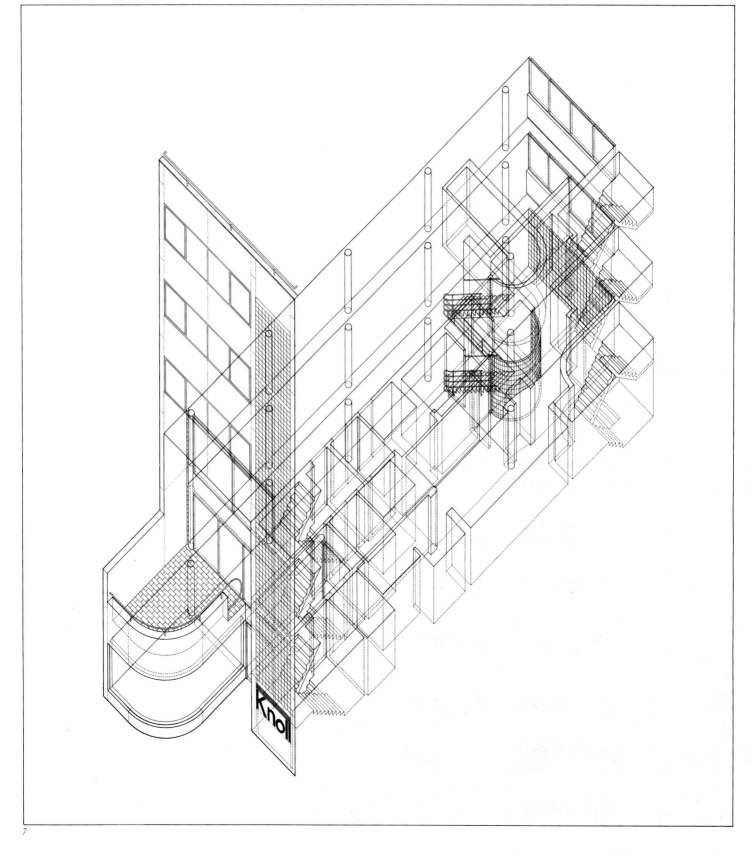

Sycamore Place
Elderly Housing
Columbus, Indiana

The problem was to design a building to contain 24 one-bedroom apartments (three of which were to be designed for handicapped occupancy), a dayroom/ common room, laundry, and beauty salon, all under HUD specifications.

The intention of the design was to transform the usual image of subsidized housing by making a building with presence that would be responsive to its inhabitants and its physical context.

The three-story stepped plan makes each vertical row of three apartments articulate, identifiable, and house-like, while acting to deinstitutionalize the building. Internally, the stepping occurs in the public corridors, creating a vestibule for every two apartments, and reinforcing the idea of entry, privacy and identity. Thus, the corridors become a sequence of rooms with natural light and views at both ends.

By adding a balcony/terrace to each apartment, the private space is extended both physically and psychologically and the facades are given a richness unusual for public housing.

The building is wood-frame construction. The exterior is horizontal cedar clapboard which is stained light gray. The site walls and benches, window trim, doors, leaders and handrails are white. The sundial was designed as the referential and spiritual sculpture/object for the project.

1.*View from southeast* 2.*View from southwest* 3.*Stair detail* 4.*Site plan* 5.*Detail of west facade* 6.*Detail of west facade* 7.*Third floor plan* 8.*Second floor plan* 9.*Ground floor plan* 10.*Typical unit* 11.*Handicap unit* 12.*Detail of north facade*

1

2

3

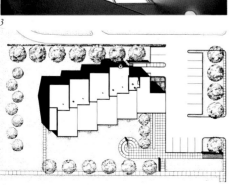

4

5

6

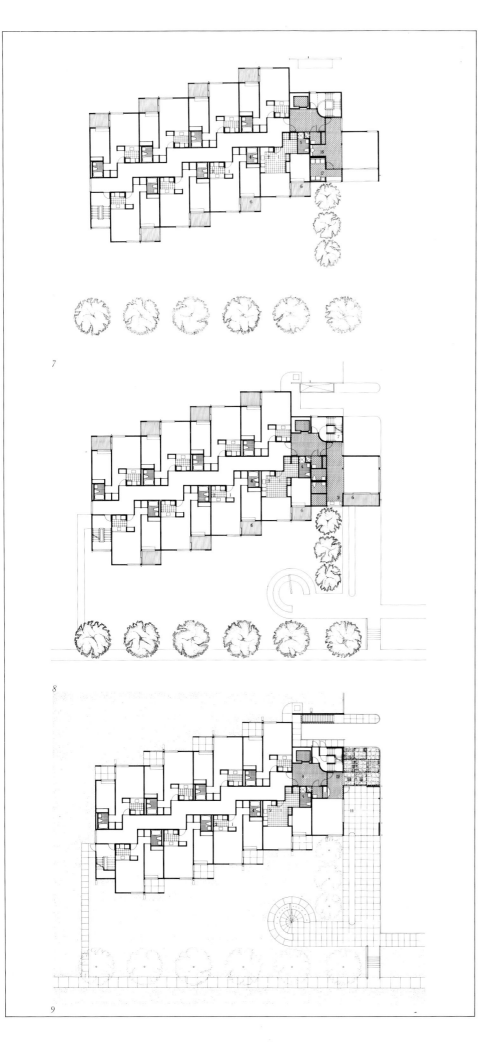

7

8

9

10

11

12

The problem was to design a family-housing project to consist of 40 two-story, three-bedroom townhouses distributed in seven building blocks. In addition there was to be a community building. The site was triangular. Two of the units are designed for the handicapped. Each townhouse has a fenced front yard, storage structure, and entry gate facing one of four pedestrian mews. The parking is consolidated at one end of the site with access to trash holding screens and the mews. As a result of the site configuration the mews vary in length and density.

The multiplicity of amenities, the identity of the individual houses and the pedestrian scale were economically feasible within the constraints of public-housing guidelines because of the overall site and building organization. By having three common walls per house, the overall exterior wall construction was minimized. An operable clerestory window is located over each stairway, affording natural light and cross ventilation in each townhouse, and the living rooms open directly to front yards.

The houses, community building, which contains a common/dayroom, office, and maintenance garage are wood frame with gray cedar clapboard exterior walls. The doors, gates, fences and window trim are painted white. The trash holding structures and site benches are painted concrete.

The landscaping is intended to complement and support the site circulation system, the courtyards and the integrated open spaces in the project.

190

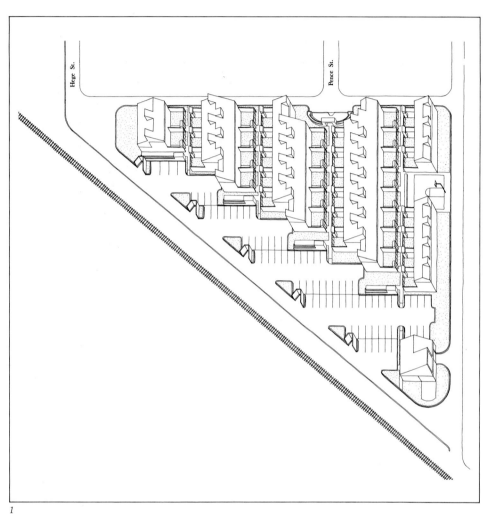

1

2

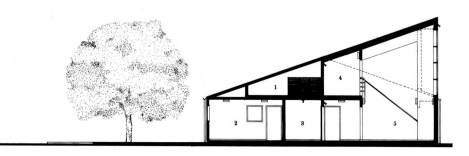

3

1.Axonometric 2.Unit A section
3.Community building section 4.Second floor
plan 5.Ground floor plan 6.Community
building second floor plan 7.Community
building ground floor plan 8.Unit A second
floor plan 9.Unit A ground floor plan

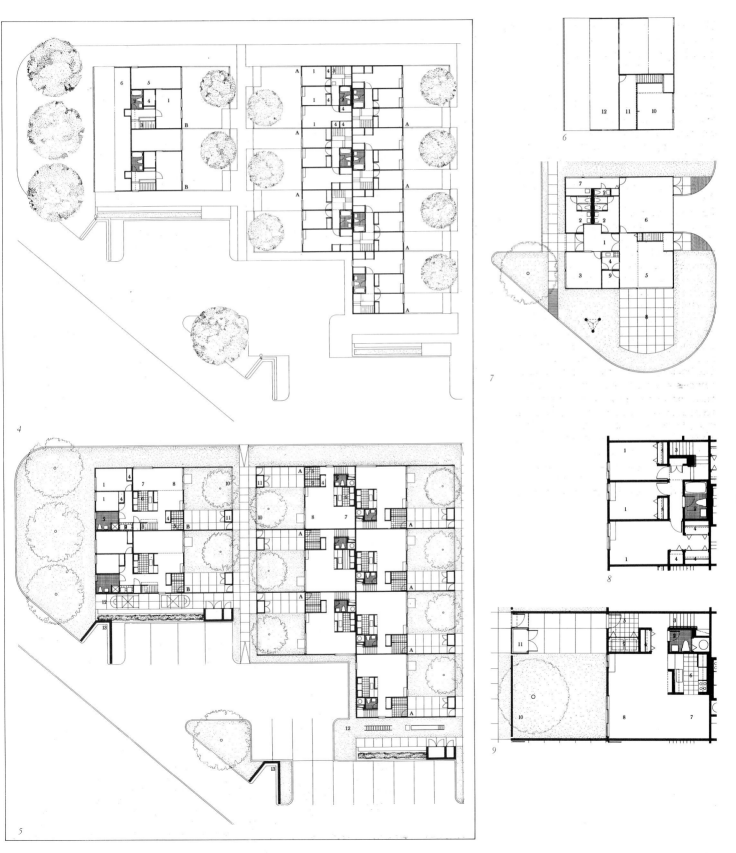

191

1

The problem was to design a Pakistani restaurant in an existing 7,500-square-foot basement space that had irregularly sized and spaced columns and no natural light or orientation.

The intention of the design was to create an environment that would eliminate the negative psychological preconceptions about basement restaurants. By manipulating the descent from the street entry into a sequence of level changes and spatial hierarchies, the sense of anticipation was intensified.

The first level change occurs at the stair landing, the second at the coat check and powder room landing, the third at the reception/waiting area and bar, separated from the initial dining space by a clear glass-block wall, and the fourth at the second larger dining room whose entire back wall is mirrored over the banquettes.

A sense of illusion and spatial enrichment was achieved through the use of a varied palette of materials, including travertine floors, oak cabinetwork, taupe suede

2

3

upholstery, mirror, glass block, gray carpeted walls, and polished aluminum ceilings. Recessed incandescent lighting fixtures are located at the glass-block dividing walls, rendering them as vertical chandeliers. Candles are located on each table, casting pattern and movement on the ceiling and transforming the environment with subtle tonal reflections.

1.Middle dining room 2.View of waiting area from stair 3.View of bar and dining room 4.View of main dining room 5.Rear dining room 6.Floor plan

4

5

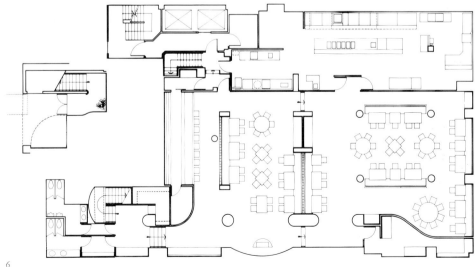

6

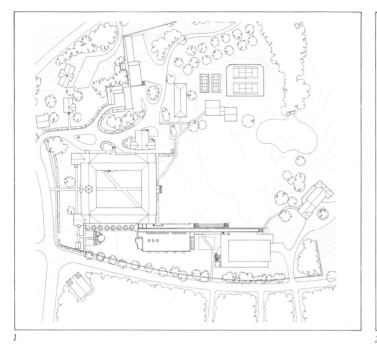

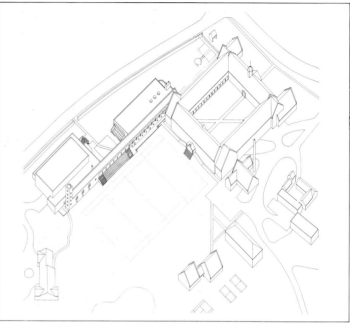

1

2

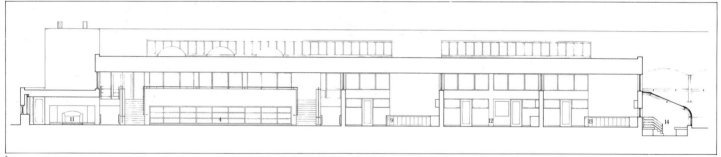

3

The problem was to design a new library/science building for a small private boarding school of 180 young women. Westover is a rural New England country campus of 150 acres. It is comprised of a series of mostly turn of the century eclectic stucco and slate roof structures linked by brick paved walks and intertwined with traditional fieldstone walls.

The project site is bounded along one edge by The Field. It is between the Main Building, with its adjacent garden, and the unsympathetic 1960 brick Student Activities Building. A large seven-foot high fieldstone wall running along a public road completes the site boundaries.

The library will eventually house 40,000 volumes including a small collection of rare books, and will provide a series of unique and quality environments for serious study, informal browsing, and music listening.

The science facility calls for three instructional laboratories: physics, chemistry and biology. A greenhouse is to augment

biological studies and an observatory is required for the permanent installation of the school's reflector telescope. Ancillary spaces necessary for the science department include faculty offices, preparation rooms and a computer science center.

The heart of the school is the Main Building—a structure designed in 1907 by one of this country's first woman architects, Theodate Pope Riddle. It is a symmetrical, arcaded, cloistered megastructure containing classrooms, administrative offices, dining room, assembly spaces and students' dormitory rooms. The central cloister opens through an axial portal to The Field, which is flanked by other campus buildings. The Field is used for intramural and interschool athletics, as well as for ceremonial occasions such as commencement.

The main organizing element of the Library and Science Center is the arcade. This elevated, covered, outdoor circulation element is, in form, function and material, an interpreted extension of the Main Building's

cloister. It begins at a bridged link to the Main Building cloister, parallels the Library and Science Center, extends itself laterally into a grandstand for viewing activities of The Field, and finally terminates at the Student Activities Building in a new lobby which overlooks an existing volleyball court. The formal concept of the Library and Science Center is that of a one-and-one-half story loft building, separate from and parallel to the arcade. Its roof floats over the rooms below, disconnected from the partitions by clerestory windows which allow a horizontal visual extension from the arcade level through the building and out to the gardens and surrounding countryside. The building is capped by the intimate, low, curving periodicals room with its fireplace mass on

1.Site plan 2.Campus axonometric
3.Longitudinal section 4.Roof axonometric
5.Arcade level axonometric 6.Ground floor
axonometric

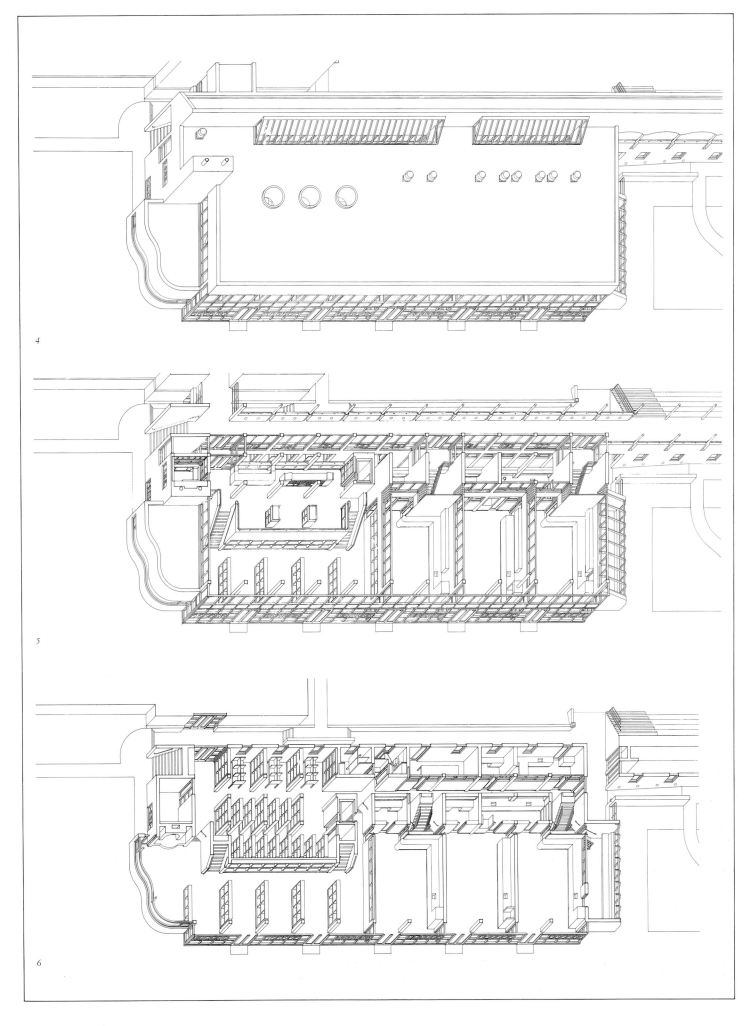

4

5

6

the north and by the Greenhouse on the south. Both these specialized forms are juxtaposed to the rigorous planar composition of the main body of the building. The west facade is a continuous curtain wall which again extends the loft spaces out into the garden to be defined ultimately by the high stone wall. The sloping arcade roof and the facade below it continue past and over the Student Activities Building, giving it a new, more sympathetic facade. This arcade element terminates in the new Observatory Tower.

From the vaulted arcade, one can enter the Library and Science Center at three locations. Each entry bridges the two-story skylighted gallery which runs the length of the building and separates the arcade as a discrete element. The entry at the library is direct to a mezzanine overlooking the main reading room one half-level down. The stacks and study carrels are located another half-level down. The other two entries lead to physics/chemistry and biology/greenhouse, all of which are on the same level as the main reading room. The entry stairs continue down another half-level to the two-story gallery and

196

1.Aerial view of campus before construction
2.View of Main Building and Student
Activities Building from field before
construction 3.View of model from southeast
4.View of Main Building from field 5.View of
Student Activities Building from Main

Building before construction 6.View of model
from northwest 7.View of Main Building
courtyard 8.View of model from northwest
9.View of model from west 10.Aerial view to
the northwest 11.Aerial view to the southwest
12.Aerial view to the southeast 13.East

elevation 14.View from sally port
15.West elevation 16.North elevation
17.Partial elevation at observatory tower
18.View at arcade 19.Partial west elevation at
courtyard 20.View from bridge

13

14

15

16

17

18

19

20

the ancillary science facilities.

The major materials of the new construction have been selected to promote the positive aspects of the existing historic campus buildings. The exterior wall material continues as polychromed stucco. The sloping roof of the arcade, which addresses The Field, is slate. Natural finished hardwood window frames, curtain walls, doors, frames, trim, cabinets and furnishings restate the existing wood interiors. Polychromed interior walls continue the exterior color scheme. Brick paving extends the existing outdoor circulation system, as do stone stairs, grandstands, copings and paving bands. Fieldstone is used externally for retaining walls which accommodate grade changes around the building, as well as internally for the recessed, traditional, periodicals room fireplace.

The entire construction is one which respects and continues the existing campus in terms of form, function and material, yet provides a spatial richness and variety of experience in keeping with the complexities and demands of the modern program.

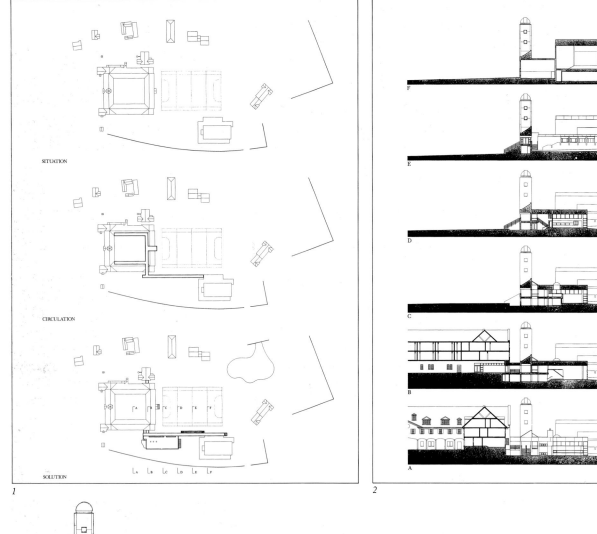

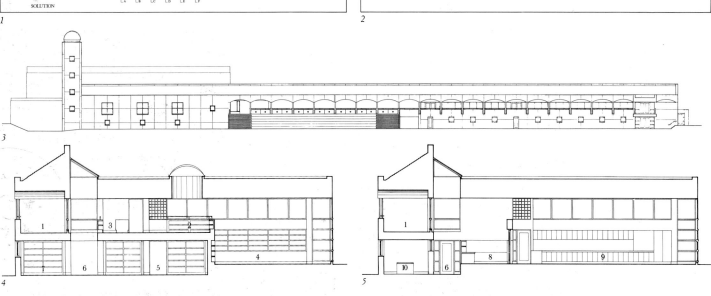

1.Design diagrams 2.Cross sections 3.East
elevation 4.Cross section at library 5.Cross
section at physics lab 6.West elevation of
arcade 7.View into lower level gallery
8.Periodicals room 9.Main reading room

10.Lower level gallery 11.Library study alcove
12.Aisle at west window wall 13.Physics
laboratory looking west 14.Physics laboratory
looking east 15.Science prep room

6

7

8

9

10

11

12

199

13

14

15

**Triangle Pacific Corporation
Office Building**
Dallas, Texas

1

2

3

The problem was to design a 60,000-square-foot corporate office building for a major kitchen cabinet manufacturer on a five-acre flat site located between two major access roads. The parti was generated by the programmatic disposition of spaces and the desire to create a unique yet unpretentious building.
The computer space, employees' cafeteria, and presentation/mock-up spaces are located on the ground floor, establishing a base. The entry is located on the second floor, accessed by a grand outside stair paralleling a reflecting pool, and articulated by a two-story high porch. The reception, main stair, and three-story high clerestory-lit lobby with balconies are located in the figural center of the building, zoning the plan and acting as the major referential space. The second and third floors contain offices, pool space, conference rooms and the executive suite. The exterior is travertine marble, butt glazed solar gray glass, aluminum, and glass block, rendering the building as solid, dense and subtly graphic.

4

5

1.Northeast facade 2.South facade detail
3.North facade 4.Southwest facade detail
5.Reception/waiting area 6.Axonometric
7.Detail of stairs 8.Atrium detail 9.View of
atrium from balcony

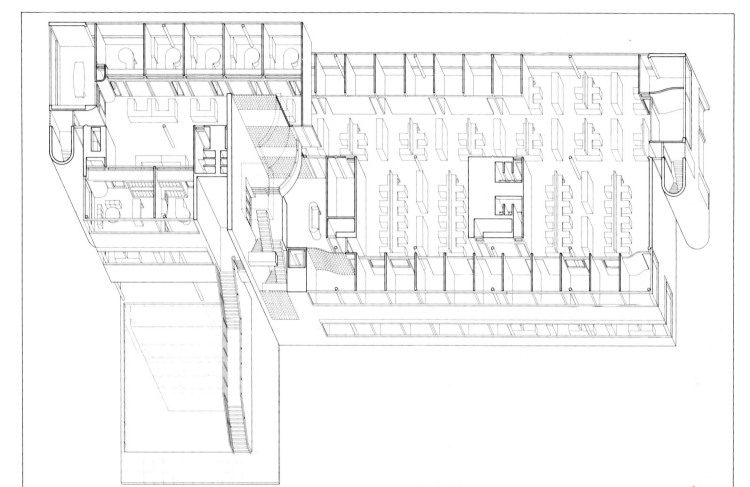

6

7

8

9

C1L CREDENZA	**C1** CREDENZA	**R2** RETURN	**R1** RETURN	**T2** TOP	**T1** TOP
T2L CREDENZA	**T1L** TOP	**SPT2L** TOP	**SPT1L** TOP	**SPT2** TOP	**SPT1** TOP
V1L VERTICAL		**V4** VERTICAL	**V3** VERTICAL	**V2** VERTICAL	**V1** VERTICAL
D1L DOOR	**D1** DOOR	**S1** SECRETARY	**P2** PEDESTAL	**P1** PEDESTAL	

202

1

The problem was to design a market-competitive wood desk and credenza system, employing existing panel and finishing technologies.

The design was generated by research into existing wood desk designs and analysis of production, assemblage, shipping, and installation characteristics.

The design conclusions were logical and cost effective while offering the flexibility of material and configuration options. The basic design is a pedestal-supported top system with an integral privacy panel. The articulation of the parts, the varying top configurations, the solid wood pull, and the mahogany standard transform the typical hollow-core door supported on two file cabinets into an object of clarity and substance.

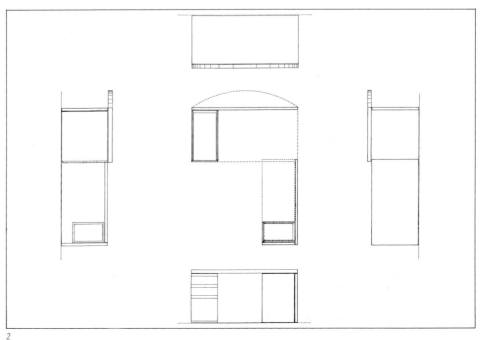

2

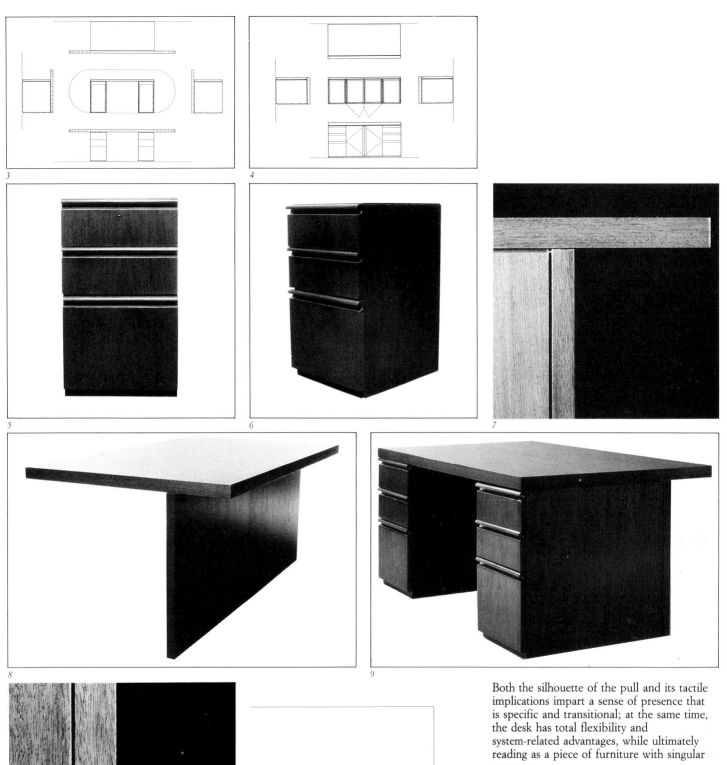

3

4

5

6

7

8

9

203

Both the silhouette of the pull and its tactile implications impart a sense of presence that is specific and transitional; at the same time, the desk has total flexibility and system-related advantages, while ultimately reading as a piece of furniture with singular presence.

1.Summary of components 2.Reception desk
3.Executive desk 4.Typical credenza
5.Pedestal front view 6.Pedestal oblique view
7.Top and pedestal side view 8.Top and modesty panel 9.Typical desk 10.Pull detail
11.Pull drawing

10

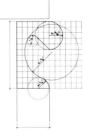

11

de Menil Residence
Houston, Texas

1

The problem was to renovate two existing structures, one a 1950s pitched-roof, indigenous, developer's ranch house, the other a two-story rectilinear "box" attached to the first by an entry link. The program required the addition of a two-car garage, storage space, pool and pool terrace, as well as the restructuring of the internal spatial organization.

The site was bounded on the south by an access road, on the north by the bayou, and on the east and west by private houses.

The solution involved reestablishing perceptual priorities and transforming the buildings through an overlay and restructuring of the site.

By painting the existing structures dark gray, their architectural anonymity was confirmed, and they in fact read as shadows of illusive objects. A major horizontal beam connects the newly built garage, auto court, and storage building. These buildings (the planter, entry gate, and walk) stand on the south in front of the original structure, on

axis to the new transparent entry link. The swimming pool and terrace stand in front of the second existing structure. The result is a reconstituted south facade and forecourt. The entry procession begins at the driveway and develops sequentially through the new spatial and structural intervention, simultaneously extending the original buildings and the site and creating a new private domain on the public side of the property.

1.West facade 2.Entry 3.View of pool and
entry gate 4.View of entry gate from residence
5.Entry gate detail 6.Entry link between
existing structures 7.Site plan

2

3

4

5

205

6

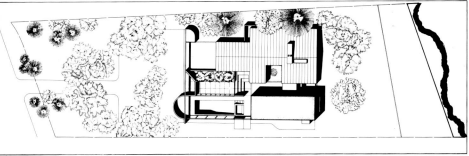

7

1.Axonometric 2.Entrance hall 3.Ground floor plan 4.Living/dining room 5.Sitting room 6.View of living/dining room and breakfast area 7.View from game room toward pool terrace 8.Game room and study above 9.Study

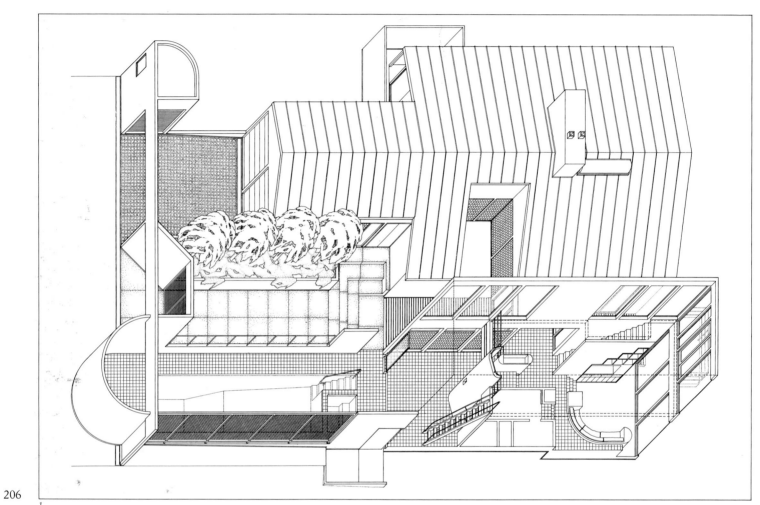

1

2

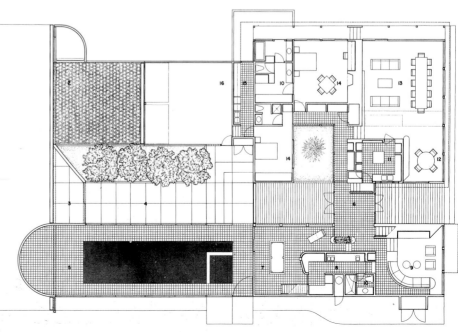

3

4

5

6

7

8

9

The problem was to build a large residence on a private dune site in East Hampton. The program was to develop seven acres with access from the north, dense woods on the east and west, and a half-mile deep dune and the ocean on the south to accommodate a main house, a guest house and garage, a pool, a tennis court, a garden and a caretaker's house.

One may recall images of the early dune houses of Southampton and East Hampton, which were of an appropriate magnitude to anchor their sites, and of a scale and presence to allow them to coexist with the ocean and the dunes. This was an attempt to reinterpret the vernacular shingle-style villa as a modern villa.

The overall strategy was to integrate the site planning and the building planning and, through the manipulation of site construct, sequence and memory, to reinforce the presentation of the architecture.

The main house had varying and specific programmatic requirements, resulting in a multifaceted, composite environment within a single structure.

The building, located at the south edge adjacent to the dune paralleling the ocean, simultaneously terminates and extends the site circulation sequence.

The plan is zoned from north to south in four articulated and modulated layers, made more complex and dense by the overlaid section manipulation.

From the cobblestone auto court to the slate entry walk, the two-story recessed entry

208

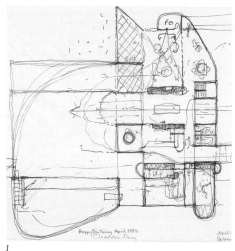

1

penetrates the first zone between the three-and-a-half-story greenhouse, which is axial to and the summation of the lawn, arbor, garden, tennis court, stair and guest suite elements. The second zone accommodates the three-story skylit entry hall and the horizontal circulation space which runs the full length of the building, paralleling the ocean, and interlocking the spatial hierarchies and site extensions. The third zone accommodates the kitchen/breakfast room, the library/den and the dining room, separated from the two-story living room by the stuccoed chimney object, which is the primary vertical element in the building. The fourth zone is the brise-soleil which accommodates the

screened porch, fronting the living room and dining room. At the west end, the circulation spine crosses the site axis at the outdoor stair and pool terrace entry, thus reestablishing the building/site overlay.

The second floor is zoned east to west around the stair-hall balcony overlooking the entry hall. The first zone to the west accommodates a two-story high game room, which is integral to the circulation zone. Adjacent to the circulation zone are the two guest-room suites of zone three. Zone four features deck extensions which overlook the dunes and ocean and which are integral to the brise-soleil. On the west end of the circulation zone, there is an extension and an interconnection to the outdoor stair, which connects down to the pool terrace and up to the roof. The first zone to the east accommodates the second level of the greenhouse. It is modulated by a study space which is an expansion north of the circulation zone, which in turn becomes a balcony overviewing the living room. Zone three accommodates the sitting room and master bedroom, which are separated from the living space by the chimney object, dressing room and bathroom. Zone four accommodates the deck overlooking the dunes and ocean, which has a stair connection to the roof in the screened porch. At the east end of zone three, there is a spiral stair and workroom overviewing the living room.

The third floor balcony loft, which overlooks the game room, and the third level of the

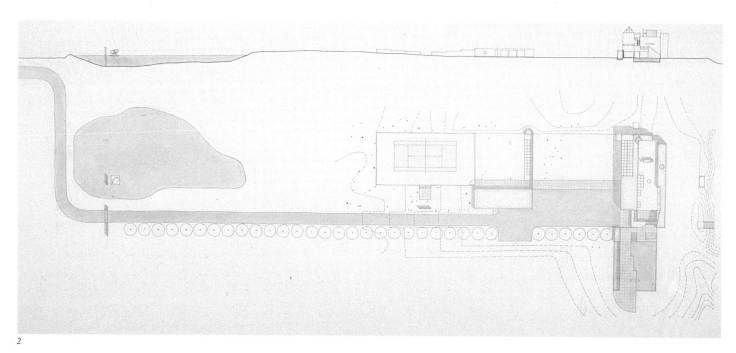

2

greenhouse, which serves as the roof over the study, constitute zone one. Zone three is the roof terrace modulated by the skylights and chimney, providing access via an outdoor stair down to the pool terrace, and extending into the brise-soleil.

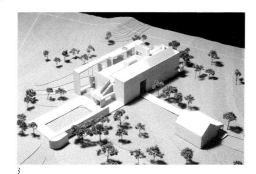

3

1.Early sketch 2.Site plan and section 3.Early schematic design 4.View of model from north 5.View of model from southeast 6.View of model from southwest 7.View of model from northwest 8.Site plan

4

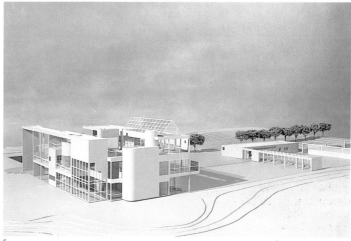

5

6

7

209

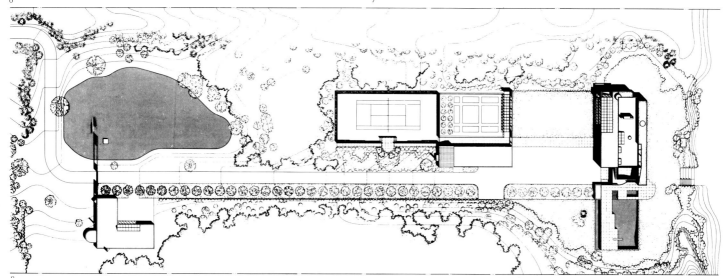

8

The guest-house garage accommodates a living/dining/kitchen space and two bedrooms, a three-car garage, workroom and storeroom. The stucco structure is extended by the arbor and garden, thus forming a second site/building reference to the main house and the pool terrace wall.

The caretaker's house (under construction) is integral to the stucco entry gate and forms the third site/building reference with the pond.

Each of the stucco site buildings is a landscape and space defining object that establishes a dialogue and recalls the overall design intentions.

The exterior and interior wall and ceiling material is cedar siding, the exterior terraces are green Vermont slate, the interior ground floor is polished black granite. The cabinetwork, and second and third floors are solid mahogany. The combination and contrasts of these materials and woods add another level of richness and meaning.

The last perception of this building is from the beach. The reference to the great shingle houses of the twenties is clear: one feels the presence of the southern facade with its

1

2

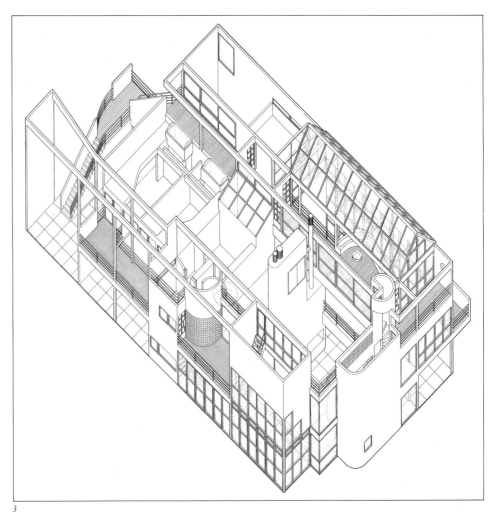

3

210

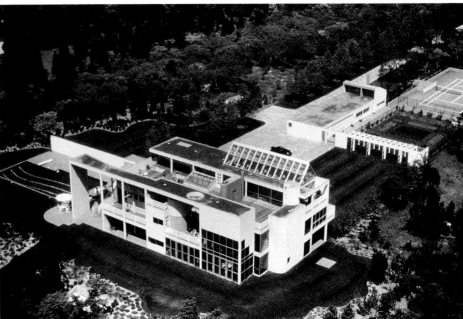

4

brise-soleil and density of layering, and its ability to claim its place on the dune and literally hold the site by its scale. The house is perceived as being much larger than it is, primarily because it is a cage, a frame being defined by its edges. The building deals with both the scale of the site (frame) and with the scales of activities (volumes). The interior and exterior rooms are proportionate to their use and activity.

In summary, this is a building which recapitulates and extends the ideal intentions of modernism. It refers to historical precedents not through literal translation, but through an understanding of organizational ideas and perceptual implications.

1.Aerial view from south 2.South facade from dunes 3.Axonometric 4.Aerial view from southeast 5.Aerial view from north 6.View of entry gate 7.Entry gate and driveway 8.View of guest house and west end of main house from driveway 9.View of guest house, garage and main house

5

6

7

8

9

211

1

2

3

4

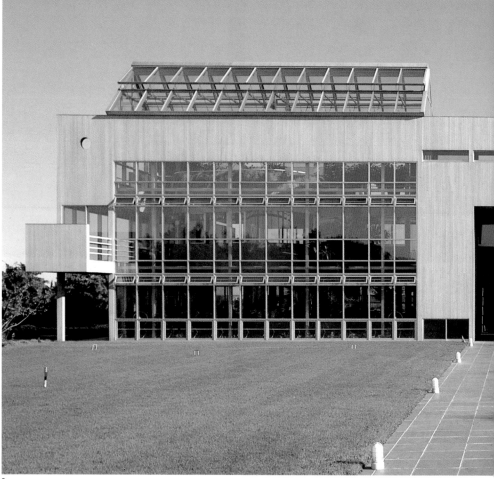

5

212

10

11

12

1.View from northwest 2.West facade
3.Southwest facade 4.View of outdoor stair
and brise-soleil from auto court 5.North
facade 6.Roof terrace 7.Northeast facade
8.East facade 9.Southeast facade 10.View of
outdoor stair and brise-soleil toward entry gate
11.View of outdoor stair deck 12.View of
swimming pool from roof 13.14.Details of
south facade 15.View from roof terrace

6

7

8

9

213

13

14

15

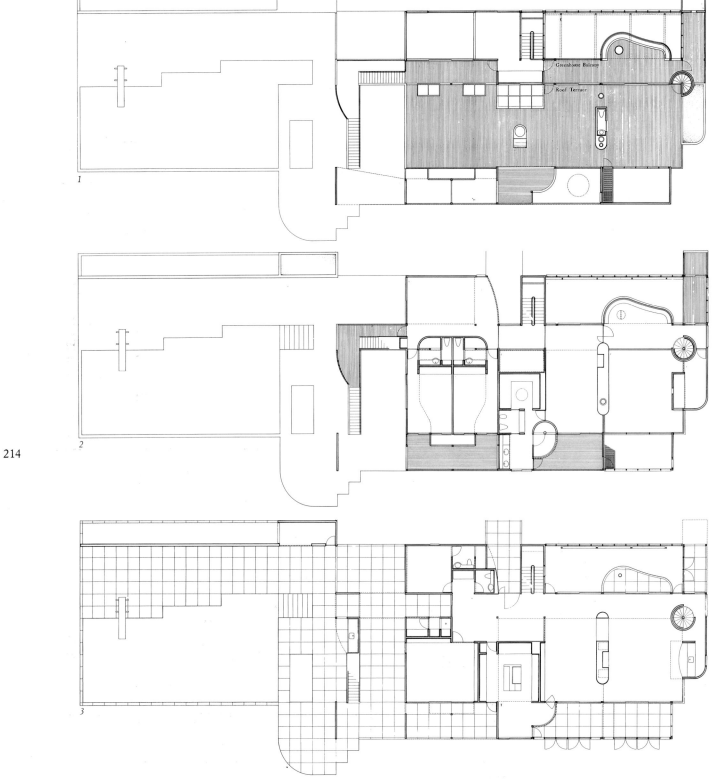

1

2

214

3

1.Third floor plan 2.Second floor plan
3.Ground floor plan 4.Section through
greenhouse, living room and screen porch
5.Section through screen porch, living room
and greenhouse 6.Section through greenhouse,
dining room and master bedroom 7.Section
through dining room, master bedroom and
greenhouse 8.Section through theater, library
and gallery 9.Section through kitchen, entry
and loft

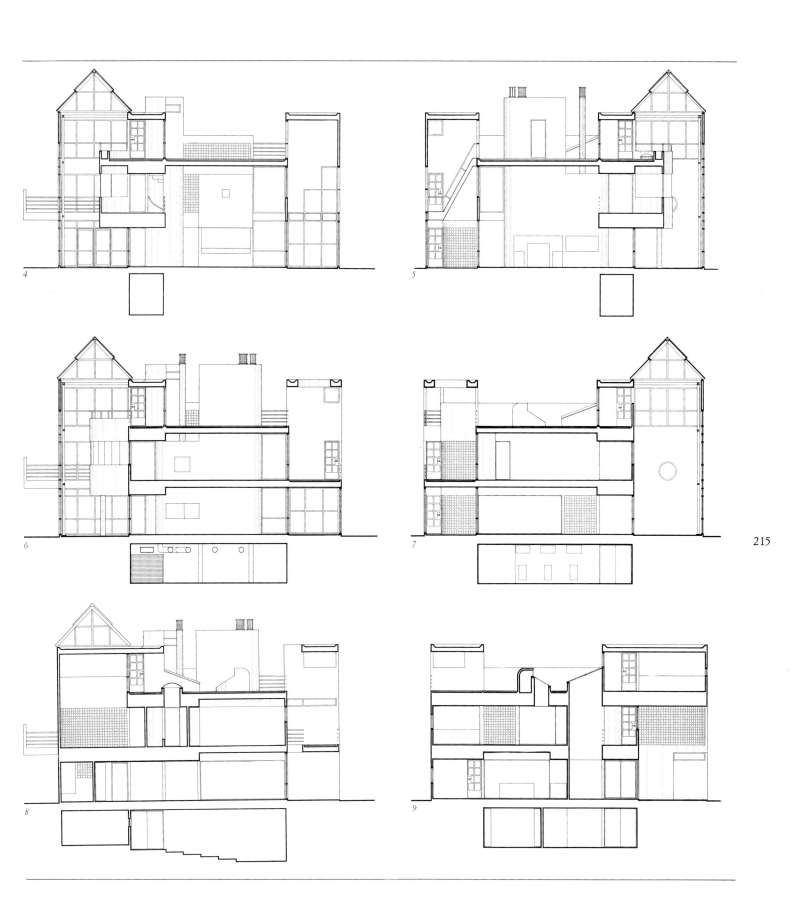

4

5

6

7

8

9

1

2

3

4

5

216

6

7

8

9

10

greenhouse from below 12.View of study in greenhouse 13.Detail of greenhouse 14.View of study 15.View of greenhouse at ground floor 16.Sectional perspective through greenhouse

11

12

13

14

15

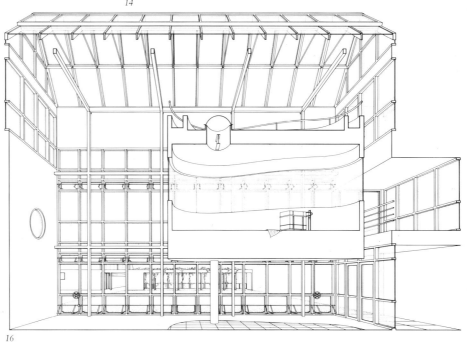

16

1

2

3

4

5

6

7

8

1.Theater 2.Master-bedroom sitting area
3.Master bedroom 4.Bedroom 5.View of
kitchen and breakfast area 6.Master bathroom
7.Master bath 8.Kitchen 9.Northwest view of
guest house and garage 10.Northeast view of
arbor, guest house, garage, garden and tennis
court from main house 11.East/garden facade
of guest house 12.View from tennis court
13.View of arbor 14.Guest house, east
elevation, west elevation, south elevation,
north elevation 15.Guest house ground floor
plan and garage Following page: north facade

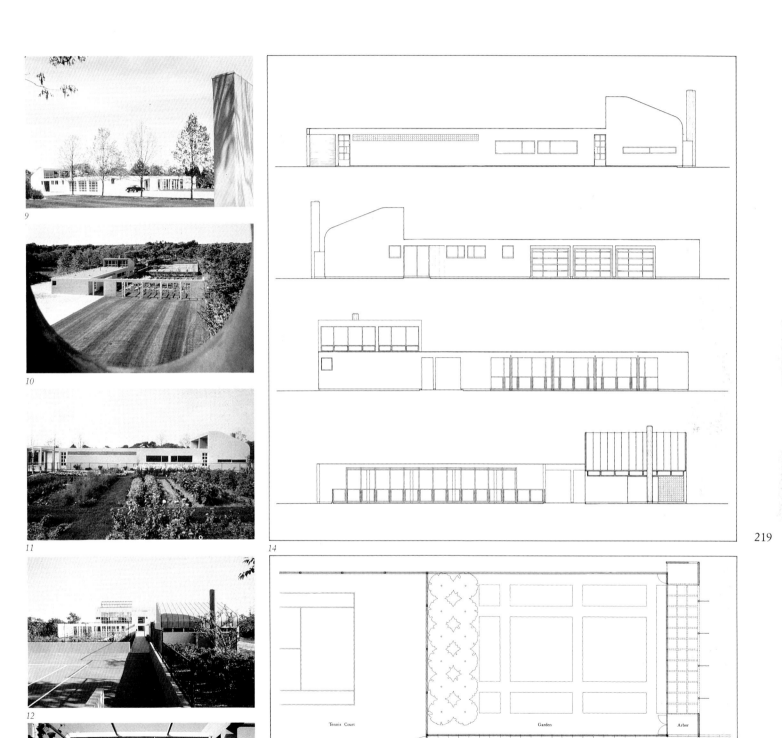

9

10

11

12

13

14

15

219

Block Residence
Wilmington, North Carolina

The problem was to design a residence on a narrow ocean-front site with road access from the north, adjacent proximate structures to the east and west, and beach and ocean to the south.

The parti makes a reference to the Geffen Residence project in Malibu.

The building becomes the site, with the ocean as land extension. The structure is divided into two buildings, connected by an outdoor ramp/arcade which parallels the pool court. The north (road) structure accommodates the entry, a three-car working garage, storage space on the ground floor and two guest bedrooms on the second floor, all connected by both the ramp and an outdoor stair from the pool terrace. The south (ocean) structure, entered off the first leg of the ramp, one half-level above grade, accommodates a two-story living space and deck extension which overlooks and gives access to the beach. It also encloses a dining room, kitchen, and, a half-level down at pool terrace grade, a library sitting room. The master-bedroom suite overlooks the deck and living room and a study balcony visually extends to the pool terrace and living room located on the second level. A screened porch and roof deck with a bridge connection to the guest-house roof deck are accommodated on a third level.

The section manipulation, the architectonic brise-soleil and spatial interlocking are more complex here than in the Geffen Residence, resulting from the formal explorations of the Taft and de Menil residences.

1.Northwest view of model 2.Southwest view of model 3.Northeast view of model 4.Ground floor plan 5.Second floor plan 6.Roof plan 7.Longitudinal section

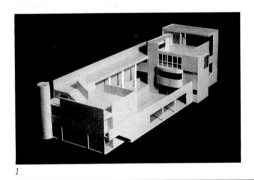

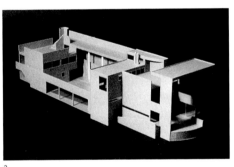

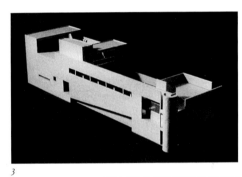

1

2

3

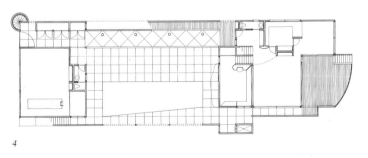

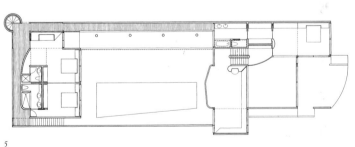

4

5

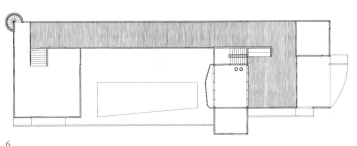

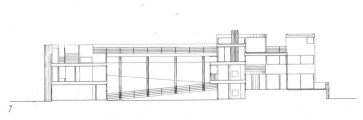

7

6

Einstein Moomjy
Showroom
New York, New York

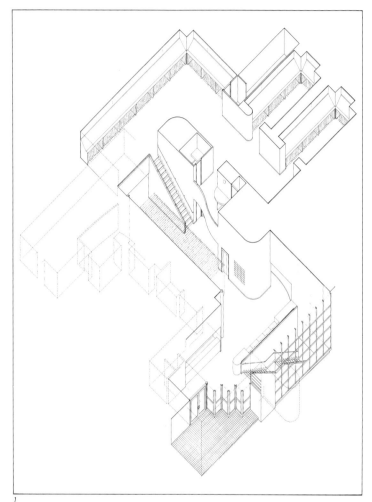

The problem was to design a carpet showroom and retail store in an awkward, three-level space, consisting of a two-story ground space, a low mezzanine which was reorganized, and a basement, all interconnected by an existing elevator. The storefront has been altered to integrate the spatial and graphic intentions, to express the two-story ground space, and to offer views down the new stair to the basement and up the second new stair to the mezzanine. Each level is designed to display different categories of merchandise.

1.Axonometric 2.View of lower level from stair 3.View of ground floor showroom from mezzanine stair 4.View of entry 5.View of entry from lower level

Greenwich Savings Bank
New York, New York

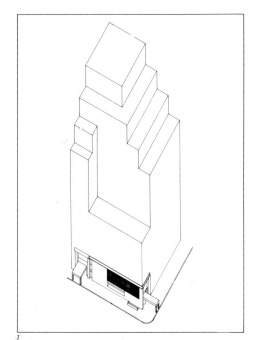

1

2

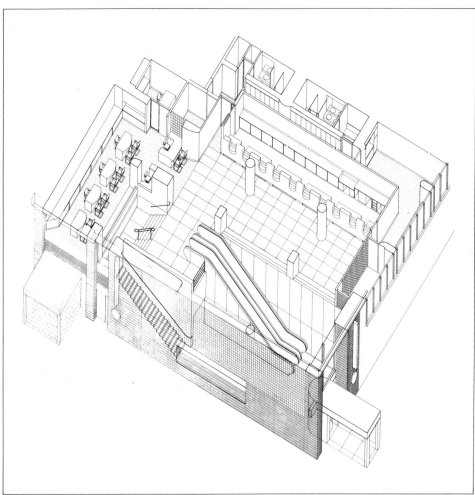

3

The problem was to design a new branch banking facility within a small existing ground-floor storefront space without direct connection to a 7,000-square-foot second floor office space. The building is located at a busy commercial intersection in Manhattan. To establish an operable and visible architectural entity, the entire exterior corner, building lobby and new bank entry were redesigned under the existing building's small-scaled turquoise and gray curtain wall. The parti was determined by the square-foot requirements of the main banking floor, which was impossible to accommodate at grade level. A portion of the second floor was removed to establish a major entry volume, accommodating escalators and a stair and

4

visually connecting the ground and second floors with a common ceiling. Both the stair and escalator arrive at a point relating to the bank officers' space, overviewing the entry and the banking floor. The open side of this space overlooks the entry space and contains a waiting area and a check-writing counter, while the closed side serves as the tellers' counter and the back office space.
The exterior materials are gray gail tile, glass block and stainless steel, with a dark green transom making a transition between the new and existing facades. The interior materials are terrazzo floors, polished aluminum strip ceilings, oak paneling and cabinetwork, stainless steel, and painted plaster.

1.Axonometric of existing building 2.View of northwest corner 3.Axonometric 4.Lobby 5.East elevation 6.South elevation 7.View toward bank officers' area 8.Banking hall 9.View from bank officers' area toward banking hall 10.Bank officers' area 11.Ground floor plan 12.Second floor plan

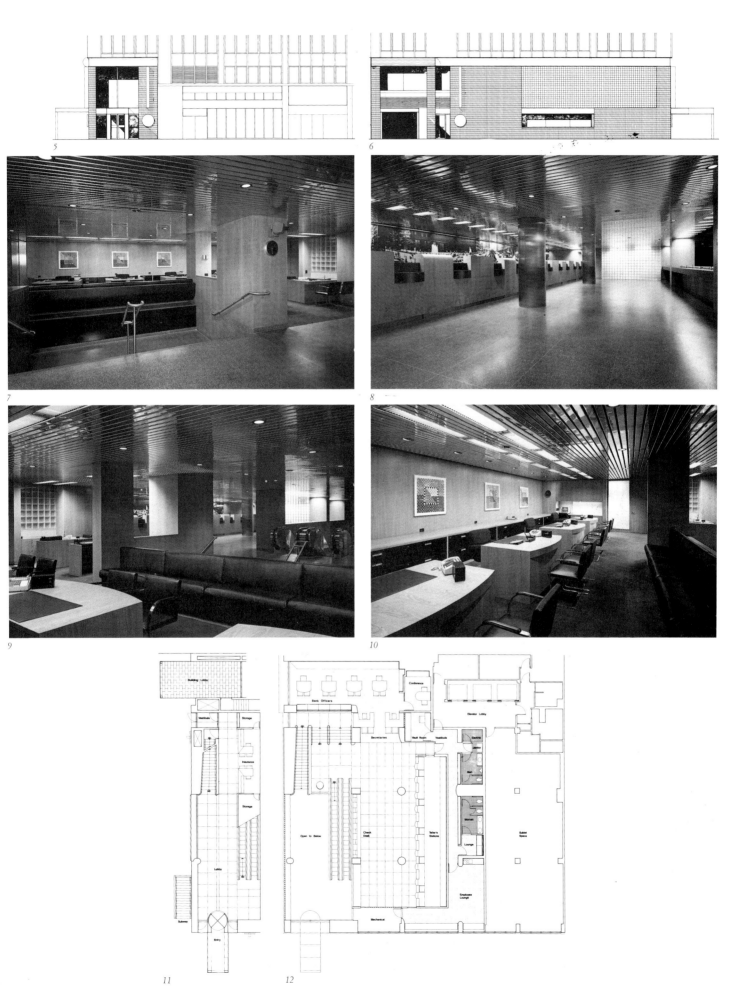

5

6

7

8

9

10

11

12

Reliance Group Holdings, Inc.
Offices
New York, New York

226

The problem was to design 75,000 square feet of corporate offices on three contiguous triangular floors in the Park Plaza Building. The program required a hierarchical office system, with offices for the chairman, president, executive vice-president, vice-presidents, and executive secretaries, as well as their support spaces, executive dining rooms, boardroom, conference rooms and specialty spaces.

The parti was generated by converting the mid-level or 29th floor into a major public space with a main interconnecting stair to the 28th and 30th floors. This space was eroded in the existing building, creating a three-story referential volume accommodating a reception, waiting, and exhibition area which offers access to all major public spaces, conference rooms and office entries.

The primary materials used are Vermont slate floors for all public spaces, oak paneling and cabinetwork for public and executive spaces, linen wall covering, velvet panels, and a plastic laminate desk and storage system for most offices. All areas are integrated by a single carpet and supportive color palette. The essential areas, aside from the public spaces, are the circulation spaces, which are intensified by their layering from exterior window wall to regulating glass transom/storage demising wall. This wall separates the perimeter offices from the interior, circulation and document filing zones, secretary stations, and glass-enclosed interior offices. At the end of each corridor, the perimeter wall with the view is exposed, thus orienting the user, both horizontally and vertically, by recall and implication.

1.Entry hall 2.Entry hall 3.Entry hall 4.30th floor plan 5.29th floor plan 6.28th floor plan 7.Entry/reception/atrium axonometric

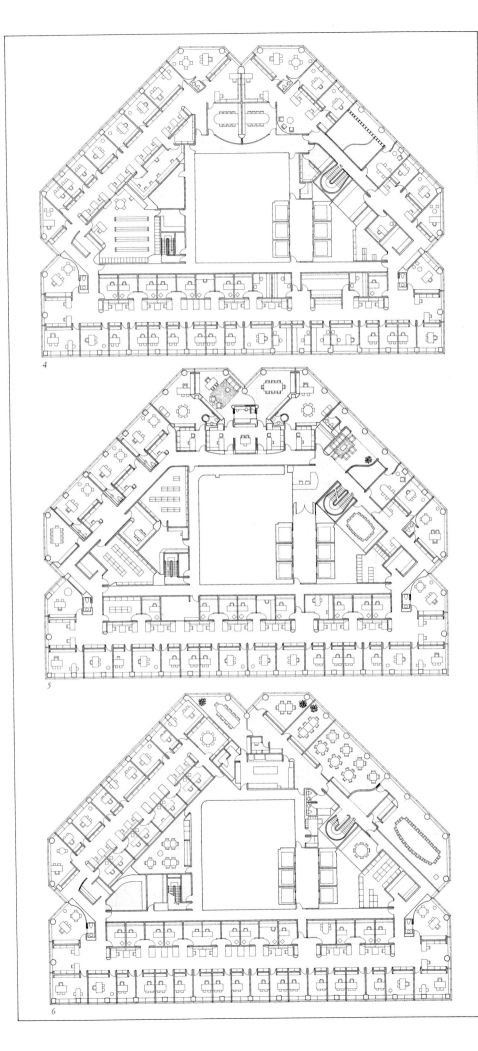

4

5

7

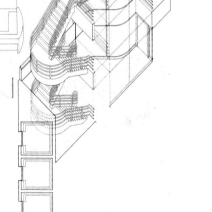

6

1

2

5

6

1.Boardroom 2.Dining room 3.Tax
library/conference room 4.Typical conference
room 5.President's office 6.Executive office

7.Typical circulation corridor 8.Executive
corridor

3

4

7

8

1

2

5

6

230

The problem was to design new offices in an existing 4,500-square-foot rectilinear space, with perimeter walls on the east and north, building core on the south, and party wall on the west.

The plan organization resulted from a logical disposition of the program, with the entry/reception space immediately adjacent to the building core, and the four executive offices on the east perimeter wall separated from the main circulation gallery by a double-faced storage wall which accommodates files in the corridor and shelving in the offices. Transom glass over the diagonal sloping shelf brings natural light into the gallery and addresses content and spatial extension. The principal's office is located on the corner; the two partners' offices are on the north facade. The conference room, bullpen and executive secretaries' offices access off the circulation gallery in the middle of the space, with a library/meeting room, kitchenette, storage and services located on the pantry wall.

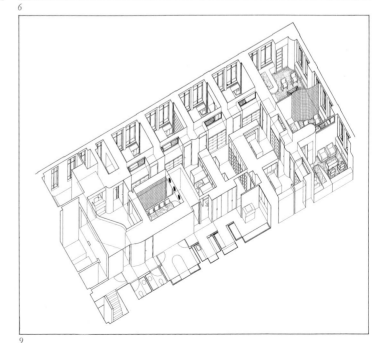

9

1.Reception and waiting area 2.Conference room 3.Partner's office 4.Partner's office 5.Secretary station with view of circulation space 6.Detail of secretary station and office entry 7.Principal's office 8.Principal's office 9.Axonometric 10.Floor plan

3

4

7

8

231

10

The problem was to renovate the existing underground concourse level at Lincoln Center. This level connects directly to the subway station, the parking garage and the Metropolitan Opera lower lobby. A new performing arts store, a new poster gallery, the tour guide service, the parking garage control, waiting, exhibition and storage all had to be accommodated on that level. Through the use of graphics, tiled and carpeted walls, polished aluminum strip ceilings, gray mirror, glass and aluminum storefront, terrazzo and oak floors, and dark gray plastic laminate store fixtures, the existing dreary concourse was transformed into a processional, articulated and participatory space. The design solved the programmatic requirements and architecturally organized the varying spatial and circulation conditions.

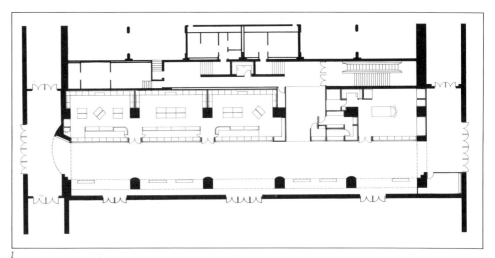

1

2

3

4

5

6

1.Floor plan 2.View of concourse 3.View of performing arts shops from concourse
4.Performing arts shop 5.Performing arts shop 6.Performing arts shop 7.View of poster gallery from concourse 8.Poster gallery
9.Concourse 10.View of Metropolitan Opera lower entry 11.View of concourse toward pedestrian tunnel 12.Pier detail

7

8

9

10

11

12

233

Viereck Residence
Amagansett, New York

1

2

3

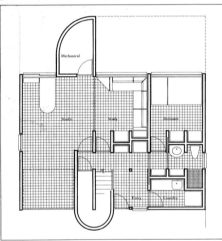
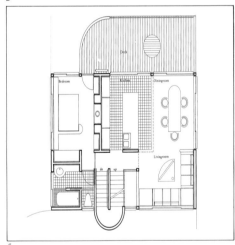
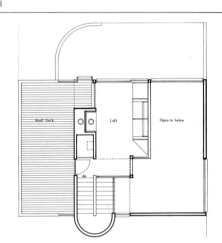

4

5

6

The problem was to design a residence on a private, sloping, wooded, six-acre site with a panoramic view of Gardner's Bay to the east. The house is located on a knoll with its access drive from the east, winding through the woods. The ground level accommodates a three-story entry and stair space, two guest rooms, a studio with eastern views and a garage. The second level accommodates a two-story living/dining space, kitchen and master bedroom, all opening to a deck

orienting east. The third level accommodates a balcony/sitting room which overlooks the living/dining space and an adjacent roof deck.

This "object" house summarizes a vertically composite, volumetric organization that exploits the knoll and views while giving a sense of total privacy.

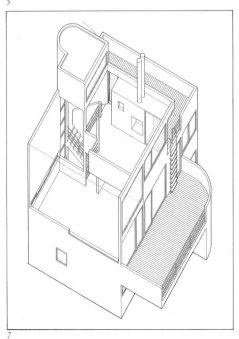

7

1.North facade 2.Southeast facade
3.Southwest facade 4.Ground floor plan
5.Second floor plan 6.Roof deck plan
7.Axonometric 8.Loft space 9.Living/dining
space 10.View of living room from stair

11.Dining room and kitchen 12.Stair
13.View of stair from living room 14.View of
dining room and kitchen with loft above
15.Site plan 16.Section

8

9

10

11

235

12

13

14

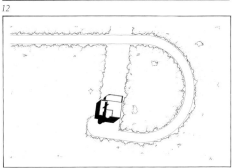

15

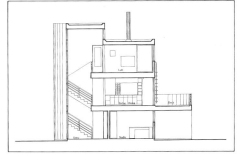

16

Ally & Gargano, Inc.
Offices
New York, New York

The problem was to design new offices for a growing advertising agency on two 25,000-square-foot contiguous floors with a central building core.

The agency organization, the systems and the proper adjacencies determined the design parti.

A panoramic view south of Manhattan is revealed upon arrival in the reception/waiting/space. This space, the executive offices and three conference/media presentation spaces are located off the south-oriented corridor. The main stair down is also accommodated in this corridor.

The offices are organized around the perimeter. Support spaces around the core are separated by the circulation gallery and rendered with oak floors, polished aluminum ceilings, and a regularized "deep wall" storage, display and niche system which is flexible to all working situations. The architectural graphic of the entire environment is purposefully neutral to encourage and support individual and group creative effort.

1.*Typical circulation space* 2.*Reception/ waiting area* 3.*Executive area circulation space* 4.*Axonometric* 5.*View of stair from 16th floor* 6.*Executive secretary area* 7.*Typical office B* 8.*Conference/presentation room* 9.*Conference/presentation room* 10.*Executive office* 11.*Typical office* 12.*16th floor plan* 13.*17th floor plan*

1

2

3

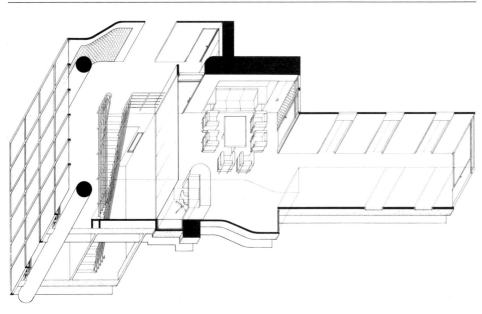

4

5

6

7

8

9

10

11

237

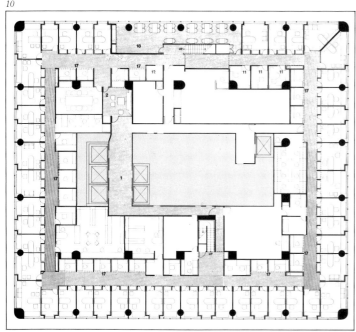

12

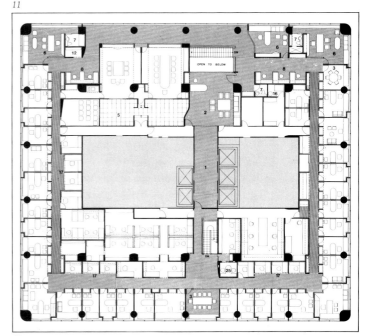

13

First City Bank
Bank and Office Building
Houston, Texas

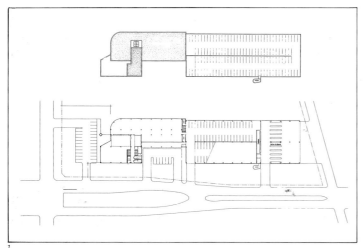

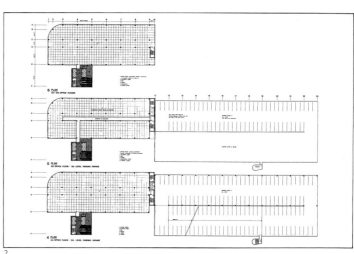

1

2

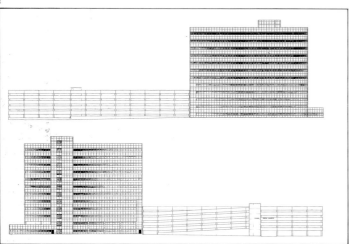

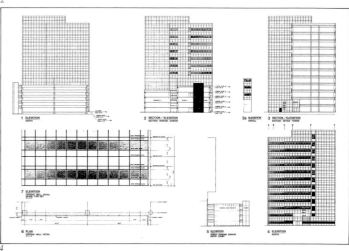

3

4

The problem was to design a 240,000-square-foot speculative office building on a corner, linear site adjacent to a major freeway. The building needed to accommodate a banking facility and a structured parking garage.

The analysis of the site, the vehicular access and parking, the required two public entries, one to the bank, the other to the office building lobby, and the development of an ideal leasing configuration determined the design parti. It articulates five major elements of the program.

The first element is the bank. Its parking and entry, which faces the highway, is rendered as a one-and-a-half story mass, articulated yet spatially integrated to the building lobby and tower.

The second element is the structured parking garage located to the rear of the site. It is connected to the building lobby by the third element, a two-story outdoor arcade, which is eroded into the base of the tower, and which fronts a visitors' parking court and forms the second required entry off the adjacent side

5

street.

The desire to create a totally flexible floor, unencumbered by a building core, determined the fourth element, a vertical core tower, which is adjacent yet integral to the building mass, housing elevators, fire stair and service spaces. At each elevator stop, there are two views, establishing a sense of orientation to both the site and the building.

The fifth element is the 12-story mass of 20,000-square-foot office floors.

The material and color palette delineates the variations of program and form through a subtle yet recognizable vocabulary. The three colors of glass—white, representing spandrel; light gray, representing structure; and dark gray, vision glass—transform the expected reading of the curtain wall into a constantly varying dialogue of color change, reflection and graphic notation. The glass colors, framed by a black aluminum grid matrix, cause a perceptual reversal, making the building both illusory and abstract in the manner of a photographic negative.

1.Site plan 2.Fourth, fifth and typical floor plans 3.Elevations 4.Sections, elevations and details 5.Northeast facade 6.East facade 7.Northwest facade 8.Southwest facade 9.West facade 10.Detail of entry arcade 11.Southwest corner detail 12.Detail of southwest corner

12

6

7

8

9

10

11

The problem was to design a 60,000-square-foot speculative office building within strict zoning ordinances, on a sloping site with a flat area adjacent to the access road.

The vehicular arrival sequence was a primary consideration in both siting the two-story building and registering its organization. The initial view is of the recessed, universally gridded south facade. Its articulated aluminum sun screen spans the expressed travertine piers which front the west facade. This facade continues the curtain wall, set flush with the travertine parapet and, without rendering floor levels, arrives parallel to the north facade. This facade features a raised entry plaza which is caught between travertine and glass-block end/core walls and a stepped-back curtain wall, revealing aluminum columns and entry vestibule. The lobby, a two-story high skylit volume which summarizes the entry sequence, is located in the center of the structure, affording easy access to the floors and offering a referential public space for the users.

1.Ground floor plan 2.Second floor plan 3.Southeast facade 4.5.Elevations 6.Northeast facade 7.Entry plaza 8.View of lobby 9.Detail of south facade 10.Northwest facade

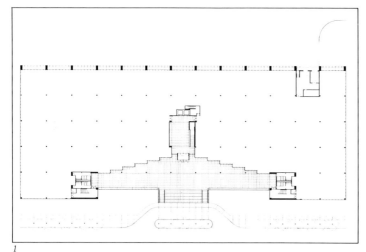

1

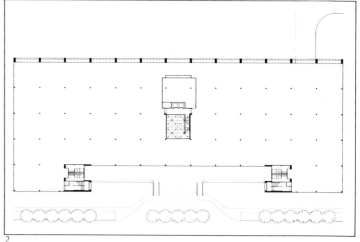

2

3

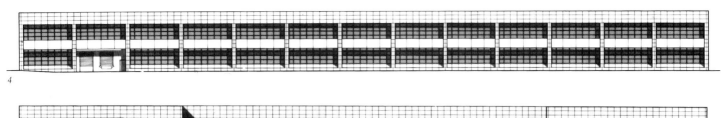

4

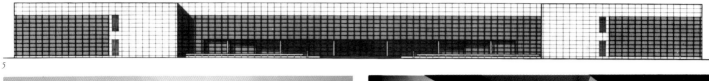

5

6

7

8

9

10

Wick Alumni Center
University of Nebraska
Lincoln, Nebraska

This project was the winning scheme in a national competition. The problem was to design, on a corner site, a new alumni center which would respond to specific and varied programmatic requirements while acknowledging contextual references and their implications.

The building massing responds to the Bertrand Goodhue Capital Building design and its axis by reframing the Historical Society Building, located at the other end of the mall opposite the Capitol Building. The garden (a programmatic requirement) was designed as an extension to the corner, negotiating the change in building/street scale from 16th Street (institutional) to R Street (residential).

The building was conceived of as a transformation of the renaissance palace model, presenting its urban exterior as primarily solid, and its interior as spatially centroidal, but layered front-to-back.

The entry/reception/waiting space and exhibition gallery, which are extended by the garden, front the two-story arcade and forecourt and open to the library and four-story, skylit center hall. The hall, which is a reinterpretation of the court, is the interior referential volume that unifies both the horizontal and vertical organization of the building. The two primary public spaces are accessible from the center hall, which is on axis to the entry. The two-story boardroom and the barrel-vaulted, three-story Great Hall, a modulated, balconied multi-use space, can accommodate large groups for a variety of events and occasions. The interconnecting balconies define an intimate sitting area with a fireplace on the ground level. This area is connected to the second-floor conference room and to a framed presentation balcony. On the long axis lies the proscenium, which accommodates projection and stage requirements. The Great Hall is a complex space in that it presents a large axial room with secondary asymmetrically modulating plan, section and facade.

The second floor accommodates the executive vice-president's office and balcony, secretary space, counselors' offices, conference room and waiting room, all relating to the center hall.

The third floor accommodates the accounting space, records staff, program staff, communications and editorial spaces and a conference room which overviews the center hall and the Great Hall.

The fourth floor contains the mechanical room and roof terrace.

The exterior materials are Roman-size brick for the primary facade, Vermont green slate for the window sills and copings, as well as for the recessions and extensions of the facade, and mahogany for the windows and doors. The interior materials are mahogany paneling in the public spaces, painted plaster walls and ceilings, and carpeted and slate floors.

The garden is framed by slate walls of various heights and by a continuous hedge, defining a space which contains a reflecting pool, trees, planted areas, paved areas and seating.

242

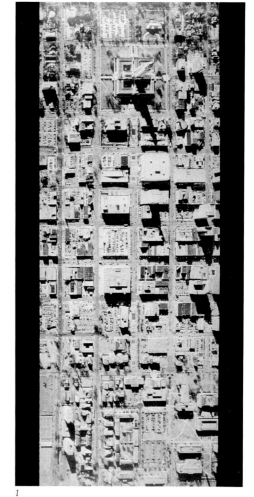

1

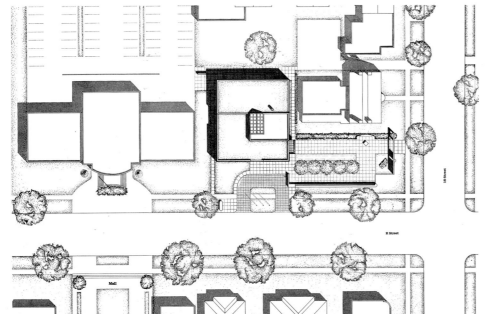

2

3

4

1.Aerial view of site 2.Site plan 3.View from
Historical Society Building toward State
Capitol Building 4.Historical Society Building
5.Axonometric 6.Axonometric 7.Southeast
view of model 8.Student Union Building
9.View of site toward west 10.East view of
model

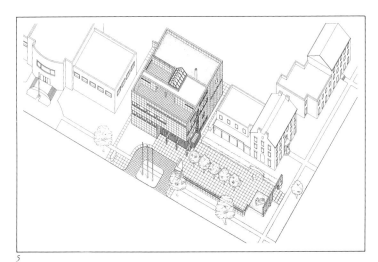

5

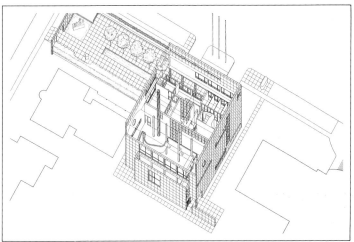

6

7

243

8

9

10

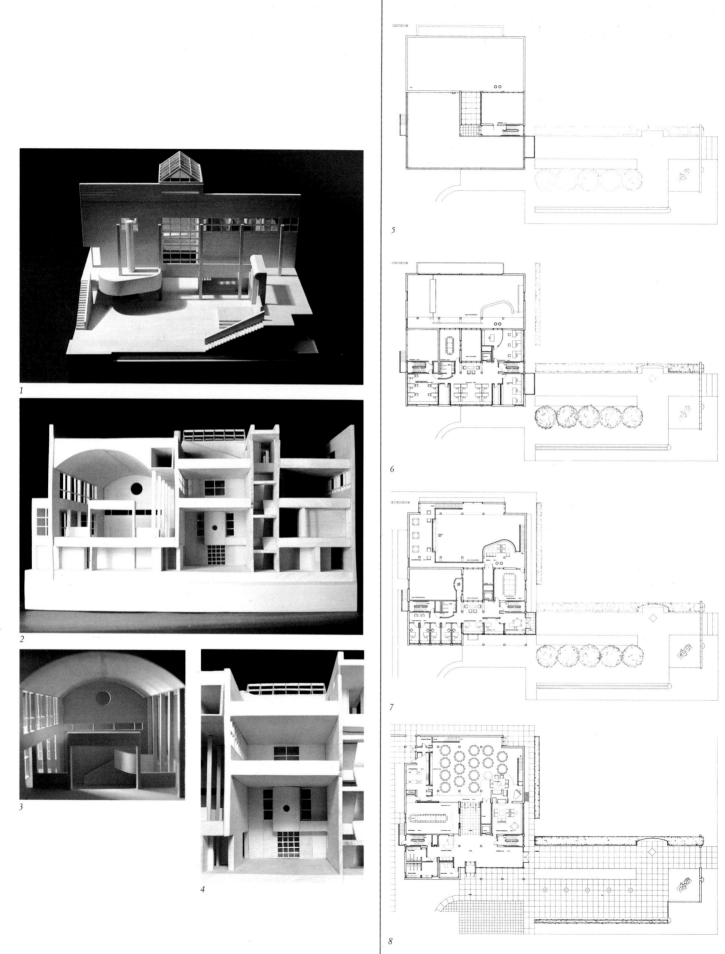

1

2

3

4

5

6

7

8

1.Model of Great Hall 2.Cross sectional view
of model 3.Model view of Great Hall
4.Model view of boardroom and conference
room 5.Fourth floor plan 6.Third floor plan
7.Second floor plan 8.Ground floor plan

9.East elevation 10.South elevation 11.West
elevation 12.North elevation 13.Wall section
at entrance and atrium 14.Section through
Great Hall and entry 15.Section through
Great Hall and exhibition area 16.Northwest
view of model

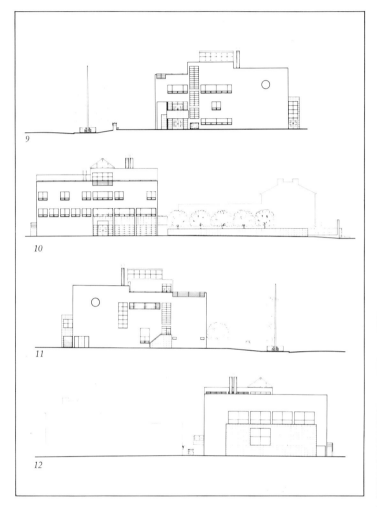

9

10

11

12

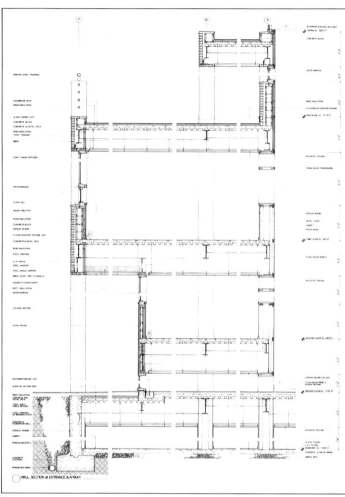

13

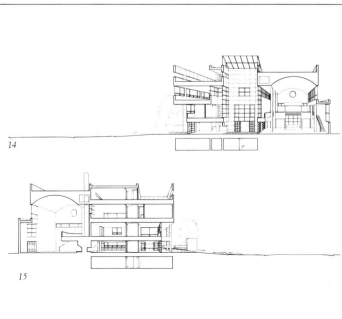

14

15

16

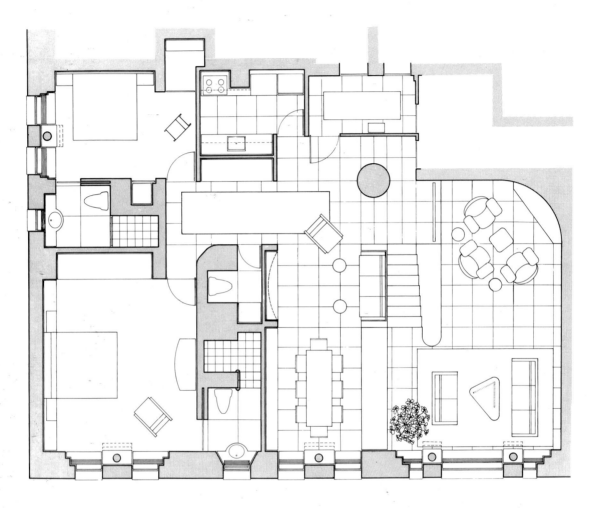

The problem was to design an apartment for an art collector in an existing, cellular, small-scale space with the living room floor six feet below that of the rest of the apartment.

The design parti was generated by the opportunity to display major works of art, the programmatic requirements to separate the two bedrooms from the living space, and the decision to exploit the existing level and volume change.

The entry hall, dining/sitting space and living room were treated as a single, complex volume modulated by the black slate stair, the dark gray lacquer cabinets and the single round column. All elements act as primary objects in a container with oak paneled walls and ceiling and green slate floors. The bedrooms are finished with oak and silk paneled walls, plaster ceilings and carpeted floors. The perimeter wall throughout the apartment, which reinforces the intended perceptual unity, is deeply recessed, with articulated oak columns integrating the black slate sills and the dropped heads with stepped capitals.

The sense of place is further reinforced by the paintings, furniture, objects, and subtle variations in texture and color. The design reaffirms the possibility of the dialogue between abstraction and traditional reinterpretation of space.

1.Floor plan 2.3.Axonometrics

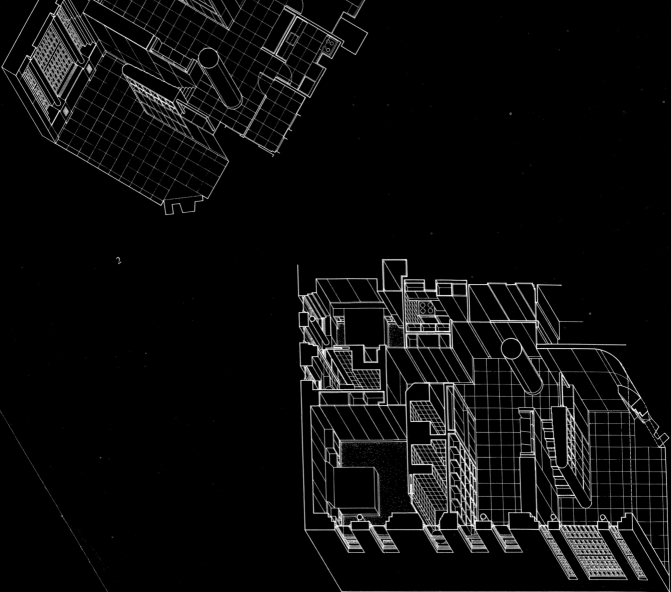

2

1

2

3

4

5

1.View of living/dining space from entry
2.Dining space 3.Sitting area from entry
4.Stair from living room toward entry

5.Living room 6.Dining space 7.View of
gallery toward entry 8.Gallery 9.Living room
10.Master bedroom

6

7

8

9

10

249

The problem was to design a new library to accommodate 140,000 volumes for a New England town with a population of 32,000. The site constraints and contextual references were the primary considerations in developing the architectural parti. The library became the anchor building in a redevelopment project and the master plan for the downtown, river edge. This was an opportunity to design a public building intended to resolve and consolidate desperate town-planning needs and issues.

By siting the building perpendicular to the existing Police Headquarters and the river, and parallel to the commercial buildings across Jesup Green, a new civic outdoor space, with its historical precedent rooted in the traditional New England green, was generated. Also, by locating the building on the existing slope, the entry from Jesup Green was made to double as a gateway. An outdoor stair to the upper library entry was covered and extended to the Levitt Pavilion. Thus, the library defines and modulates a layered sequence of new public outdoor spaces from Main Street to the peninsula, while establishing an architectural presence and reference to the town.

The program is distributed on three levels. The lower level, at Jesup Green, accommodates the public meeting room and adjacent lobby functions, the staff lounge and service spaces, the mechanical room and the outdoor stair. The second level, at the new parking area and Levitt Pavilion grade, accommodates a covered outdoor porch which faces the river and resolves the intersection of the outdoor stair and the library entrance. The information and circulation desk, reference room, periodical area, main reading room, stacks, picture collection, audio-visual library and work spaces are located on this level. The third level, which is a balcony overlooking the main reading room, offers views north over Jesup Green, to the town, and through the upper clerestory windows. It accommodates the children's library and story room, two seminar rooms, the director's office, staff offices and workrooms.

The primary exterior materials were selected to support the existing contextual references and to present a public building image. The walls are two colors of brick, rendering a base and horizontal banding, reinforced by cast stone sills, copings and stairs, white aluminum windows and doors, and a terne-metal roof over the main reading room volume.

In summary, the library was designed as a discrete object with four articulate facades, as well as a site anchor, definer and place marker. The main reading room volume, conceived of as a traditional referential space, reveals the clarity, spatial ordering and hierarchies of the building, its image and its memory.

1.Existing site plan 2.Site plan 3.Second floor plan 4.Main floor plan 5.Lower level plan 6.West elevation 7.East elevation 8.9.10.11.Sections

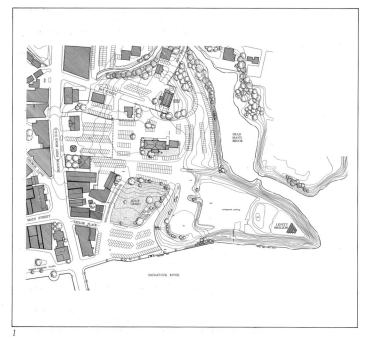

1

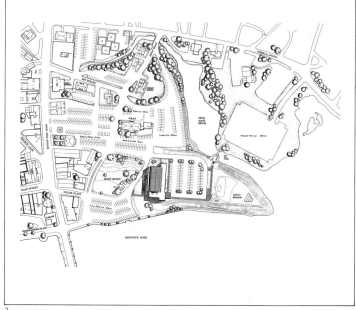

2

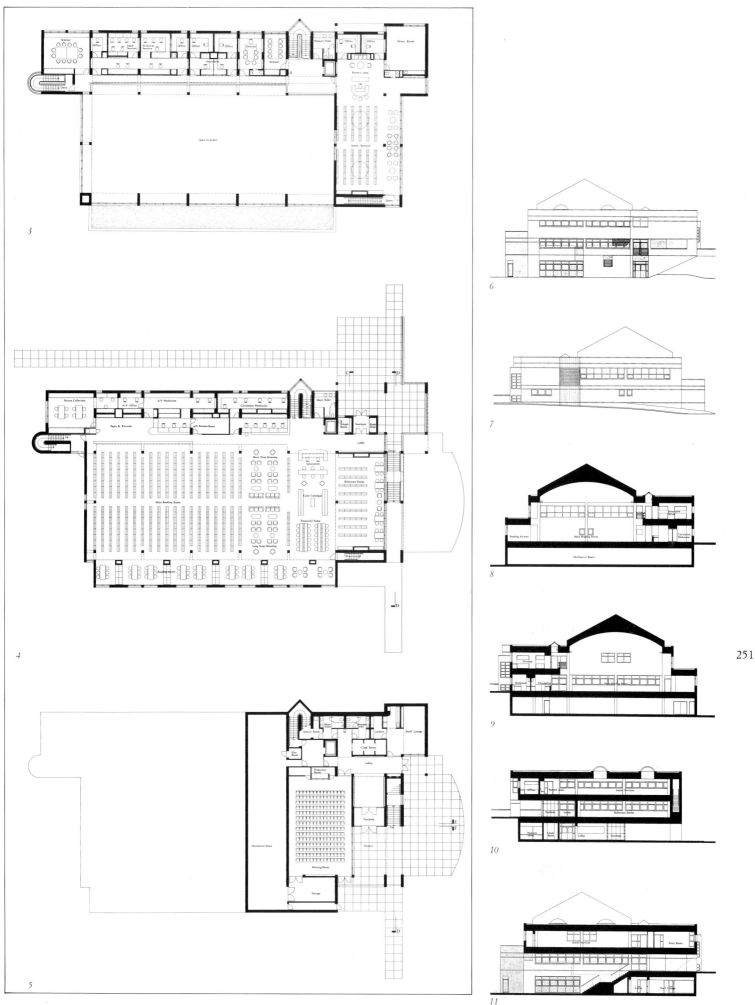

3

4

5

6

7

8

9

10

11

251

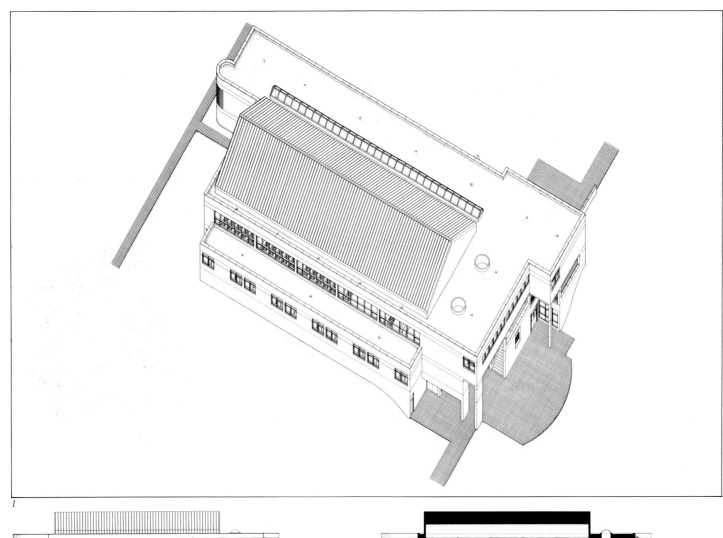

1

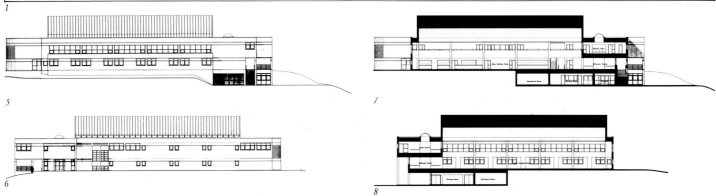

5

6

1

8

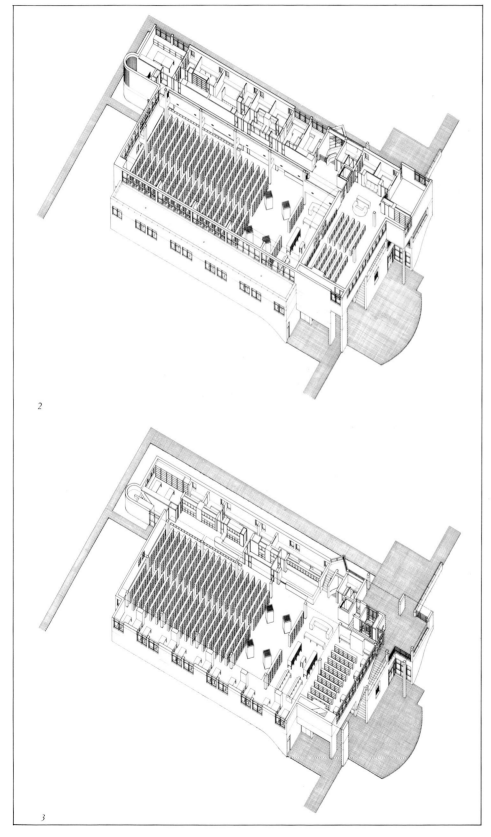

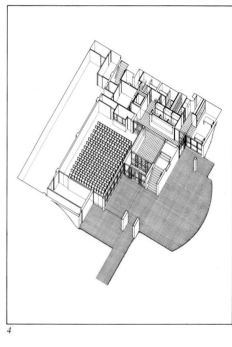

2

4

3

de Menil Residence
Santa Monica, California

254

1

The problem was to renovate a residence designed by Richard Neutra in 1938 (originally the Lewin Residence), while maintaining the basic interior organization and exterior configuration.

The two-story horizontal building's only vertical or sectional development was in the two stairs, rendering the ground and second floors as separate layers, both functionally and perceptually. The various plan configurations seemed to be singular and local, and, with the exception of the orientation to the ocean view, unhierarchical. The new design interpretation clarified the original building through the formal manipulation of transparency, extension, layering and color. A new perceptual order and unity was achieved by realigning vertically major referential walls, by establishing planar hierarchies, articulating simultaneous exterior and interior planes through color coding, refining and visually extending the stairwells, and extending the court with a terrace and a pool. The spatial

2

3

hierarchy informs the original parti with a new sense of calm and serenity.

1.Southwest facade 2.Study 3.Living room
4.Longitudinal section 5.View of living room
and sitting/library space from entry hall
6.Sitting/library space 7.View of living room,
dining room and entry hall 8.Dining room
9.Stairway detail 10.Second floor plan
11.Ground floor plan

4

5

6

7

8

9

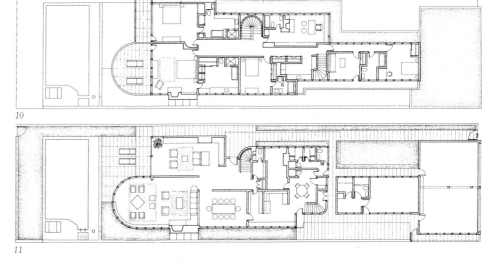

10

11

Gimelstob Residence
New Vernon, New Jersey

The problem was to design a large residence on a 17-acre open site modulated by a longitudinal ridge. The site encompassed a natural 10-foot grade change from north to south. The client was an athletic family with three sons.

The parti referred to the court house precedent with the massing relating to programmatic disposition, grade change and integrated outdoor spaces.

The front (north) wing, with its parabolic curved roof, recalls the Hines Residence project, and accommodates the two-story entry and stair, the two-story balconied living/dining area and the music room, kitchen/breakfast room, and study/den on the ground floor. The children's library/study overlooks the entry; the master bedroom overviews the living/dining room, which is under the curved roof on the second floor; and a screened porch overviews the court off the living/dining balcony. The east wing accommodates the guest room and game room on the ground floor, three children's bedrooms on the second floor, and a three-story high gymnasium on the lower ground floor with balcony overviews, integral stair and access to both the court and lower level outdoor playing areas. The south wing accommodates master bedrooms, dressing rooms, a separated guest room on the second floor, and the two-story family room, which is connected to the kitchen service spaces and garage on the ground floor. The single-story west wing accommodates a pool house and service structure which defines the third side of the court. The south wall of the court, which overviews the lower grade, is connected to basketball and tennis courts and is reached by a grand stair.

The exterior materials are gail tile—cream, terra-cotta and putty—which articulate the primary, secondary and tertiary volumes of the massing composition while reinforcing the architectural intentions. The window frames are teak and the court paving is blue stone. The interior has painted plaster walls and ceilings with granite and oak floors and ash cabinetwork.

This design attempts to interpret "house" through cubist transformations rather than traditional vernacular, with informed awareness of historical precedents and organizational principles.

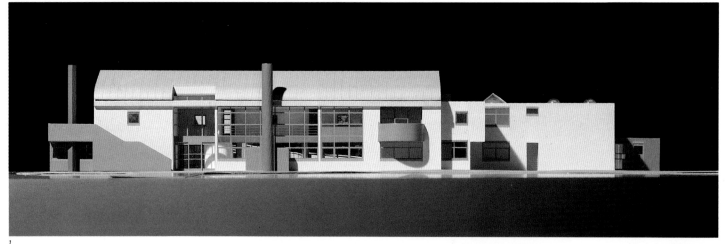

1

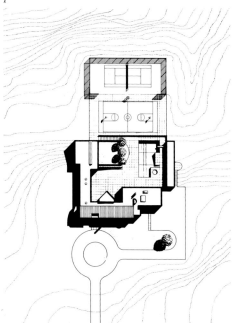

2

3

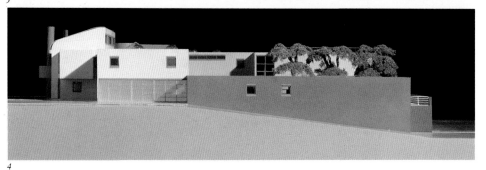

4

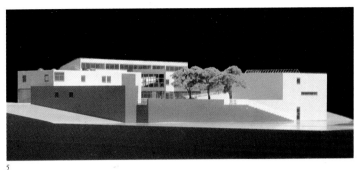

5

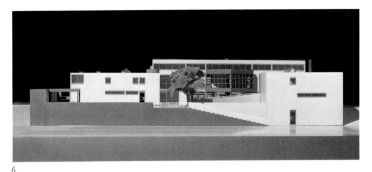

6

7

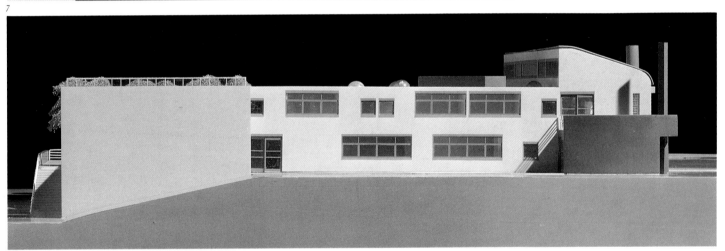

8

257

1.North view of model 2.Site plan
3.Northwest view of model 4.West view of
model 5.Southwest view of model 6.South
view of model 7.Southeast view of model
8.East view of model 9.Aerial view of model
from southeast
(model photos from schematic phase)

9

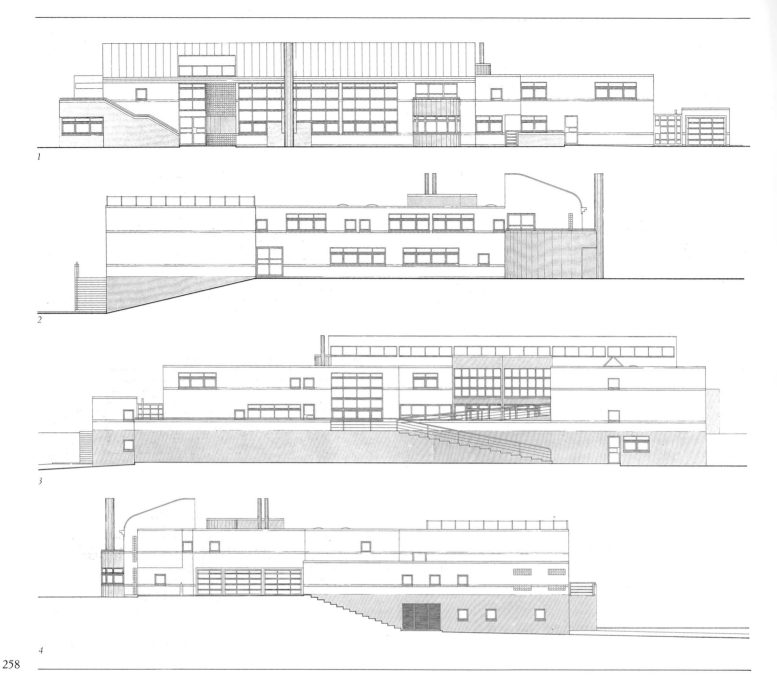

1

2

3

4

1.North elevation 2.East elevation 3.South
elevation 4.West elevation 5.Section C
6.Section D 7.Section A 8.Section B
9.Ground floor plan 10.Second floor plan

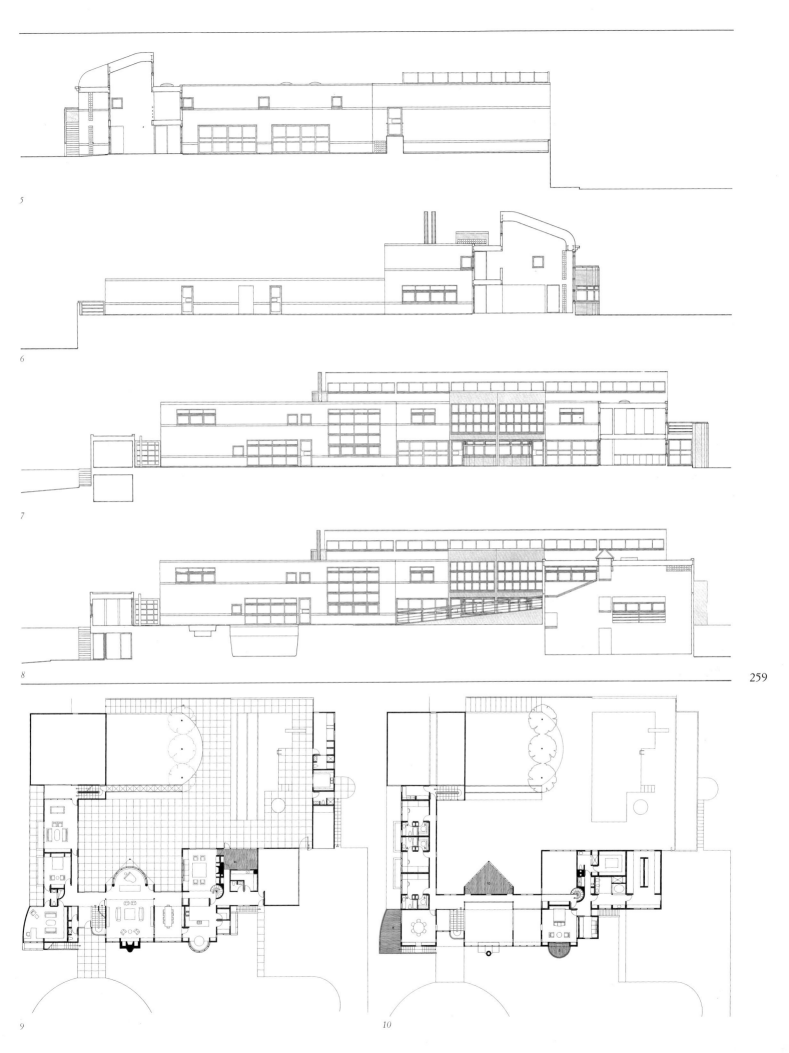

5

6

7

8

9   10

Gwathmey Siegel & Associates Architects
Offices
New York, New York

The problem was to accommodate an architect's office within an existing loft space of 17,000 square feet.

The loft was stripped with the exception of the sprinkler system, radiators, columns, and existing windows facing east, south and north. The location of passenger elevators on the northwest wall and service elevators on the west wall was instrumental in determining the circulation and planning parti.

The existing ceiling height of 14 feet was the uppermost vertical datum. The new window head reference of 10 feet established the second datum, which accommodated the air conditioning and the general lighting system. The door height of 7.5 feet established the third datum, the 6-foot height of the loft partitions the fourth, and the 3-foot height of window sills and shelving the fifth.

Entry is from the elevators into a low-ceilinged, small foyer with frosted glass gridded doors. The foyer then opens into the reception, waiting and exhibition area, presenting the initial loft volume. The two conference/presentation spaces and the partners' office are the closed spaces on the east facade, separated from the open loft by the reception/exhibition space and the office supply/printing and mail rooms. The north aisle accommodates present job files and archives, the south aisle accommodates catalogues, reference material, three meeting alcoves and the samples room. The rear houses the service elevator, model shop and kitchen.

The working loft area contains four associates' spaces, two per module, and 48 drafting stations, all semicontained with individual task lighting and reference boards. The entire area was conceived as a single complex furniture/space modulating object.

1

2

3

1.Entry/reception area 2.Reception/waiting
area 3.View of reception/waiting area toward
entry 4.Partners' office 5.Conference room

4

5

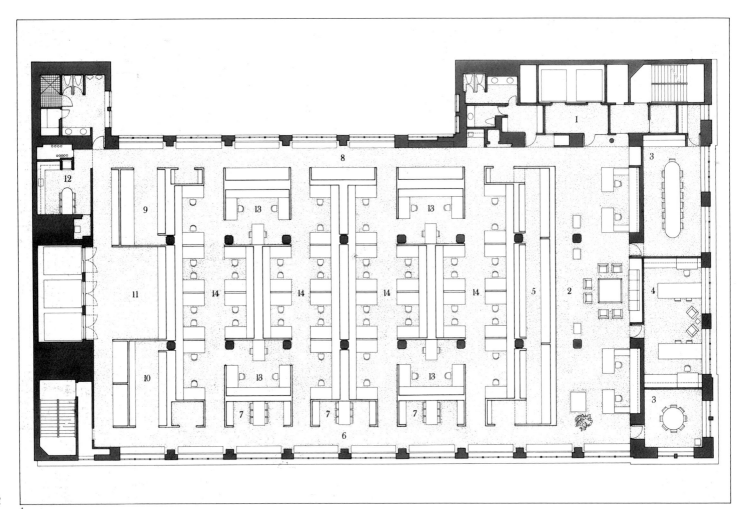

1

2

3

1.Floor plan 2.View of circulation gallery
from entry 3.View toward reception area and
office workroom 4.Drafting and associates'
space 5.Drafting space 6.View of circulation
gallery from conference room

4

5

6

**Guggenheim Museum
Renovation and Addition**
New York, New York

Built in the late 1950s, Frank Lloyd Wright's museum is located on Fifth Avenue between 88th and 89th Streets facing Central Park. It contains one of the great major spaces of the twentieth century, a five-story cylindrical ramped volume of reinforced concrete. The permanent collection of abstract art, together with one of the largest impressionist and post-impressionist collections in the world, must be kept in storage because the major part of the space is allocated for changing exhibits.

The addition and renovation would permit a major portion of the existing collection to be permanently exhibited. This scheme would return the entire original building to public access, enlarge on-site storage facilities, double the size of administration facilities

and double the capacity of the restaurant and bookstore. The new addition would also include the library, which is now off-site, and expand space for maintenance, conservation and restoration.

The first and existing four-story addition to the original structure was built in 1965 by the Taliesin Fellowship, on the northeast corner of the site. It has proved to be too small and inefficient. Fortunately, the foundations of the addition were designed to accommodate added construction.

The three phases of this proposal would occur sequentially, thus allowing change without major disruption. A 10,000-square-foot vault would be constructed under the Fifth Avenue sidewalk for expansion of all existing basement service

and shop spaces. The new building would be built on top of the existing addition, extending its structure. The stair and exterior walls would be removed and rebuilt, and six floors would be added. The ground floor would accommodate the enlarged bookstore, as well as administrative and service entries. The second, third and fourth floors would house the expanded permanent collection and tie directly into the original building in both plan and section. The fifth and sixth floors would accommodate the art storage and conservatory, the seventh floor would become the library, the eighth and ninth floors would serve the administration, and the tenth floor, with its double-height space, would accommodate the restaurant and special museum functions. The tenth floor

1

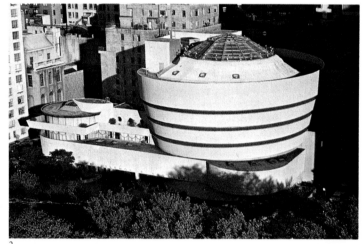

2

3

4

5

1.Northwest facade before annex construction
2.Aerial view from southwest before annex construction 3.North facade before annex
construction 4.Existing view from 89th street
5.Southwest view of model 6.Existing section
7.Proposed north elevation 8.Proposed south
elevation 9.Proposed section 10.North view
of model 11.South view of model
12.Northwest view of model

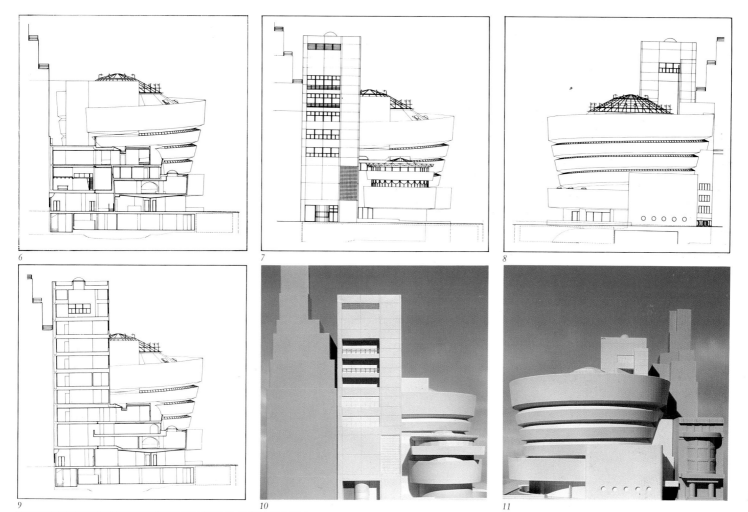

265

would also overlook the roofscape of the original building and Central Park beyond. Following the completion of this addition, the original structure would be renovated accordingly.

Respecting both the scale and character of the street, the new addition would address 89th Street, with its north facade acting as a negotiator to the existing urban fabric. The west facade, facing Fifth Avenue and the Park, would offer a more neutral facade to the original building's articulated sculptural forms, and allow it for the first time to be perceived as both an object and contextual building.

1

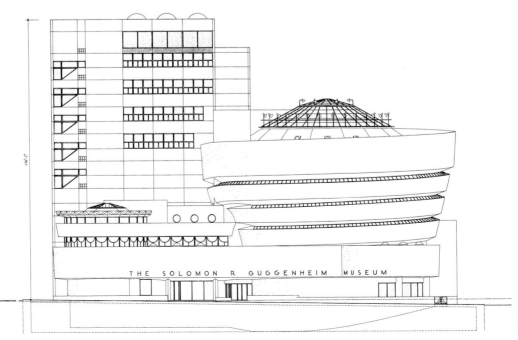

THE SOLOMON R GUGGENHEIM MUSEUM

2

1.West view of model 2.West elevation   3.Basement floor plan 4.Ground floor plan   floor plan 10.Seventh floor plan 11.Eighth
5.Second floor plan 6.Third floor plan   floor plan 12.Ninth floor plan 13.Tenth floor
7.Fourth floor plan 8.Fifth floor plan 9.Sixth   plan

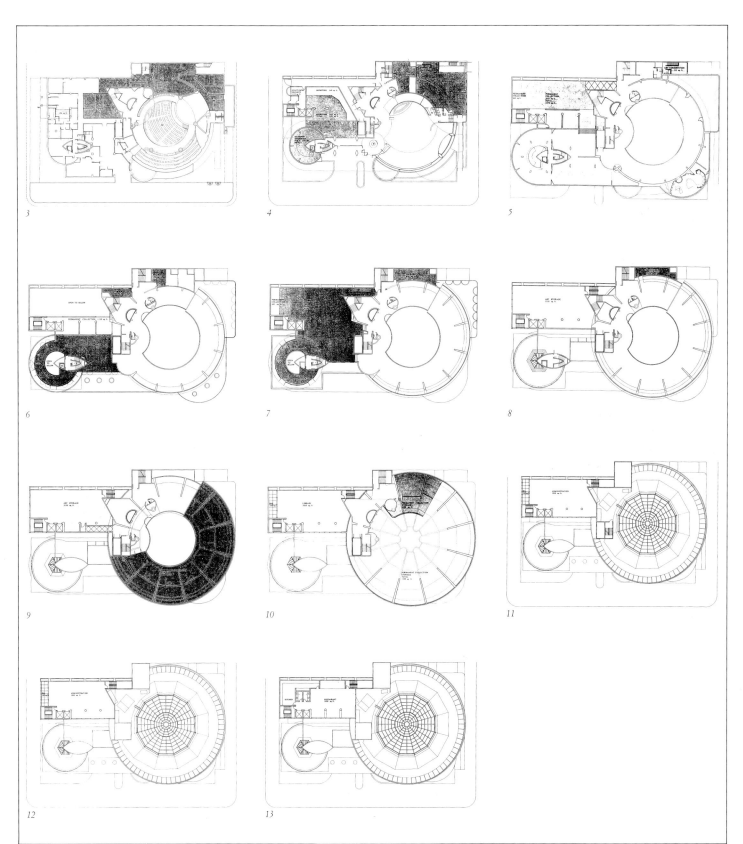

3

4

5

6

7

8

9

10

11

12

13

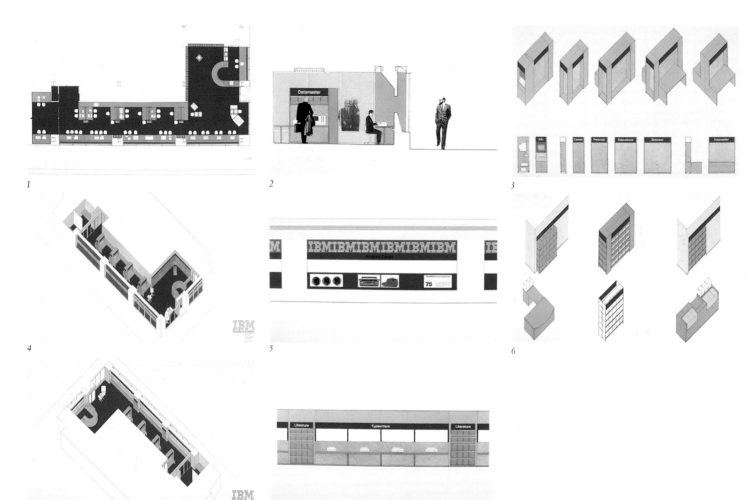

1

2

3

4

5

6

7

8

The problem was to evaluate the design parameters of the existing product centers and propose an alternative solution which would be implemented in a variety of spaces across the country. Aside from the architecture, there was a requirement to design product and software display alternatives, sales counters, work stations and graphics.

Each store's area would be divided into two zones: the front, or selling area, which would accommodate the sales and display counter, software display, product display, sales demonstration area, work area and manager's office; and the back, or support area, which would accommodate administrative, storage and service spaces, accessible to the front. The storefronts were designed to accommodate two types of display. The graphic window is divided into three

horizontal zones, an easel display bottom panel for changing graphics, a slot window at pedestrian eye level, affording a horizontal view of the space, and an upper frieze with a repetitive IBM graphic. In all cases, this installation is backed internally by work counters and display stations to intensify the window reference and to eliminate street distraction for those working. The floor-to-ceiling window wall which accommodates the entry vestibule and the varying pedestal product display elements affords full-store visibility.

All display elements, graphics, work stations, shelving units, software display shelves and sales counters are modular and adaptable to any installation. The floor is red carpet, the front ceiling is polished aluminum tile, the fixtures are dark gray plastic laminate, the walls are varying tones of gray paint and the

lighting is general flourescent.

The intention was to create an environment that would present the products directly but subtly; one that would be perceptually organized but varying; dignified, yet clearly commercial; one which would engender a sense of expectation and security.

The Albany Product Center was the first installation and it was basically successful. At the time of publication, through reevaluation and user comments, modifications in the graphics and additional display elements are being implemented.

1.Plan of prototype 2.Section through typical storefront 3.Modular components
4.Axonometric 5.Storefront elevation
6.Modular components 7.Axonometric
8.Interior elevation at perimeter ledge

IBM Product Center
Albany, New York

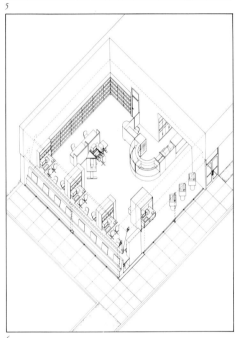

269

1.*View of center from access road* 2.*View toward entry and display pedestals* 3.*Sales counter* 4.*Floor plan* 5.*Store front* 6.*Axonometric* 7.*Open window display at entry facade* 8.*Interior view of software display niche and sales counter* 9.*Interior view from sales counter*

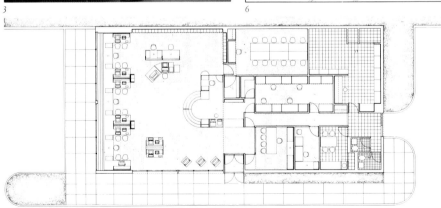

The Evans Partnership
Office Building
Rutherford, New Jersey

The problem was to design a
240,000-square-foot speculative office
building on a compacted fill site. The
location was a major highway intersection
adjacent to the New Jersey Meadowlands
Sports Complex.
The pile foundations and the 28-foot by
28-foot structural bay fixed the building's
footprint. A precast concrete exterior wall
was designed to present the building from a
highway vehicular scale as well as a user
pedestrian scale. Thus, the west facade,
which is centered on the site entry location
on axis to the pedestrian tree alley, was
eroded and set back in a vertical and
horizontal stepping sequence for four stories,
rendering a major entry notation that is both
formal and literal. The precast horizontal
panels are further articulated by an extended
curved sill and by recessed horizontal
stripping in the structural zone of the panel.
A three-dimensional rendering and changes
in texture are produced, adding secondary
and tertiary readings to the intention.

*1.Model view of west facade 2.Model view of
east facade 3.Model detail of west facade
4.Site plan 5.Typical floor plan 6.Ground
floor plan*

1

2

3

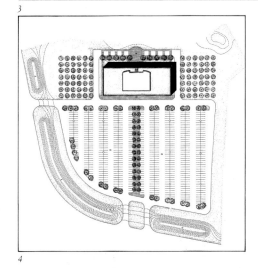

4

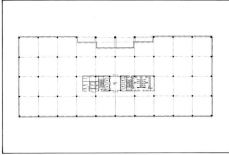

5

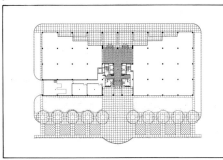

6

The Evans Partnership
Office Building
Paramus, New Jersey

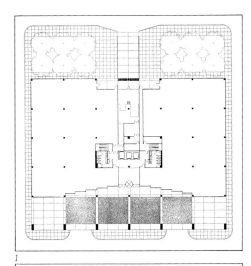

1

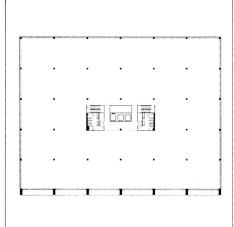

2

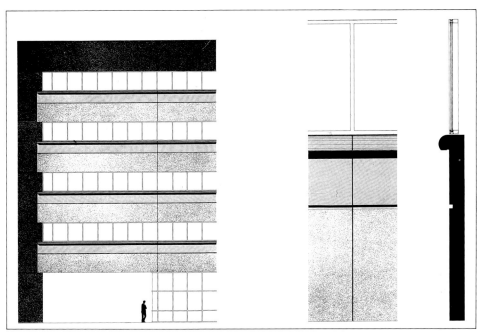

3

4

5

The problem was to design a 200,000-square-foot speculative office building on a cul-de-sac with adjacent structures on all sides.

The design parti was generated by the coincidence of orientation and entry. The south facade, with its recessed entry and covered automobile drop-off, became an integral frontal brise-soleil. The precast concrete exterior wall was developed from the investigation for the Rutherford Building. This wall contributes a unique sense of quality, weight and density that is intensified by a green glass and black aluminum curtain wall infill.

1.Ground floor plan 2.Typical floor plan
3.Precast concrete design details 4.Model view
of north facade 5.Model view of south facade
6.View from southeast 7.Detail of south
facade 8.Southwest precast corner detail
9.Detail of west facade

6

7

8

9

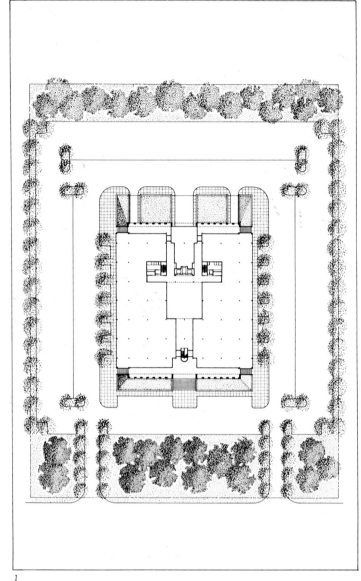

1

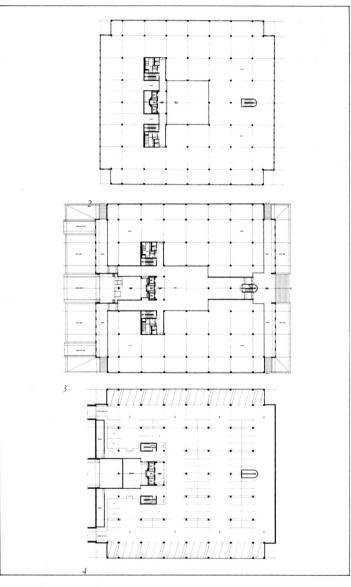

2

3

4

The problem was to design a
150,000-square-foot speculative office
building on a restrictive site. The structure
and exterior wall were predetermined as
precast concrete.

The design parti was generated by the
structural implications, parking limitations
and multiple entry requirements. A building
base was developed with parking one
half-level below grade. This generated raised
covered arcades on the front and back
facades, and accessed entries consolidated in
a center three-story skylit court. The arcade

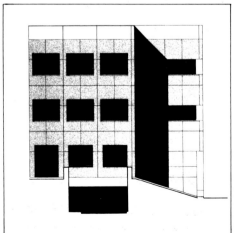

5

facades were constructed of 40-foot by
10-foot, punched window, vertical, precast
panels resting on a bermed and
stair-articulated base. The side facades were
constructed of 30-foot horizontal precast
panels with green glass and black aluminum
curtain wall infill between the columns and
horizontal open ventilation slots at the base.
The dual facade renders the structural
integrity and reinforces the formal notations
of base, entry and frontality unique to
low-rise speculative office buildings.

1.Site plan 2.Typical floor plan 3.Ground
floor plan 4.Garage floor plan 5.Elevation of
corner detail 6.Model view of east corner

7.Model view of west corner 8.Model view of
northwest facade 9.North elevation
10.South elevation 11.East elevation

6

8

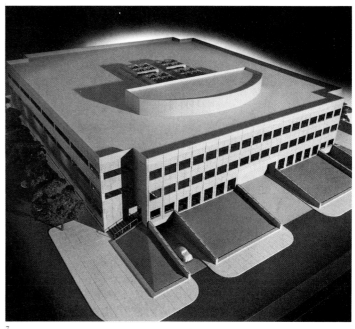

7

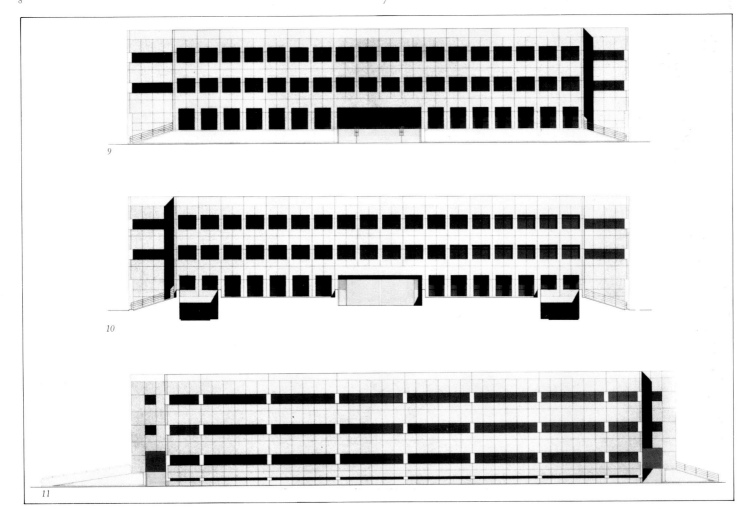

9

10

11

**Beverly Hills Civic Center
Competition**
Beverly Hills, California

1

2

3

4

5

6

This project was the result of a national competition. The problem was to design new buildings and renovate existing structures to form a new civic center. The 10-acre site was adjacent to and included the existing city hall building, which was maintained as an object in the park. The proposed city hall park was formally generated by the transverse axis of the city hall and the termination of the Burton Wave greenbelt, which created a major civic outdoor space.

The ceremonial city hall entrance and covered secondary entry were provided from Rexford Drive. The main foyer, located under the tower dome, was conceived as the gateway to the new civic center complex. By establishing the east/west city hall axis as the major cross-site connection via the proposed Rexford Drive Bridge, all city services, community facilities, library and parking areas are interconnected and can be reached under cover. The east-west axis is terminated by an outdoor court and community auditorium facility. The Rexford Drive Bridge is a referential symbol which reinforces the identity of the new civic center. Rexford Drive is the major participatory street of the complex. From a vehicle, one can view the entire civic center. A continuous covered automobile drop-off exists for all facilities.

The upper level of the arcade provides flexible office space which can be used as future expansion space for the city hall or for other government services. Architecturally, this level, with its curved roof, establishes a site cornice. The mid-level of the arcade

connects to the city hall entry level via the bridge and contains community activity spaces, covered exhibition galleries, auditorium lobby, as well as entrances to the fire and police buildings.

Alpine Drive serves as the vehicular access to the public parking garage, police department building and jail, fire department, vehicle return, and library services. Each building has its own frontage and image along Alpine Drive.

By making the buildings separate yet contiguous, the planning precedent of downtown Beverly Hills is extended. The Alpine Drive facades and the Rexford Drive arcade support the idea of a civic center, rather than a series of separate object buildings which compete with each other and with the original city hall building.

The proposal calls for the connection of Alpine Drive to Santa Monica Boulevard for a more efficient vehicular circulation system. One assumes that any future expansion of the civic center will occur to the east of Alpine Drive in the industrial zone. To establish this connection, an outdoor mall is provided from Rexford Drive to Alpine Drive between the police and library buildings. Public parking is centralized and located below grade to minimize its visual impact. From the parking levels, all facilities can be reached under cover.

A public terrace on the southern roof of the renovated library is reached from the community activity level. Access from Rexford Drive and the upper arcade level via stairs and elevators is also provided. The

library staff lounge, dining facility and major community meeting space open directly to this terrace.

The civic center courtyard, on axis with the Rexford Drive Bridge, is a paved arcaded cloister enclosed by the police, fire, and auditorium buildings. It contains a grand stair which ascends to the community activity level and auditorium lobby. In addition to its entrance and symbolic functions, it could function as a small outdoor theater or meeting place.

The civic center park contains a fountain/plaza defined by zones of landscaping and paving. An arbor, garden zone and hedge row establish the southern site edge.

In summary, this proposal has direct references to the Library and Science Building at the Westover School. The arcade, or spine, is in both cases the major site organizer and referential structure, acting here as a facade to separate existing and new structures, while reinforcing the existing city hall.

1.Aerial site 2.View of existing city hall 3.Overall view of model from west 4.Overall view of model from south 5.Overall view of model from east 6.Overall view of model from north 7.View of model from north 8.Site plan 9.Ground floor plan 10.Second floor plan 11.Third floor plan 12.North elevations 13.Cross sections 14.East elevation 15.Section 16.West elevation 17.South elevation 18.Cross section 19.Partial west elevation 20.Section detail

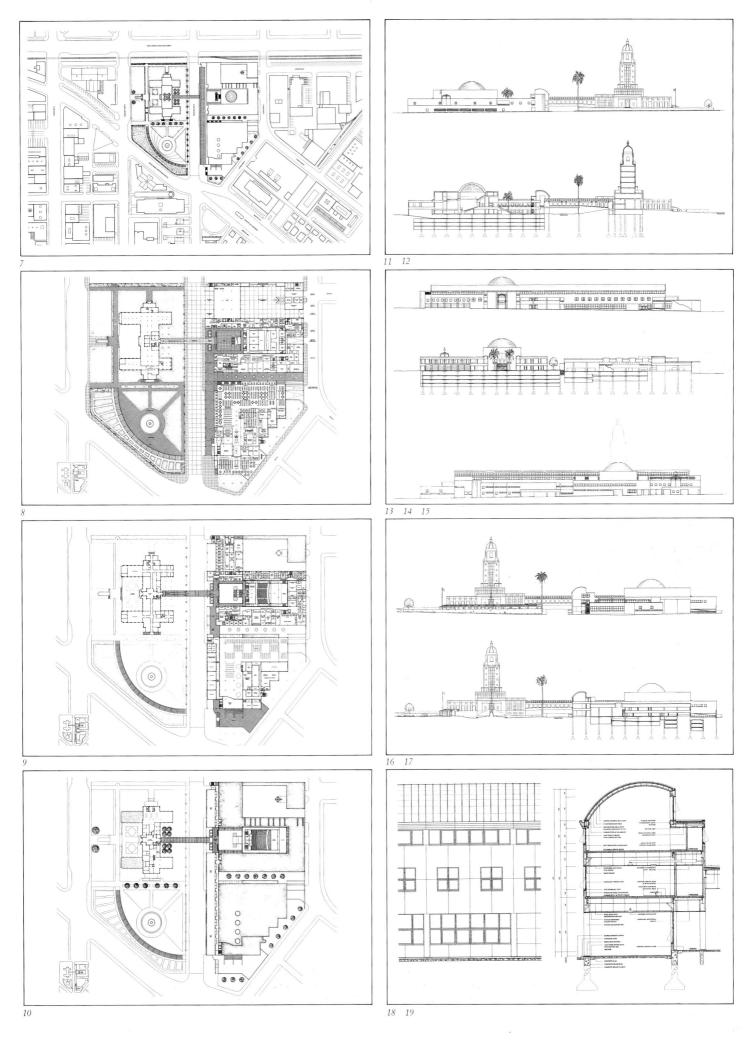

7

8

9

10

11 12

13 14 15

16 17

18 19

275

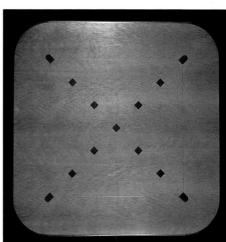

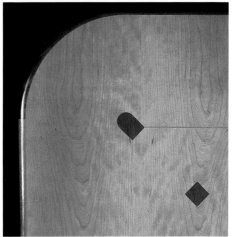

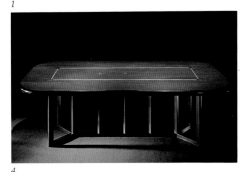

The inspiration for the de Menil Table Series came from our mutual involvement in furnishing a major residence with Austrian Secessionist furniture.

The parti of this wood table series was determined by a clear expression of structure and form that was articulated in the base and the top simultaneously.

The vertical base supports penetrate the top and describe the structure graphically, adding a richness of expression. By using two wood types that are basically interchangeable, the articulation is made distinctive. The base, the bull-nosed edge and the penetrations are one solid wood type and the top surface is a veneer of another wood type. The final addition of the brass edge in the visual middle of the table offers one more layer of density.

The proposed woods are mahogany, cherry, ash and ebony, reestablishing a wood and craft furniture aesthetic.

1.Coffee table 2.Coffee table top 3.Coffee table detail 4.Dining table

The purpose of this design was to document, in a composite and graphic technique, a summary of design intention sensibilities and references.
The geometric references were the golden section, the square and circle, real and implied diagonals, and cubist form, all rendered through color density and overlay, transforming the literal into the implied.

1."Soleil Couchant" tapestry, 5' × 7' 2.Sketch

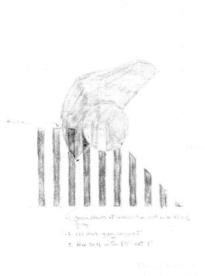

2

The Evans Partnership
Office Building
Piscataway, New Jersey

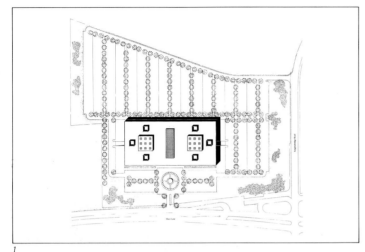

1

2

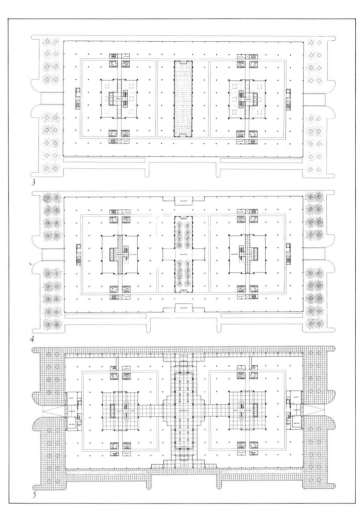

3

4

5

The problem was to design a 450,000-square-foot, three-story speculative office building on a corner site.

The building is 575 feet long and 270 feet wide, with entrances from covered arcades on the long facades into a central, linear, barrel-vaulted, skylit space. Punched windows, side aisles and granite facades recall the public mall space. At the center, two halls extend north and south to two central skylit lobbies with an articulated core object containing elevators, expressed stair and bridges to the office space. Thus, the maximum dimension from exterior perimeter to the interior skylight is 90 feet, creating an optimum flexible design standard and a strategy for offering three major interior referential volumes in a 150,000-square-foot floor.

The exterior is gray glass with black mullions, rendered in a general grid similar to the AT&T Building in Parsippany, with the interior granite walls and floors of the central volume extending out to the set-back wall of the arcade.

1.Site plan 2.Entry hall 3.Third floor plan
4.Second floor plan 5.Ground floor plan
6.East elevation 7.Section A through hall
8.Section B through atrium 9.Entry hall
section and elevation 10.Atrium wall section
and elevation 11.Axonometric of atrium
12.South elevation 13.Longitudinal section
14.North elevation

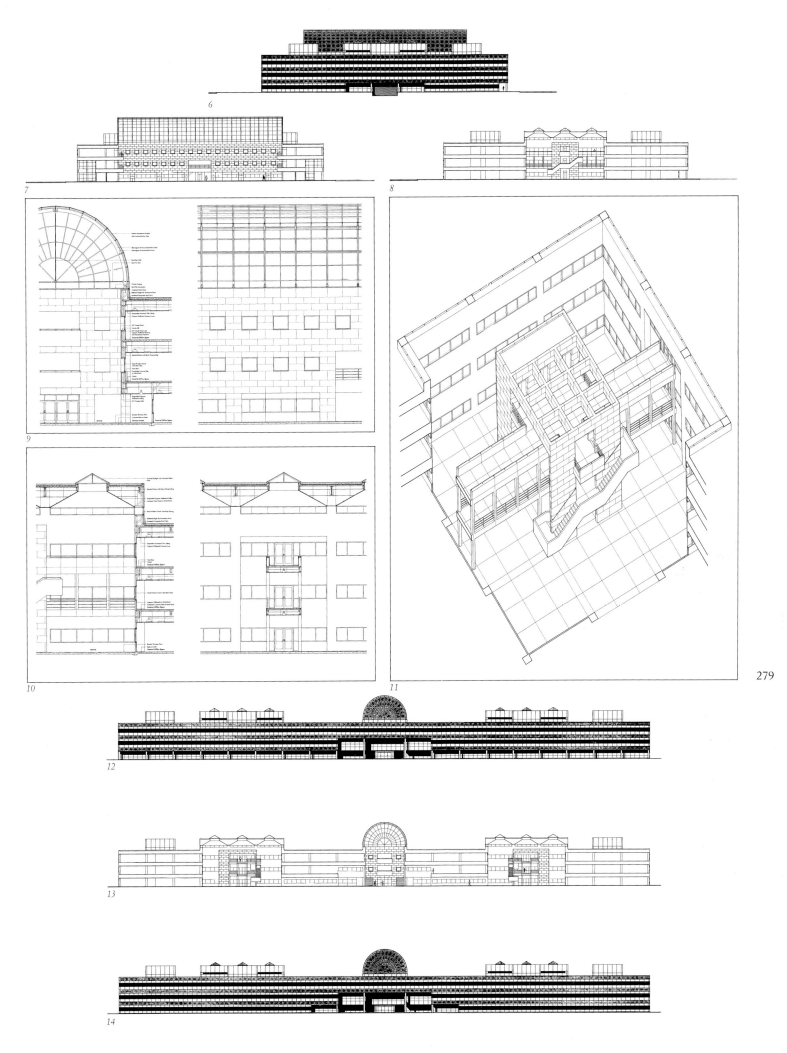

6

7

8

9

10

11

12

13

14

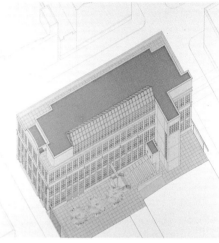

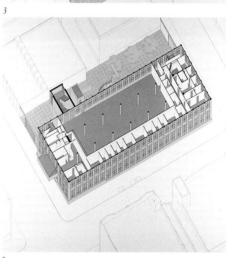

The problem was to design a specialized museum in an existing 45,000-square-foot, three-story 1920s loft building adjacent to the Astoria Motion Picture Studio Complex. The design proposes reglazing the existing window openings and repairing the stucco masonry exterior to support its listing on the National Registration of Historic Buildings. The public entrance and box office, demarcated by a new movie-house marquee, will be located on 36th Street off the pedestrian plaza, central to the complex. The ground floor accommodates the lobby, reception desk, museum store, café/gallery, an exhibition space facing and opening to the museum courtyard, a state of the art, 200-seat movie theater, offices for the local community board, and loading dock and service facilities. The landscaped courtyard accommodates an outdoor theater and stage, plus the new monumental stair tower, which accesses all floors. The second floor accommodates the administrative offices, the curatorial staff, a library and flexible exhibition galleries. The third floor accommodates an orientation theater, a two-story high balconied sound stage and flexible exhibition space. The fourth floor addition on the roof contains a "greenhouse" studio, flexible exhibition space, a major reception room with catering kitchen and a roof terrace offering views of the Manhattan skyline.

The design deals primarily with an interior environment which, with the exception of specific spaces, is totally flexible and multi-programmable.

280

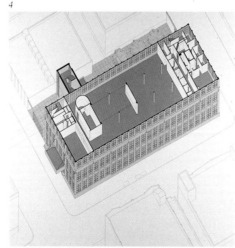

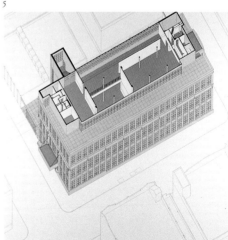

1.Site plan 2.Axonometric view from southwest 3.Axonometric view from northeast 4.Ground floor axonometric 5.Second floor axonometric 6.Third floor axonometric 7.Penthouse floor axonometric 8.View of existing building 9.Ground floor plan 10.Second floor plan 11.Third floor plan 12.Penthouse plan 13.West and north elevation 14.East and south elevation

8

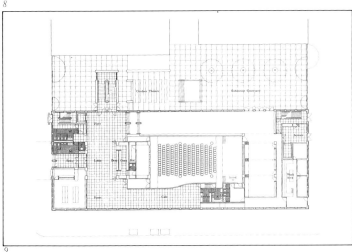

9

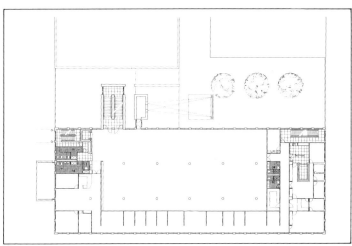

10

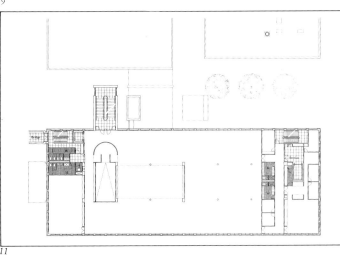

11

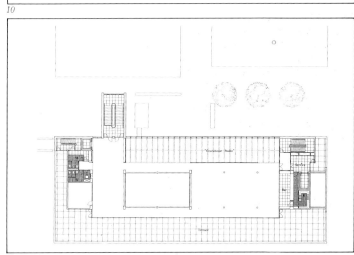

12

281

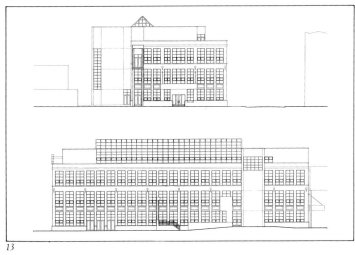

13

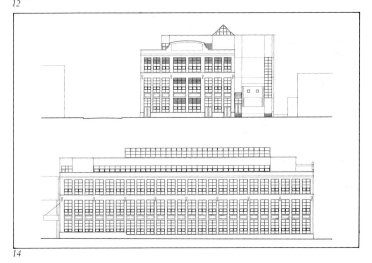

14

Charles Gwathmey was born in 1938 in Charlotte, North Carolina. He attended the University of Pennsylvania and Yale University, where he received a master of architecture degree in 1962. Upon graduation he was awarded the William Wirt Winchester Traveling Fellowship for "the outstanding graduating student in architecture." During the year 1962–1963, he continued his studies under a Fulbright Grant in France.

Since 1964 Mr. Gwathmey has been a professor of architectural design, maintaining faculty positions at Yale, Princeton, Columbia and Harvard universities and the Cooper Union. He has lectured widely and has served on numerous design award juries.

In 1970, after four years of private practice, Mr. Gwathmey became the youngest architect to receive the Arnold W. Brunner Prize from the American Institute and Academy of Arts and Letters. This award is presented annually to "an architect who has made a significant contribution to architecture as an art." In 1974, Mr. Gwathmey was the only architect named in the Leadership in America issue of *Time* magazine.

In 1976 Charles Gwathmey was elected to membership in the American Institute and Academy of Arts and Letters; in 1978 he was named a trustee of the Institute of Architecture and Urban Studies; in 1979 he was elected president of the Board of Trustees; and in 1981 he became a fellow in the American Institute of Architects.

Robert Siegel was born in 1939 in New York City. He received a bachelor of architecture degree from Pratt Institute in 1962 and a master of architecture degree from Harvard University in 1963.

Prior to the formation of Gwathmey Siegel & Associates Architects, Mr. Siegel was an associate with Edward L. Barnes and Associates, Architects, in New York City.

In 1979 he was elected vice-president of the New York Chapter of the American Institute of Architects.

In their 16 years as a firm, Gwathmey Siegel & Associates Architects has won over 45 design awards including National AIA Honor Awards for the Straus Residence in Purchase, New York; Whig Hall at Princeton University; the Dormitory, Dining and Student Union Facility at the State University College at Purchase, New York; and the Taft Residence in Cincinnati, Ohio.

The American Institute of Architects awarded their highest honor to Gwathmey Siegel & Associates Architects, the 1982 Architectural Firm Award; and in 1983, the New York AIA celebrated Charles Gwathmey and Robert Siegel with the Gold Medal.

Miller Residence
Fire Island, New York

Dorr, Maude. "A Place in the Sun: Vacation Houses." *Progressive Architecture*, November 1965, pp. 128–133.

"Maison Miller, Fire Island, New York 1963." *Aujourd'hui*, nos. 55–56 (1967), pp. 32–33.

Kaspar, Karl. *International Vacation Houses.* Stuttgart: Verlag Gerd Hstje, 1967, pp. 126–129.

Herlinger-Bristol Ltd.
Showrooms and Offices
New York, New York

"Offices, New York, Architects. Gwathmey and Henderson." *The Architectural Review*, May 1968, pp. 373–374.

Gwathmey Residence and Studio
Amagansett, New York

"Geometry by the Sea." *The Architectural Forum*, April 1966, pp. 52–55.

Plumb, Barbara. "Cylinders and Cubes for Building Blocks." *The New York Times Magazine,* April 10, 1966, pp. 60–61.

Sverbeyeff, Elizabeth. "Geometry at the Beach." *House Beautiful*, July 1966, pp. 54–58.

40 Under 40: An exhibition of young talent in architecture. New York: The Architectural League, 1966, p. 10.

"Replicated Residence." *Architectural Forum*, vol. 126, no. 1 (January/February 1967), p. 81.

"Homes for All Seasons." *Holiday,* October 1967, p. 63.

"Maison Robert Gwathmey, Amagansett, New York 1965." *Aujourd'hui*, nos. 55–56 (1967), pp. 32–33.

Plumb, Barbara. *Young Design for Living.* New York: Viking Press, 1969, pp. 118–119.

Lewin, Susan. "It's a Dream." *House Beautiful,* July 1972, pp. 23–27.

Johnson, Philip. "The State of the Art." *Inland Architect,* vol. 17, no. 2 (February 1973), pp. 14–19.

Goldberger, Paul. "Architecture's '5' Make Their Ideas Felt." *The New York Times,* November 26, 1973, p. 23.

Skurka, Norma. "Housing Out of Tune with the Times." *The New York Times Magazine,* February 24, 1974, pp. 74–75.

"Gwathmey Henderson Siegel, Amagansett, Long Island." *Global Interior,* no. 6 (1974), p. 49.

Hunter, Sam and Jacobus, John. *American Art of the 20th Century.* New York: Harry N. Abrams, Inc., 1974.

"Autour d'un tennis. Amagansett, New York." *Architecture Française,* no. 393 (October 1975), pp. 112–115.

"New York: House at Long Island." *The Toshi-Jutaku Quarterly,* no. 11 (Autumn 1975), pp. 91–97.

Tafuri, Manfredo. "'European Graffiti.' Five × Five = Twenty-five." Translated by Victor Caliandro. *Oppositions 5* (1976), pp. 35–74.

Breslow, Kay and Paul. "Charles Gwathmey and Robert Siegel: Residential Works 1966/77." *ADA Edita.,* Tokyo, 1977, pp. 22–27.

Goldberger, Paul. "A Design for Orderly Living." *The New York Times Magazine,* December 11, 1977, pp. 146–148, 163–167.

Stern, Robert, A.M. *New Directions in American Architecture,* revised edition. New York: George Braziller, 1977, p. 120.

Five Houses Gwathmey Siegel Architects, Catalogue 7, The Institute for Architecture and Urban Studies, 1977–78, pp. 5–6.

Drexler, Arthur. *Transformations in Modern Architecture.* New York: The Museum of Modern Art, 1979.

The Architecture of Suffolk County. New York: Heckscher Museum, 1979, pp. 28–29, 32.

Diamondstein, Barbaralee. *American Architecture Now.* New York: Rizzoli, 1980, pp. 63–77.

Howard, Jane. "East Hampton." *Travel & Leisure,* vol. 11, no. 5 (May 1981), pp. 80–81.

"Gwathmey Siegel: Winner of AIA's Firm Award." *AIA Journal,* February 1982.

"The Gwathmey House and Studio, 1967, Amagansett, New York, USA." *Toshi Jutaku Urban Housing,* July 1983, pp. 96–99.

Goldberger, Paul. "The Strangling of a Resort." *The New York Times Magazine,* September 4, 1983, p. 17.

Straus Residence
Purchase, New York

"Suburban House: Purchase, New York." Record Houses of 1968, *Architectural Record,* vol. 143, no. 6 (Mid-May 1968), pp. 34–37.

"The 1968 Honor Awards." *AIA Journal,* vol. XLIX, no. 6 (June 1968), p. 106.

Sverbeyeff, Elizabeth. "The Sculptured House." *House Beautiful,* September 1968, pp. 86–91.

"Sculpture for Living In." *House Beautiful's Building Manual,* no. 57 (Spring/Summer 1969), pp. 150–153.

"Four Centuries of American Style: A Ten Page Preview of U.S. Architectural Exhibit at Osaka Expo '70." *American Home,* February 1970, p. 40.

Moholy-Nagy, Sybil. "Maison privée dans le Connecticut." *USA: Architecture Formes Functions.* Lausanne, Switzerland: Editions Anthony Krafft, 1971, pp. 336–337.

Chermayeff, Ivan. *Observations on American Architecture.* New York: Viking Press, 1972, p. 35.

Wagner, Walter. *Great Houses.* New York: McGraw Hill, Inc., 1976, pp. 56–59.

Breslow, Kay and Paul. "Charles Gwathmey and Robert Siegel: Residential Works 1966/77." *ADA Edita.,* Tokyo, 1977, pp. 28–33.

Sedacca Residence
East Hampton, New York

"Buildings in the News." *Architectural Record,* February 1969, p. 40.

"A Glowing House." *House Beautiful,* September 1969, pp. 91–95.

"Focus on Form." *Building Manual,* no. 59 (Spring/Summer 1970), pp. 136–139.

"Gwathmey Henderson Siegel, East Hampton, Long Island." *Global Interior*, no. 6 (1974), p. 50.

Breslow, Kay and Paul. "Charles Gwathmey and Robert Siegel: Residential Works 1966/77." *ADA Edita.*, Tokyo, 1977, pp. 34–41.

Five Houses Gwathmey Siegel Architects, Catalogue 7, The Institute for Architecture and Urban Studies, 1977–78, pp. 16.

Goldberg Residence
Manchester, Connecticut

Architectural Record Houses of 1969. *Architectural Record,* Mid-May 1969, pp. 40–43.

Plumb, Barbara. "All Line and Light." *The New York Times Magazine*, November 23, 1969, pp. 126–127.

"Approdata nel bosco." *Ville Giardini*, December 1970, pp. 6–11.

Sartogo, Adriana. "America America." *La Rivista dell' Arredamento Interni*, no. 50 (February 1971), pp. 6–7.

Breslow, Kay and Paul. "Charles Gwathmey and Robert Siegel: Residential Works 1966/77." *ADA Edita.*, Tokyo, 1977, pp. 42–47.

Five Houses Gwathmey Siegel Architects, Catalogue 7, The Institute for Architecture and Urban Studies, 1977–78, pp. 8–9.

Cooper Residence
Orleans, Massachusetts

"A House of Cylinders and Cubes." *House & Garden*, January 1970, pp. 66–67.

Architectural Record Houses of 1970. New York: McGraw-Hill, 1970, pp. 62–65.

Sartogo, Adriana. "A Cape Cod nella Nuovo Inghilterra." *La Rivista dell' Arredamento Interni*, no. 62 (February 1972), pp. 2–70.

Sartogo, Adriana. "Volumni Estroversi." *Ville Giardini*, no. 60 (December 1972), pp. 10–13.

Sartogo, Adriana. "Volumni Estroversi." Tuttoville (Quaderni di) *Ville Giardini.* Milan: Gorlich Editore, S.P.A., 1973.

Abercrombie, Stanley. "Whigs of Whig Hall." *Architecture Plus*, vol. 1, no. 4 (May 1973), pp. 32–43.

The Architectural Record Book of Vacation Houses, second edition. New York: McGraw Hill, 1977, pp. 190–193.

Breslow, Kay and Paul. "Charles Gwathmey and Robert Siegel: Residential Works 1966/77." *ADA Edita.*, Tokyo, 1977, pp. 48–53.

Steel Residence I
Bridgehampton, New York

(Previously published as Residence in Bridgehampton #2)

"Gwathmey/Siegel: House No. 1, Long Island, New York." *A + U*, September 1972, pp. 16–30.

"Mare e Brughiera." *Ville Giardini 89*, May 1975, pp. 26–35.

Tafuri, Manfredo. "'European Graffiti.' Five × Five = Twenty-five." Translated by Victor Caliandro. *Oppositions 5* (1976), pp. 35–74.

Stern, Robert, A.M. *New Directions in American Architecture,* revised edition. New York: George Braziller, 1977, p. 120.

Breslow, Kay and Paul. "Charles Gwathmey and Robert Siegel: Residential Works 1966/77." *ADA Edita.*, Tokyo, 1977, pp. 60–63.

The Architecture of Suffolk County. New York: Heckscher Museum, 1979, p. 32.

Sarnitz, August. "Bemerkungen zu Gwathmey & Siegel." *UM BAU 2*, Vienna, July 1980, pp. 47–56.

Five Houses Gwathmey Siegel Architects, Catalogue 7, The Institute for Architecture and Urban Studies, 1977–78, pp. 16–17.

Steel Residence II
Bridgehampton, New York

(Previously published as Residence in Bridgehampton #1)

Espanet, Marta Siemek. "La piscina in casa e le pareti di legno." *La Revista Dell' Arredamento Interni*, no. 60 (December 1971), pp. 10–13.

Stagg, Anne. "All Year Vacation Houses: A Surge of Space." *House & Garden*, March 1971, pp. 114–121.

"Gwathmey/Siegel: House No. 2, Long Island, New York." *A + U*, November 1973, pp. 108–111.

"Mare e Brughiera." *Ville Giardini*, no. 89 (May 1975), pp. 26–35.

Tafuri, Manfredo. "'European Graffiti.' Five × Five = Twenty-five." Translated by Victor Caliandro. *Oppositions 5* (1976), pp. 35–74.

Breslow, Kay and Paul. "Charles Gwathmey and Robert Siegel: Residential Works 1966/77." *ADA Edita.*, Tokyo, 1977, pp. 64–73.

Five Houses Gwathmey Siegel Architects, Catalogue 7, The Institute for Architecture and Urban Studies, 1977–78, p. 13.

Stern, Robert, A.M. *New Directions in American Architecture,* revised edition. New York: George Braziller, 1977.

Dunaway Apartment
New York, New York

Corbin, Patricia. "Water: Great Therapy for What Ails You." *House & Garden,* May 1970.

"Classic Modern Setting for a Fascinating Woman." *House & Garden*, July 1971, pp. 60–63.

Tollerton, Richard Henry. "The cool world of Faye Dunaway." *House & Garden*, February 1972, pp. 52–53.

Carlsen, Peter. "Design: Charles Gwathmey." *Avenue*, April 1977, pp. 44–48.

Goldberger, Paul. "A Design for Orderly Living." *The New York Times Magazine,* December 11, 1977, p. 147.

Five Houses Gwathmey Siegel Architects, Catalogue 7, The Institute for Architecture and Urban Studies, 1977–78, pp. 6–7, 9.

Breslow, Kay and Paul. "Charles Gwathmey and Robert Siegel: Residential Works 1966/77." *ADA Edita.*, Tokyo, 1977, pp. 54–59.

Service Buildings & Heating Plant
State University College at Purchase
Purchase, New York

"Service Buildings." *Architecture Plus*, May 1973, p. 37.

"Works of Gwathmey Siegel, Service Group and Boiler Plant." *A + U*, no. 46 (October 1974), pp. 122–125.

Dormitory, Dining and Student Union Facility
State University College at Purchase
Purchase, New York

Heyer, Paul. *Architects on Architecture, New Directions in America.* Walker Publishing Company, 1966, p. 411.

"Academic Village." *Architectural Forum*, November 1970, pp. 34–41.

Architecture for the Arts: State University of New York College at Purchase. New York: The Museum of Modern Art, 1971, pp. 40–41.

"College Dormitory." *Architecture Plus*, May 1973, pp. 40–43.

"Student Dining and Dormitory Facilities, State University of New York at Purchase." *Interiors*, November 1974, pp. 70–72.

"Gwathmey Siegel, Student Residential Complex and Dining Facility, New York State University, Purchase, New York." *A + U*, April 1975, p. 81.

"USA: Universita', Dormitories and Dining Hall, New York State University, Purchase, New York." *Domus*, no. 547 (June 1975), pp. 4–7.

Dean, Andrea. "Honor Awards: Six New Buildings, Four Recyclings and Mies." *AIA Journal*, April 1976, pp. 20–21.

"Charles Gwathmey, Residence universitaire à Purchase." *Architecture d'Aujourd'hui*, no. 186 (August, September 1976).

Goldberger, Paul. "A Design for Orderly Living." *The New York Times Magazine,* December 11, 1977.

Marlin, William. "A Section Through the Thinking of Gwathmey Siegel Architects." *Architectural Record*, September 1979, pp. 91–102.

Abercrombie, Stanley. *Gwathmey Siegel Monographs on Contemporary Architecture.* New York: Whitney Library of Design, 1981, pp. 32–39.

Wright, Sylvia Hart. *Highlights of Recent American Architecture.* Metuchen (N.J.): The Scarecrow Press, Inc., 1982, p. 43.

Gwathmey Siegel Architects
Offices
New York, New York

"Gwathmey Siegel's Own Offices transformed from lofty studio space at New York Carnegie Hall and a history of the firm." *Interiors*, July 1972, pp. 74–76.

Eskilson Residence
Roxbury, Connecticut
(project)

Breslow, Kay and Paul. "Charles Gwathmey and Robert Siegel: Residential Works 1966/77." *ADA Edita.*, Tokyo, 1977, pp. 74–81.

Five Houses Gwathmey Siegel Architects, Catalogue 7, The Institute for Architecture and Urban Studies, 1977–78, pp. 9–11.

Sarnitz, August. "Bemerkungen zu Gwathmey & Siegel." *UM BAU 2*, Vienna, July 1980, pp. 47–56.

Whig Hall
Princeton University
Princeton, New Jersey

"Citations, Whig Hall, Princeton, New Jersey." *Progressive Architecture,* January 1973, pp. 82–83.

"1973 P/A Citation Winner completed." *Progressive Architecture*, April 1973, p. 23.

Abercrombie, Stanley. "Whigs of Whig Hall." *Architecture Plus*, May 1973, pp. 32–43.

"Whig Hall, Princeton, New Jersey." *Progressive Architecture*, June 1973, pp. 122–125.

Morgan, William D. "Modern Lecture Hall is Constructed in 80 Year Old Shell." *American School & University*, June 1973, pp. 56–57.

"Whig Hall, Princeton, New Jersey, Gwathmey & Siegel." *Space Design*, no. 120 (August 1974), pp. 40–50.

"Works of Gwathmey Siegel, Whig Hall." *A + U*, no. 46 (October 1974), pp. 110–117.

Dean, Andrea. "Honor Awards: Six New Buildings, Four Re-cyclings and Mies." *AIA Journal*, April 1976, pp. 6–7.

Tafuri, Manfredo. "'European Graffiti.' Five × Five = Twenty-five." Translated by Victor Caliandro. *Oppositions 5* (1976), pp. 35–74.

Stern, Robert, A.M. *New Directions in American Architecture,* revised edition. New York: George Braziller, 1977, p. 123.

Goldberger, Paul. "A Design for Orderly Living." *The New York Times Magazine,* December 11, 1977, pp. 147.

"Five Frontiersmen." *Newsweek*, November 6, 1978, p. 86.

Drexler, Arthur. *Transformations in Modern Architecture.* New York: The Museum of Modern Art, 1979, p. 15.

"Images of the 70's." *AIA Journal*, vol. 69, no. 1 (1979).

"Big in the 70's: Recycling and Restoration." *AIA Journal*, January 1980, pp. 55–56.

Diamondstein, Barbaralee. *American Architecture Now.* New York: Rizzoli, 1980, pp. 63–77.

Abercrombie, Stanley. *Gwathmey Siegel Monographs on Contemporary Architecture.* New York: Whitney Library of Design, 1981, pp. 20–25.

"Gwathmey Siegel: Winner of AIA's Firm Award." *AIA Journal*, February 1982.

Wright, Sylvia Hart. *Highlights of Recent American Architecture,* Metuchen (N.J.): The Scarecrow Press, Inc., 1982, p. 43.

Tolan Residence
Amagansett, New York

Lewin, Susan. "It's a Dream." *House Beautiful*, July 1972, pp. 23–27.

"Gwathmey-Siegel Architects: Freedom of line, form, and space in a residence with an ocean view at Amagansett, Long Island." *Interiors*, July 1972, pp. 68–71.

"Vacation Retreats: Rising dramatically in wide open spaces." *Vacation Homes*, 1973 edition, pp. 88–93.

Skurka, Norma. "Housing Out of Tune with the Times." *The New York Times Magazine*, February 24, 1974, pp. 74–75.

"Gwathmey Henderson Siegel, Amagansett, New York." *Global Interior*, no. 6 (1974).

"Tolan House, Eastern Long Island, New York, Record Houses." *Architectural Record,* May 1975.

"New York: House at Long Island." *The Toshi-Jutaku Quarterly*, no. 11 (Autumn 1975), pp. 91–97.

"Autour d'un tennis. Amagansett (New York)." *Architecture Française,* no. 393 (October 1975), pp. 112–115.

"House at Long Island." *Urban Housing*, Autumn 1975, pp. 91–97.

Tafuri, Manfredo. "'European Graffiti.' Five × Five = Twenty-five." Translated by Victor Caliandro. *Oppositions 5* (1976), pp. 35–74.

The Architectural Record Book of Vacation Houses, second edition. New York: McGraw-Hill, Inc., 1977, pp. 34–37.

Breslow, Kay and Paul. "Charles Gwathmey and Robert Siegel: Residential Works 1966/77." *ADA Edita.*, Tokyo, 1977, pp. 82–89.

Five Houses Gwathmey Siegel Architects, Catalogue 7, The Institute for Architecture and Urban Studies, 1977–78, pp. 9, 11 & 13.

Drexler, Arthur. *Transformations in Modern Architecture.* New York: The Museum of Modern Art, 1979, p. 42.

Meenan, Monica. "At Home, A View From the Top." *Town & Country*, June 1980, p. 136.

Abercrombie, Stanley. *Gwathmey Siegel Monographs on Contemporary Architecture.* New York: Whitney Library of Design, 1981, pp. 14–19 & 66.

Stucchi, Silvano. "Cultura a Professione Negli USA." *L'Industria Delle Construzioni*, October 1983, p. 7.

New York Apartment
New York, New York

Yee, Tom. "Apartment designed for Books and Art. *House & Garden*, March 1975, pp. 68–73.

Fitzgibbons, Ruth Miller. "Mini building within a shell." *Interiors*, vol. 10 (October 1975), pp. 132–135, 164.

"Una casa per due collezionisti d'arte africana." *Casa Vogue,* November 1976, pp. 172–177.

"Long walls hold African art and books." *Decorating: A House & Garden Guide*, 1976, pp. 134–139.

Breslow, Kay and Paul. "Charles Gwathmey and Robert Siegel: Residential Works 1966/77." *ADA Edita.*, Tokyo, 1977, pp. 108–117.

Cogan Residence
East Hampton, New York

"Tailored to One Family's Lifestyle." *The New York Times Magazine,* January 21, 1973, pp. 52–53.

Skurka, Norma. "A Matter of Space." *The New York Times Magazine,* January 28, 1973, pp. 50–51.

"Private Residence in East Hampton, New York, Record Houses of 1973." *Architectural Record,* vol. 153, no. 6 (Mid-May 1973), pp. 84–87.

"Private Housing." *Architecture Plus*, May 1973, p. 38.

Lewin, Susan. "True Drama Well Cast." *House Beautiful,* September 1973, pp. 115–121.

"House at East Hampton." *Urban Housing Magazine*, Tokyo, December 1973, pp. 2–9.

"Cogan House, East Hampton, New York, U.S.A." *A + U*, no. 46 (October 1974), pp. 79–89.

"The Making of a Seaside Refuge." *House Beautiful's Building Manual*, no. 68 (Fall/Winter 1974/1975).

"Gwathmey Siegel East Hampton, Long Island." *Global Interior*, no. 6 (1974), pp. 42–63.

"Nave de Prato." *Ville Giardini,* no. 99 (March 1976), pp. 2–7.

Allen, Gerald. "The Comforts of Tradition." *Mainliner/United Airlines Magazine,* April, 1977, pp. 28–72.

Art and Contemporary Architecture, Gwathmey Siegel Architects, catalogue. New York: David Findlay Galleries, September 22, 1977 to October 15, 1977, p. 4.

Goldberger, Paul. "A Design for Orderly Living." *The New York Times Magazine,* December 11, 1977.

Breslow, Kay and Paul. "Charles Gwathmey and Robert Siegel: Residential Works 1966/77." *ADA Edita.*, Tokyo, 1977, pp. 90–101.

Five Houses Gwathmey Siegel Architects, catalogue 7, The Institute for Architecture and Urban Studies, 1977–78, pp. 6–7, 9.

Abercrombie, Stanley. *Gwathmey Siegel Monographs on Contemporary Architecture.* New York: Whitney Library of Design, 1981, pp. 26–31 & 67.

"Gwathmey Siegel: Winner of AIA's Firm Award." *AIA Journal,* February 1982.

Elia-Bash Residence
Califon, New Jersey

Allen, Gerald. "Three Projects by Gwathmey Siegel Architects." *Architectural Record,* July 1974, pp. 105–112.

"Works of Gwathmey Siegel, Elia Bash Residence Project." *A + U*, no. 46 (October 1974), pp. 100–101.

Tafuri, Manfredo. "'European Graffiti.' Five × Five = Twenty-five." Translated by Victor Caliandro. *Oppositions 5* (1976), pp. 35–74.

Breslow, Kay and Paul. "Charles Gwathmey and Robert Siegel: Residential Works 1966/77." *ADA Edita.*, Tokyo, 1977, pp. 102–107.

Five Houses Gwathmey Siegel Architects, Catalogue 7, The Institute for Architecture and Urban Studies, 1977–78, pp. 12–13.

Sarnitz, August. "Bemerkungen zu Gwathmey & Siegel." *UM BAU 2,* Vienna, July 1980, pp. 47–56.

Cohn Residence
Amagansett, New York

"Works of Gwathmey Siegel, Cohn Residence." *A + U*, October 1974, pp. 90–97.

"New York State's Building of the Year." *Empire State Architect*, December 1974, p. 18.

Five Houses Gwathmey Siegel Architects, Catalogue 7, The Institute for Architecture and Urban Studies, 1977–78, pp. 9, 13.

Goldberger, Paul. "A Design for Orderly Living." *The New York Times Magazine,* December 11, 1977.

Hurtt, Steve, McDermott, John J., and Nory Miller. "A Critical View of Modern American Houses." *Process Architecture,* Tokyo, no. 7 (1978), pp. 26–29.

Breslow, Kay and Paul. "Charles Gwathmey and Robert Siegel: Residential Works 1966/77." *ADA Edita.,* Tokyo, 1977, pp. 118–127.

Meenan, Monica. "At Home, A View from the Top." *Town & Country,* June 1980, p. 137.

Whitney Road Housing
Perinton, New York

"Public Housing." *Architecture Plus,* May 1973, p. 39.

Allen, Gerald. "Three Projects by Gwathmey Siegel Architects." *Architectural Record,* July 1974, pp. 105–112.

"Works of Gwathmey Siegel, Perinton Housing Project." *A + U,* no. 46 (October 1974), pp. 104–107.

Frampton, Kenneth. "Gwathmey Siegel & Associates Perinton Housing Project, New York, 1975." *Modern Architecture and the Critical Present.* Architectural Design Profile, 1982, pp. 86–91.

Tafuri, Manfredo. "'European Graffiti.' Five × Five = Twenty-five." Translated by Victor Caliandro. *Oppositions 5* (1976), pp. 35–74.

"Perinton Housing, Rochester, New York." The Toshi-Jutaku. *Process Architecture,* no. 12 (1980), pp. 13–19.

Abercrombie, Stanley. *Gwathmey Siegel Monographs on Contemporary Architecture.* New York: Whitney Library of Design, 1981, pp. 44–49.

Gwathmey Barn
Greenwich, Connecticut

"Renovated Barn, Greenwich Connecticut." *Architectural Record,* January 1974, pp. 114–115.

Skurka, Norma. "A Dumb Barn Gets Smart." *The New York Times Magazine,* September 15, 1974.

"Works of Gwathmey Siegel, Barn Renovation." *A + U,* October 1974, pp. 98–99.

"U.S.A.: Ex grannaio." *Domus,* no. 547 (June 1975), pp. 22–24.

Fisher, Karen. "Blow-up." *New York Magazine,* April 28, 1975, p. 58.

"Barn Renovation: Greenwich, Connecticut," 1976, C.S.A. Honor Awards.

Schwab, Gerard Von. "Wonhous, Gwathmey Greenwich, Connecticut, U.S.A." *Living In One's Own House: One Family Houses,* Stuttgart: Karl Krämer Verlag, 1977, pp. 37–40.

Burden, Ernest. *Living Barns.* Boston: New York Graphic Society, 1977, pp. 156–157.

"Restoration of a Barn, Greenwich, Connecticut." *Connecticut Architect,* January/February 1977, p. 13.

Five Houses Gwathmey Siegel Architects, Catalogue 7, The Institute for Architecture and Urban Studies, 1977–78, pp. 8–9.

Lewin, Susan Grant. "A Grand New Barn Raising." *House Beautiful,* March 1978, pp. 114–119.

"Grand New Barns." *Building Manual,* Summer 1980, pp. 120–123.

Pearl's Restaurant
New York, New York

Goldberger, Paul. "The Restaurant's Design Succeeds Elegantly." *The New York Times,* November 6, 1973.

"A Sliver of Oriental Serenity on 48th Street." *Interiors,* March 1974, pp. 86–87.

"Works of Gwathmey Siegel, Pearl's Restaurant." *A + U,* no. 46 (October 1974), pp. 118–119.

Goldberger, Paul. "Design for Dining: Feasts for the Eye, Too." *The New York Times,* July 30, 1976.

"Three Interiors by Gwathmey Siegel for Difficult Spaces and Complex Programs." *Architectural Record,* September 1976, pp. 103–110.

Carlsen, Peter. "Design." *Avenue,* April 1977, pp. 44–48.

Abercrombie, Stanley. *Gwathmey Siegel Monographs on Contemporary Architecture.* New York: Whitney Library of Design, 1981, pp. 40–43, 68.

Heyne, Pamela. *Today's Architectural Mirror, Interiors Buildings and Solar Designs.* Van Nostrand Reinhold Company, 1982, pp. 35–37.

"Interview, Charles Gwathmey." *Restaurant and Hotel Design,* March/April 1983, pp. 36–39, 87.

Sagner Residence
West Orange, New Jersey
(project)

Allen, Gerald. "Three Projects by Gwathmey Siegel Architects." *Architectural Record,* July 1974, pp. 105–112.

"Works of Gwathmey Siegel, Sagner Residence Project." *A + U,* no. 46 (October 1974), pp. 102–103.

Tafuri, Manfredo. "'European Graffiti.' Five × Five = Twenty-five." Translated by Victor Caliandro. *Oppositions 5* (1976), pp. 35–74.

Five Houses Gwathmey Siegel Architects, Catalogue 7, The Institute for Architecture and Urban Studies, 1977–78, pp. 12–13.

Breslow, Kay and Paul. "Charles Gwathmey and Robert Siegel: Residential Works 1966/77." *ADA Edita.,* Tokyo, 1977, pp. 134–139.

Sarnitz, August. "Bemerkungen zu Gwathmey & Siegel." *UM BAU 2,* Vienna, July 1980, pp. 47–56.

Geffen Residence
Malibu, California
(project)

Five Houses Gwathmey Siegel Architects, Catalogue 7, The Institute for Architecture and Urban Studies, 1977–78, pp. 6–7, 9, 13.

Diamondstein, Barbaralee. *American Architecture Now.* New York: Rizzoli, 1980, pp. 63–77.

St. Casimir Housing
Yonkers, New York
(project)

"St. Casimir." *Architecture Plus,* October 1974.

"Works of Gwathmey Siegel, St. Casimir Housing Project." *A + U*, no. 46 (October 1974), pp. 108–109.

Buettner Residence
Sloatsburg, New York

Breslow, Kay and Paul. "Charles Gwathmey and Robert Siegel: Residential Works 1966/77." *ADA Edita.*, Tokyo, 1977, pp. 162–169.

Transammonia Corporation Offices
New York, New York

Ryder, Sharon Lee. "Two By Four." *Progressive Architecture,* June 1975, pp. 66–71.

Charof Residence
Montauk, New York

Breslow, Kay and Paul. "Charles Gwathmey and Robert Siegel: Residential Works 1966/77." *ADA Edita.*, Tokyo, 1977, pp. 140–147.

Kislevitz Residence
Westhampton, New York

Goldberger, Paul. "A Design for Orderly Living." *The New York Times Magazine,* December 11, 1977.

Breslow, Kay and Paul. "Charles Gwathmey and Robert Siegel: Residential Works 1966/77." *ADA Edita.*, Tokyo, 1977, pp. 152–161.

Five Houses Gwathmey Siegel Architects, Catalogue 7, The Institute for Architecture and Urban Studies, 1977–78, pp. 1, 3.

Hurtt, Steve, McDermott, John J. and Miller, Nory. "A Critical View of Modern American Houses." *Process Architecture*, Tokyo, no. 7 (1978), pp. 20–25.

"Una nuova architettura nel respeto di un antico volume." *Abitare*, no. 165 (June 1978), pp. 6–13.

Stephens, Suzanne. "Casa Moderna." *Progressive Architecture*, July 1978, pp. 72–75.

"Gwathmey Siegel." *A + U*, no. 96 (September 1978), pp. 145–157.

Hughes, Robert. "U.S. Architects, Doing Their Own Thing." *Time,* January 4, 1979, pp. 52–59.

Lewin, Susan Grant. "1920's Spanish Colonial Gone Modern." *House Beautiful*, April 1979, pp. 114–119.

"Moving into the Present." *Housing*, July 1979, pp. 82–83.

"Modern Houses in America." *Process Architecture,* no. 7 (1979), pp. 20–25.

"Boxes Unboxed." *Building Manual*, Fall 1980.

Diamondstein, Barbaralee. *American Architecture Now.* New York: Rizzoli, 1980, pp. 63–77.

"Charles Gwathmey on a Personal Approach to Architecture." *Architectural Digest*, November 1983, p. 48.

Vidal Sassoon Salon
La Costa, California

"Three Interiors by Gwathmey-Siegel for Difficult Spaces and Complex Programs." *Architectural Record*, September 1976, pp. 103–110.

"Other Spatial Realms." *Progressive Architecture*, February 1977, pp. 72–82.

Carlsen, Peter. "Design." *Avenue*, April 1977, pp. 44–48.

"Sassoon Strategy." *Interior Design*, December 1978, pp. 128–130.

Vidal Sassoon Salon
New York, New York

"Three Interiors by Gwathmey-Siegel for Difficult Spaces and Complex Programs." *Architectural Record*, September 1976, pp. 103–110.

"Other Spatial Realms." *Progressive Architecture,* February 1977, pp. 72–82.

Carlsen, Peter. "Design." *Avenue,* April 1977, pp. 44–48.

"Sassoon Strategy." *Interior Design,* vol. 49, no. 13 (December 1978), pp. 128–130.

Vidal Sassoon Salon
Chicago, Illinois

"Other Spatial Realms." *Progressive Architecture,* February 1977, pp. 72–82.

Heyne, Pamela. "Today's Architectural Mirror." *Interiors, Buildings, and Solar Designs.* Van Nostrant Reinhold Company, 1982, pp. 66–67.

"Sassoon Strategy." *Interior Design,* vol. 49, no. 13 (December 1978), pp. 128–130.

Vidal Sassoon Salon
Beverly Hills, California

"Vidal Sassoon Salon, Beverly Hills, California." *Architectural Record*, January 1978, pp. 80–83.

"Vidal Sassoon, Beverly Hills, California, U.S.A." *Nikkei Architecture,* May 1978, pp. 104–105.

"Sassoon Strategy." *Interior Design*, vol. 49, no. 13 (December 1978), pp. 128–130.

Abercrombie, Stanley. *Gwathmey Siegel Monographs on Contemporary Architecture.* New York: Whitney Library of Design, 1981, pp. 56–59.

"Gwathmey Siegel: Winner of AIA's Firm Award." *AIA Journal,* February 1982.

Vidal Sassoon Corporate Offices
Los Angeles, California

Klein, Judy Graf. "Elements of Design." *The Office Book.* New York: Facts on File, Inc., 1982, p. 77.

"Sassoon Strategy." *Interior Design*, vol. 49, no. 13 (December 1978), pp. 128–130.

Student Apartment Housing
State University College at Purchase
Purchase, New York

"Apartment Housing Project, New York State University College at Purchase." *L'Industria Delle Construzioni*, April 1978, pp. 75–80.

"Purchase Apartment Housing Project." *Architectural Record*, October 1978, pp. 116–117.

"Purchase Housing." *The Toshi-Jutaku Urban Housing*, March 1979, pp. 50–53.

"Purchase Housing, State University College at Purchase, New York." *The Toshi-Jutaku-Process Architecture*, no. 12 (1980), pp. 20–25.

Island Walk Cooperative Housing
Reston, Virginia

Coyone, Dierdre C. and Kunze, Carl. "Section 11(b) Financing Used by Reston, Virginia to Get Section 8 Cooperative Units Built." *Journal of Housing*, October 1978.

"Reston Housing, Reston Virginia." *The Toshi-Jutaku Process Architecture*, no. 12 (1980), pp. 26–31.

Bower & Gardner
Law Offices
New York, New York

"Other Spatial Realms." *Progressive Architecture*, February 1977, pp. 72–82.

Yee, Roger. "Law Offices of Bower & Gardner." *Interiors*, March 1977, pp. 90–93.

The Evans Partnership
Prototype Office Building

"USA 'Campus' Per Uffici." *L'Industria Delle Construzioni*, no. 84 (October 1978), pp. 53–59.

Gordon, Barclay. "Low-Rise Office Buildings." *Architectural Record*, September 1980.

The Evans Partnership
Office Building
Piscataway, New Jersey

"USA 'Campus' Per Uffici." *L'Industria Delle Construzioni*, no. 84 (October 1978), pp. 53–59.

"Gwathmey Siegel: Winner of AIA's Firm Award." *AIA Journal*, February 1982.

Unger Apartment
New York, New York

"Three Interiors by Gwathmey Siegel for Difficult Spaces and Complex Programs." *Architectural Record*, September 1976, pp. 108–110.

"Living Swell: The House that Kay Unger Built." *Mademoiselle*, February 1977, pp. 158–161.

Breslow, Kay and Paul. "Charles Gwathmey and Robert Siegel: Residential Works 1966/77." *ADA Edita.*, Tokyo, 1977, pp. 148–151.

Damson Oil Corporation
Office Building
Houston, Texas

"What's a High-Style Design Firm Like Gwathmey Siegel Doing Designing Speculative Office Buildings Along Freeways and in Office Campuses?" *Architectural Record*, December 1977, pp. 108–115.

Cataldi, Giancarlo. "USA-Uffici Sull' Autostrada." *L'Industria Delle Construzioni*, no. 83 (September 1978), pp. 60–65.

U.S. Steakhouse Restaurant
New York, New York

"Other Spatial Realms." *Progressive Architecture*, February 1977, pp. 72–82.

Yee, Roger. "U.S. Steakhouse Company." *Interiors,* February 1977, pp. 76–79.

Goldberger, Paul. "A Design for Orderly Living." *The New York Times Magazine,* December 11, 1977.

The Interiors Book of Shops & Restaurants by the Editors of Interiors Magazine. New York: Whitney Library of Design, 1981, pp. 76–77.

Northpoint
Office Building
Houston, Texas

"What's a High-Style Design Firm Like Gwathmey Siegel Doing Designing Speculative Office Buildings Along Freeways and in Office Campuses?" *Architectural Record*, December 1977, pp. 108–115.

Cataldi, Giancarlo. "USA-Uffici Sull' Autostrada." *L'Industria Delle Construzioni*, no. 83 (September 1978), pp. 60–65.

Barber Oil Corporation
Offices
New York, New York

Klein, Judy Graf. "Designing Office Space." *The Office Book.* New York: Facts on File, Inc., 1982, p. 133.

East Campus Student Housing & Academic Center
Columbia University
New York, New York

Katz, James C. "Columbia College Renaissance: The East Campus Complex." *Columbia College Today,* Summer 1977, pp. 6–8.

Diamondstein, Barbaralee. *American Architecture Now.* New York: Rizzoli, 1980, pp. 63–77.

Doubilet, Susan. "Gwathmey Siegel: East Campus Complex." *Skyline*, January 1981, pp. 18–19.

Abercrombie, Stanley. *Gwathmey Siegel Monographs on Contemporary Architecture.* New York: Whitney Library of Design, 1981, pp. 71, 108–113.

Huxtable, Ada Louise. "An Ingenious Advance in Housing Design." *The New York Times*, October 4, 1981.

"Gwathmey Siegel: Winner of AIA's Firm Award." *AIA Journal*, February 1982.

"Expanding Horizons: The East Campus Complex by Gwathmey Siegel and Associates." *Architectural Record,* February 1982.

"East Campus Complex, Columbia University, by Gwathmey Siegel and Associates." *Space Design*, Tokyo, July 1982, pp. 59–66.

Dinelli, Fiamma. "USA-Nuovo Campus Per La Columbia University." *L'Industria Delle Construzioni*, no. 139 (May 1983), pp. 54–61.

"Columbia University, Student Housing and Academic Center." *A + U*, May 1983, pp. 72–77.

"Charles Gwathmey on a Personal Approach to Architecture." *Architectural Digest,* November 1983, pp. 48–49.

Haupt Residence
Amagansett, New York

Five Houses Gwathmey Siegel Architects, Catalogue 7, The Institute for Architecture and Urban Studies, 1977–78, pp. 18–29.

"Gwathmey Siegel, Haupt Residence." *Global Architecture, Houses*, no. 6 (1979), pp. 110–115.

Szenasy, Susan S. "Microcosm on the Dunes." *Residential Interiors,* vol. IV, no. 2 (March/April 1979), pp. 88–93.

"Haupt House, Amagansett, New York, Record Houses of 1979." *Architectural Record*, Mid-May 1979, pp. 88–91.

"Gwathmey Siegel Haupt Residence, Amagansett, New York, 1977–1979." *G.A. Houses,* June 1979, pp. 110–115.

Meenan, Monica. "At Home, a View from the Top." *Town & Country*, June 1980, p. 138.

"Gwathmey/Siegel Haupt Residence." *The Toshi-Jutaku Urban Housing,* February 1982, p. 6.

"Gwathmey/Siegel." *A + U*, no. 118 (July 1980), pp. 101–106.

Weitz Residence
Quogue, New York

Five Houses Gwathmey Siegel Architects, Catalogue 7, The Institute for Architecture and Urban Studies, 1977–78, pp. 30–43.

"Gwathmey Siegel." *A + U*, September 1978, p. 159.

Marlin, William. "A Section through the Thinking of Gwathmey Siegel Architects." *Architectural Record*, September 1979, pp. 91–102.

Herzig, Doris. "Modern Traditional vs. Modern Modern." *Newsday,* October 27, 1979, pp. 6–7.

Lewin, Susan Grant. "A Self-Contained Oasis That Reaches Out to the Surf." *House Beautiful,* June 1980.

Meenan, Monica. "At Home, a View from the Top." *Town & Country*, June 1980, p. 139.

"Gwathmey Siegel." *A + U*, no. 118 (July 1980), pp. 93–100.

Smetana, Donnatella. "La Casa Sulla Duna." *Casa Vogue*, July/August 1980, pp. 48–53.

Abercrombie, Stanley. *Gwathmey Siegel Monographs on Contemporary Architecture.* New York: Whitney Library of Design, 1981, pp. 78–83.

Thomas & Betts Corporation
Office Building
Raritan, New Jersey

"What's a High-Style Design Firm Like Gwathmey Siegel Doing Designing Speculative Office Buildings Along Freeways and in Office Campuses?" *Architectural Record*, December 1977, pp. 108–115.

"U.S.A. 'Campus Per Uffici." *L'Industria Delle Construzioni*, no. 84 (October 1978), pp. 53–59.

Marlin, William. "A Section through the Thinking of Gwathmey Siegel Architects." *Architectural Record*, September 1979, pp. 91–102.

Abercrombie, Stanley. *Gwathmey Siegel Monographs on Contemporary Architecture.* New York: Whitney Library of Design, 1981, pp. 90–95.

Benenson Residence
Rye, New York

Five Houses Gwathmey Siegel Architects, Catalogue 7, The Institute for Architecture and Urban Studies, 1977–78, pp. 44–59.

"Private House, Rye, New York." *Architectural Record Houses*, (Mid-May 1980), pp. 62–65.

"Gwathmey/Siegel." *A + U*, no. 118 (July 1980), pp. 85–91.

"Benenson Residence Rye, New York, USA." *The Toshi-Jutaku Process Architecture*, no. 18 (December 1980), pp. 13–18.

Swirl Inc.
Showrooms and Offices
New York, New York

Filler, Martin. "Two for the Show." *Progressive Architecture*, March 1978, pp. 76–79.

"Swirl Showrooms, New York, New York." *Process Architecture*, no. 13, March 1980, pp. 50–51.

Hyatt Hotel & Casino
Aruba, Antilles
(project)

"Playboy Resort, Aruba, 1976." *A + U*, January 1977, pp. 94–95.

Swid Apartment
New York, New York

Lewin, Susan Grant. "The Art of Space Sculpture." *House Beautiful*, September 1978, pp. 106–111.

"An Apartment of Ideas." *Interior Design*, vol. 50, no. 1 (January 1979), pp. 170–179.

"Dove l'arte e di casa, A New York in Un Grattacielo Del 1912." *Abitare*, no. 179 (November 1979), pp. 20–29.

"Swid Apartment, New York, New York." *Process Architecture*, no. 13 (March 1980), pp. 58–61.

Abercrombie, Stanley. *Gwathmey Siegel Monographs on Contemporary Architecture.* New York: Whitney Library of Design, 1981, pp. 60–65.

Heyne, Pamela. *Today's Architectural Mirror, Interiors Buildings and Solar Designs.* Van Nostrand Reinhold Company, 1982, p. 40.

Emery, Sherman R., ed. "An Apartment of Ideas, Architects Gwathmey/Siegel Rebuild a Manhattan Cooperative." *Styled for Living.* Interior Design Books, 1983, pp. 99–105.

Poster Originals, Ltd.
New York, New York

"Other Spatial Realms." *Progressive Architecture*, February 1977, pp. 72–82.

Mun, David. *Shops, A Manual of Planning and Design.* London: The Architectural Press, 1981, p. 65.

Garey Shirtmakers
Showrooms and Offices
New York, New York

Filler, Martin. "Two for the Show." *Progressive Architecture*, March 1978, pp. 76–79.

Klein, Judy Graf. "Elements of Design." *The Office Book.* New York: Facts on File, Inc., 1982, pp. 67, 71.

Crowley Residence
Greenwich, Connecticut

"Gwathmey Siegel." *A + U*, no. 96 (September 1978), p. 158. (Published as project.)

Geffen Apartment
New York, New York

Bethany, Marilyn. "Shaping Space with Color." *The New York Times Magazine*, March 18, 1979, pp. 84–85, 92.

"Geffen Apartment, New York, New York." *Process Architecture*, no. 13 (March 1980), pp. 62–64.

Abercrombie, Stanley. *Gwathmey Siegel Monographs on Contemporary Architecture.* New York: Whitney Library of Design, 1981, pp. 84–89.

"A Sign of the Times." *Architectural Record*, Mid-February, 1981.

"Architectural Approach, Inventive Spatial Solution for an Apartment in Manhattan." *Architectural Digest*, June 1983, pp. 150–153.

Also in Japanese edition of *Architectural Digest*, no. 5 (March 1984), pp. 102–109.

Taft Residence
Cincinnati, Ohio

Five Houses Gwathmey Siegel Architects, Catalogue 7, The Institute for Architecture and Urban Studies, 1977–78, pp. 60–69.

"Gwathmey Siegel." *A + U*, no. 96 (September 1978), p. 160.

"Space, Place and Object: Gwathmey/Siegel Architects." *Skyline*, February 1980, pp. 6–7.

Goldberger, Paul. "Modernist Villa in Ohio." *The New York Times Magazine*, December 28, 1980, pp. 36–37, 50.

Abercrombie, Stanley. *Gwathmey Siegel Monographs on Contemporary Architecture.* New York: Whitney Library of Design, 1981, pp. 70, 102–107.

"Ohio Residence." *A + U*, June 1981, pp. 23–30.

"Gwathmey Siegel Architects—Private House, Cincinnati, Ohio." *Architectural Record,* Mid-May 1981, pp. 86–91.

Donovan, Carrie, ed. "Modernist Villa in Ohio." *Living Well. The New York Times Book of Home Design and Decoration*, 1981, pp. 156–161.

"Clarity behind a Projecting Facade, House near Cincinnati, Gwathmey Siegel Architects." *AIA Journal*, Mid-May 1981, pp. 167–174.

"Gwathmey Siegel: Winner of AIA's Firm Award." *AIA Journal*, February 1982.

"Ohio Residence, Cincinnati, Ohio USA, Gwathmey Siegel & Associates Architects." *Toshi-Jutaka*, Monthly Journal of Urban Housing, February 1982, pp. 5–11.

Wiser, Ann. "A Vision Made Clear, A Contemporary Look at the American Dream." *United Airlines Magazine*, May 1982, pp. 58–63, 103–109.

"Gwathmey Siegel: Winner of AIA's Firm Award." *AIA Journal*, February 1982.

"East Campus Complex, Columbia University by Gwathmey Siegel & Associates." *Space Design*, Tokyo, July 1982, p. 66.

"Residence in Southern Ohio." *Global Architecture*, no. 13 (March 1983), pp. 32–41.

"The Seventh Annual Review of New American Architecture," National A.I.A. Awards. *Architecture*, May 1984, p. 166.

"Casa Taft, Cincinnati, Ohio, Estados Unidos, 1978." *La Casa Unifamiliar.* Barcelona: Editorial Gustavo Gili, S.A., pp. 80–83.

Northgate Housing
Roosevelt Island, New York
(project)

Goldberger, Paul. "A Broader Horizon is in the Offing for Roosevelt Island." *The New York Times*, September 26, 1977, p. 33.

Freiberg, Peter. "Action on Roosevelt Island." *Skyline*, January 1983, p. 4.

Lincoln Center for the Performing Arts
Administrative Offices
New York, New York

"Brightening Dark Corners." *AIA Journal,* October 1979, p. 46.

FDM Productions
Offices
New York, New York

Constantine, Eleni. "A Corner on the World." *Progressive Architecture*, September 1979, pp. 140–143.

AT&T
Office Building
Parsippany, New Jersey

"What's a High-Style Design Firm Like Gwathmey Siegel Doing Designing Speculative Office Buildings Along Freeways and in Office Campuses?" *Architectural Record*, December 1977, pp. 108–115.

Gordon, Barclay. "Low-Rise Office Buildings." *Architectural Record,* September 1980.

"Gwathmey Siegel: Winner of AIA's Firm Award." *AIA Journal*, February 1982.

The Evans Partnership
Office Building and Offices
Parsippany, New Jersey

Gordon, Barclay. "Low-Rise Office Buildings." *Architectural Record,* September 1980.

"Offices: Honorable Mention: Evans Partnership/Evans Shure Construction Company, Parsippany, New Jersey." *Interior Design*, November 1980, p. 200.

Abercrombie, Stanley. *Gwathmey Siegel Monographs on Contemporary Architecture*. New York: Whitney Library of Design, 1981, pp. 96–101.

Klein, Judy Graf. *The Office Book*. New York: Facts on File, Inc., 1982, pp. 54–55.

Yee, Roger and Gustafson, Karen. *Corporate Design*. Interior Design Books, 1983, p. 208.

The Evans Partnership
Offices
New York, New York

Constantine, Eleni. "A Corner on the World." *Progressive Architecture,* September 1979, pp. 140–143.

Heyne, Pamela. *Today's Architectural Mirror, Interiors, Buildings and Solar Designs*. Van Nostrand Reinhold Company, 1982, p. 68.

Knoll International
Showroom and Office Building
Boston, Massachusetts

Prokopoff, Stephen. *Boston: Forty Years of Modern Architecture.* Institute of Contemporary Art and William J.R. Curtis, 1980, pp. 15, 46–47.

Schlefer, Jonathan. "Back Bay Boon & Bust." *The Real Paper,* March 1, 1980.

"Architects Gwathmey Siegel bring new life to Newbury Street while respecting its historical tradition." *Interior Design,* May 1980.

"Die Postmoderne Bei Knoll." *Architektur, Innenarchitektur Technischer Ausbau*, June 1980, pp. 554–555.

Miller, Nory. "Knoll Makes Its Move, The Boston Showroom." *Progressive Architecture*, July 1980, pp. 79–81.

Huxtable, Ada Louise. "An Architectural Shot Heard 'Round the World." *The New York Times*, September 28, 1980, pp. 37, 51.

Centre d'Exposittion Knoll, Boston." *Architecture d'Aujourd'hui*, no. 210 (September 1980), pp. 58–59.

Dinelli, Fiamma. "Knoll Showroom, Boston." *L'Industria Delle Construzioni*, no. 114 (April 1981), pp. 60–67.

Abercrombie, Stanley. *Gwathmey Siegel Monographs on Contemporary Architecture*. New York: Whitney Library of Design, 1981, pp. 72–77.

"Gwathmey Siegel: Winner of AIA's Firm Award." *AIA Journal*, February 1982.

Sycamore Place
Elderly Housing
Columbus, Indiana

"Apartments for Senior Citizens Opened." *The Republic,* Columbus, Indiana, November 1, 1982.

Shezan Restaurant
New York, New York

"Great Looking Dining Places, Shezan." *The New York Times Magazine*, December 20, 1976, pp. 59–61.

"Elegance without Opulence." *Interior Design*, vol. 48, no. 1 (January 1977), pp. 108–111.

"Other Spatial Realms." *Progressive Architecture,* February 1977, pp. 72–82.

Carlsen, Peter. "Design." *Avenue,* April 1977, pp. 44–48.

Goldberger, Paul. "A Design for Orderly Living." *The New York Times Magazine,* December 11, 1977, p. 147.

"Design '78, Shezan Restaurant." *Mainliner Magazine,* May 1978, p. 67.

"The Interior Decade: A Summary of the 1970's." *Progressive Architecture*, September 1979, p. 135.

"Shezan Restaurant, New York, N.Y." *Process Architecture*, no. 13 (March 1980), pp. 52–55.

Abercrombie, Stanley. *Gwathmey Siegel Monographs on Contemporary Architecture*. New York: Whitney Library of Design, 1981, pp. 50–55, 69.

Heyne, Pamela. *Today's Architectural Mirror, Interiors, Buildings and Solar Designs*. Van Nostrand Reinhold Company, 1982, p. 47–48.

"Interview, Charles Gwathmey." *Restaurant and Hotel Design,* March/April 1983, pp. 36–39, 87

Library and Science Building
Westover School
Middlebury, Connecticut

"The Science/Library Center: The Architects' Plan." *Westover School Alumnae Magazine,* vol. 19, no. 2 (Winter 1981–1982).

"Raise Now to Westover: A New Science/Library Center." *School Self-Mailer,* fund-raising letter, Westover School, Summer 1982.

Boraks, David. "Past and future linked." *The Sunday Republican*, May 6, 1984, sect. 5, pp. 1, 5.

Triangle Pacific Corporation
Office Building
Dallas, Texas

"Triangle Pacific Offices, Gwathmey Siegel Architects." *Texas Architect*, November/December 1980, p. 44.

"Gwathmey Siegel: Winner of AIA's Firm Award." *AIA Journal*, February 1982.

Dillon, David. "Gwathmey Siegel Wins AIA Prize, The Triangle Pacific Building in Dallas is among Firm's Work." *The Dallas Morning News*, Wednesday, June 16, 1982.

Knoll International
Desk and Credenza System

Klein, Judy Graf. "Elements of Design." *The Office Book*. New York: Facts on File, Inc., 1982, pp. 101.

Halliday, Sarah. "Meier and Gwathmey/Siegel at Knoll." *Skyline*, April 1983, p. 21.

Yee, Roger and Gustafson, Karen. *Corporate Design.* Interior Design Books, 1983, p. 174.

de Menil Residence
Houston, Texas

Nisselson, Jane. "The Surprise of Color—New Dimension in Classic Design." *House & Garden*, April 1981, pp. 162–167.

"Texas Residence." *A + U*, June 1981, pp. 36–39.

McKay, Gary. "Color Conversion, An Architect's Bold Redesign." *Home and Garden*, January 1982, pp. 142–144.

"Harlequin Colours in a Logical Spatial Plan." *House & Garden* (British edition), January 1982, pp. 48–51.

"Gwathmey Siegel: Winner of AIA's Firm Award." *AIA Journal*, February 1982.

"Gwathmey Siegel Houston Residence." *G.A. Houses, ADA Edita,* Tokyo, no. 11 (May 1982), pp. 40–45.

"East Campus Complex, Columbia University, by Gwathmey Siegel & Associates." *Space Design*, Tokyo, July 1982.

"Charles Gwathmey on a Personal Approach to Architecture." *Architectural Digest,* November 1983, p. 49.

de Menil Residence
East Hampton, New York

Five Houses Gwathmey Siegel Architects, Catalogue 7, The Institute for Architecture and Urban Studies, 1977–78, pp. 70–81.

Diamondstein, Barbaralee. *American Architecture Now.* New York: Rizzoli, 1980, pp. 63–77.

G.A. Document 4, "Gwathmey Siegel & Associates, Long Island Residence, Long Island, New York." *ADA Edita,* Tokyo, 1981, pp. 84–87.

Abercrombie, Stanley. *Gwathmey Siegel Monographs on Contemporary Architecture.* New York: Whitney Library of Design, 1981, pp. 114–117.

"On Style II," Gwathmey Siegel's Beach House, discussed at I.A.U.S. *Skyline,* March 1983, pp. 8–9.

Tinsman, Elizabeth Robertson. "'Toad Hall' in East Hampton." *The Hamptons,* June 1983, pp. 27–30.

Davis, Douglas. "Elegant New Geometry." *Newsweek,* June 27, 1983, pp. 88–93.

Morton, David. "Hampton House." *Progressive Architecture*, December 1983, pp. 47–57.

Scully, Vincent. "Architecture: Gwathmey Siegel and Associates." *Architectural Digest*, December 1983, pp. 120–131.

Architectural Digest (Italian edition), no. 33 (February 1984), pp. 62–68.

"Home Sweet Home, Yesterday, Today, and Tomorrow." *Ladies Home Journal* (100th Anniversary issue), January 1984, pp. 108–113.

"de Menil Residence, East Hampton, New York." *G.A.,* no. 15 (January 1984), pp. 26–49.

"In Praise of Modernism." *Domus,* no. 647 (February 1984), pp. 27–37.

"Alla Deriva, Una Casa di Charles Gwathmey, a Long Island." *Harper's Italia Gran Bazaar*, no. 3 (March 1984), pp. 92–101.

Sikes, Gini. "Casa Role." *Metropolis*, April 1984, p. 25.

Dean, Andrea Oppenheimer. "An Abstract Language Made Comprehensible and Comfortable." *Architecture*, May 1984, pp. 302–313.

Einstein Moomjy
Showroom
New York, New York

"Soaring Tri-Level Carpet Store Sets Exciting Pace in Retail Design." *Contract,* December 1980, pp. 54–59.

Reliance Group Holdings, Inc.
Offices
New York, New York

Yee, Roger and Gustafson, Karen. *Corporate Design.* Interior Design Books, 1983, pp. 116–117, 136–137, 147, 160–161.

"Reliance Group Holdings, Inc. Three Contiguous Floors for the Corporate Headquarters of a Major Conglomerate." *Interior Design*, January 1983, pp. 208–215.

Morton L. Janklow & Associates
Offices
New York, New York

"Gwathmey Siegel & Associates Offices for Morton L. Janklow & Associates." *Architectural Record, Interiors,* Mid-February 1982.

Viereck Residence
Amagansett, New York

"The Viereck House Long Island by Gwathmey Siegel." *Architectural Record Houses of 1982* and *Architectural Record,* Mid-May 1982, pp. 116–120.

"Viereck Residence." *Nikkei Architecture,* August 1982, pp. 59–62.

"Viereck House." *Toshi-Jutaku Urban Housing,* February 1983, pp. 29–35.

Garey, Carol Cooper. "Small House on a Grand Scale." *House Beautiful,* October 1983, pp. 102–105.

First City Bank
Bank and Office Building
Houston, Texas

"Gwathmey Siegel: Winner of AIA's Firm Award." *AIA Journal*, February 1982.

"Chapter Awards Program." *Oculus*, journal of the New York Chapter of the American Institute of Architects, vol. 45, no. 9 (May 1984), p. 6.

Wick Alumni Center
University of Nebraska
Lincoln, Nebraska

Murphy, Jim. "Wick Center Architects Gwathmey & Siegel...Their Designs are 'Impeccable, Disciplined and Rigorous.'" *Nebraska Alumnus*, September/October 1981, pp. 18–20.

"Projects-Nebraska Competition." *Skyline,* October 1981, p. 15.

G.A. Document 4. "Gwathmey Siegel & Associates, Wick Alumni Center, University of Nebraska, Lincoln, Nebraska." *ADA Edita*, Tokyo, 1981, pp. 80–83.

Architectural Design Citation: Gwathmey Siegel & Associates Architects. *Progressive Architecture,* January 1982.

Arango Apartment
New York, New York

Cross, Parthenia. "Charles Gwathmey Builds a High-Level Cabinet." *Avenue,* April 1984, pp. 120–127.

Westport Public Library
Westport, Connecticut

Kazzi, John, "Library Design Plans Submitted." *The Hour Suburban,* July 8, 1983, p. 13.

Hines, Patricia. "Architect: Library Plan Has a Place in Westport." *Westport News,* September 30, 1983.

de Menil Residence
Santa Monica, California

Hines, Thomas S. "Architectural Treasure Renewed, Revitalizing Neutra Lewin's House in Southern California." *Architectural Digest,* October 1983, pp. 176–182.

Gwathmey Siegel & Associates Architects
Offices
New York, New York

Slesin, Suzanne. "Architects Bridge the Gap between Home and Office." *The New York Times*, May 27, 1982.

"Moving West, Gwathmey Siegel & Associates, New Loft Headquarters on Tenth Avenue." *Interior Design,* January 1983, pp. 196–202.

Dietsch, Deborah. "General Office Winner." *Interiors*, January 1983, pp. 108–109.

Stucchi, Silvano. "New Architect's Office on 10th Avenue, New York." *L'Industria Delle Construzioni*, October 1983, pp. 60–62.

Beverly Hills Civic Center
Competition
Beverly Hills, California

"In Competition, Beverly Hills, California, Civic Center." *Skyline*, November 1982, pp. 4–6.

de Menil Table Series
ICF

"Technology and Tradition Mark Chicago Show." *The New York Times*, June 16, 1983, p. C1, C6.

"ICF's deMenil Tables." *Interior Design*, January 1984, pp. 146–147.

Tapestry
V'Soske

"Floored." P/A News Report. *Progressive Architecture,* January 1984, p. 24.

International Design Center
Showroom Buildings
Long Island City, New York

Slesin, Suzanne. "Queens Site to be Converted into International Design Center." *The New York Times*, March 10, 1983, p. C1.

"An International Design Center Planned for New York." *Interior Design*, April 1983, p. 86.

"Dineen Heads International Design Center, New Long Island City Development." *Contract*, May 1983.

Abercrombie, Stanley. "Does New York Need a Design Center?" (editorial). *Interior Design*, July 1983, pp. 176–177.

"Un prestigieux centre international d'exposition." *Club Maison*, September 1983.

"Design Leaders Rally Around New York's International Design Center." *Interiors,* December 1983.

Museum of the Moving Image
Astoria, New York

Bennetts, Leslie. "Astoria Studio Revives Film Era in New York." *The New York Times*, August 3, 1983, p. C17.

Exhibitions

The Architectural League of New York
"40 under 40"
September 1966

School of Visual Arts
"7 Architects and 7 Sculptors"
November 1967

Princeton University
"Retrospective 1968"
November 1968

The Museum of Modern Art
"State University College at Purchase, New York"
May 1971

The Heckscher Museum
"The Architecture of Suffolk County"
April 1971

The Museum of Modern Art
"Another Chance for Housing: Low-rise Alternative"
June–August 1973

Triennale 15
International Exposition
Milan, Italy
September 20–November 20, 1973

Institute for Architecture and Urban Studies
"Five Houses"
Gwathmey Siegel Architects
December 1977–January 1978

Institute for Architecture and Urban Studies
"Toad Hall," East Hampton, New York
January–February 1983

We thank the following people who have worked in the office and contributed to the projects.

Senior Associates
Jacob Alspector
Joel Bargmann
Richard Gould
Bruce Nagel
Thomas Phifer
Gustav Rosenlof

Associates
Paul Aferiat
Jose Coriano

Architects
Robert Anderson
Tulga Alpay
Marla Applebaum
Henry Ayon
Lynn Bensel
Christopher Chimera
John Chimera
John Choi
Richard Clark
John Colamarino
Stephen Domries
Bruce Donnally
Christoper Egan
Jeffry Feingold
Margaret Fitzpatrick
Steven Forman
Glen Fries
David Fukui
Millan Galland
William Garbus
Howard Goldstein
Susan Green
Tim Green
Peter Guggenheimer
Victoria Hage
Steven Harris

Durwood Herron
David Hingston
Debbie Ingsler
Karen Jacobson
Margaret Jann
Johannes Kastner
David King
Eleanor Klein
David Knowlton
Dirk Kramer
Jude Le Blanc
Renny Logan
Frank Lupo
Richard Manna
Dean Marchetto
Barry McCormick
Jay Measley
John Meder
Jo Merriman
Andrew Minchun
Marvin Mitchell
Michael Monsky
Reed Morrison
Vincent Mulcahey
David Murphy
John Nambu
Fuensanta Nieto
Reese Owens
Andrew Pettit
John Petrarca
Elisabeth Post
Stephen Potters
Thomas Pritchard
Goerge Raustiala
Karen Renick
Daniel Rowen
Joseph Ruocco
Barry Silberstang
Marc Simon
David Steinman
James Swan
Earl Swisher
Peter Szilagyi

Tsun-Kin Tam
Nick Toecheff
Irene Torroella
Alexandra Villegas
Edward Walsh
Thomas Whitrock
Timothy Wood
George Wu
Ivan Zaknic

Student Interns
Nancy Barrett
Paul Bentel
Theodora Betow
Richard Brennan
Tracy Brown
David Buckman
Kathleen Byrne
Pierre Catacuzene
Robert Choeff
Chris Coe
Dianna Lee Coronato
Vincent Cortina
Long Diep
Pamela Donnelly
Tip Housewright
Darragh Kelvie
Jeffrey Matz
Carlene Ramus
Brian Reiff
Joseph Rosa
Eric Steel
James Stevens
Susan Watt
Peter Wheelwright

Administrative Staff
Cathaline Cantalupo
Adrienne Catropa
Dinah Shammaa Modiano
Robin Noble
Nikky Radlick
Kimberly Ross

Susan Scott
Courtney Steel
Mimi Taft
Sandra Volts
Theresa Watkins

Photographers
Peter Aaron
Jaime Ardiles-Arce
Otto Baitz
Hedrich-Blessing
Orlando Cabanban
Louis Checkman
Goerge Cserna
David Fanzen
Yukio Futagawa
David Hirsch
Timothy Hursley
John Kisch
Balthazar Korab
Nathaniel Lieberman
Bill Maris
Norman McGrath
Peter Paige
Richard Payne
Marvin Rand
Steven Rosenthal
Mark Ross
Roberto Schezen
Ezra Stoller
Tom Yee

Model Makers
George Awad
Lawrence Callender
David Diamond
Dale Flick
Albert Maloof
George Raustiala
Curtis Vasquez